THE PRESIDENTIAL
ELECTION OF 1996

THE PRESIDENTIAL ELECTION OF 1996

Clinton's Incumbency and Television

E. D. Dover

PRAEGER

Westport, Connecticut
London

Library of Congress Cataloging-in-Publication Data

Dover, E. D.
    The presidential election of 1996 : Clinton's incumbency and
television / E. D. Dover.
      p. cm.
    Includes bibliographical references and index.
    ISBN 0–275–96259–8 (alk. paper)
    1. Presidents—United States—Election—1996. 2. Television
broadcasting of news—Political aspects—United States.
3. Television and politics—United States. I. Title.
JK526 1998g
324.7'3'097309049—DC21   98–4946

British Library Cataloguing in Publication Data is available.

Library of Congress Catalog Card Number: 98–4946
ISBN: 0–275–96259–8

First published in 1998

Praeger Publishers, 88 Post Road West, Westport, CT 06881
An imprint of Greenwood Publishing Group, Inc.

Printed in the United States of America

The paper used in this book complies with the
Permanent Paper Standard issued by the National
Information Standards Organization (Z39.48–1984).

10 9 8 7 6 5 4 3 2 1

TO MOLLY

CONTENTS

Tables   ix

1.   Presidential Elections in the Television Age   1

2.   Clinton Becomes a Strong Incumbent   47

3.   The Battle for the Republican Nomination   91

4.   The Seven Month General Election Campaign   133

5.   Conclusions and Epilogue   177

Bibliography   183

Index   195

TABLES

2.1 Partisan Distribution of Congressional Districts prior to the 1994 Election by Presidential Election Results   69

2.2 Partisan Distribution of Congressional Districts after the 1994 Election by Presidential Election Results   70

2.3 Gallup Poll Recorded Support for Clinton and Dole in 1995   73

4.1 Clinton's Strongest States   173

4.2 Clinton's Weakest States   173

4.3 Support for Candidates by Selected Social Groups   174

4.4 Support for Candidates by Selected Attitudes   175

The Presidential Election of 1996

CHAPTER 1

PRESIDENTIAL ELECTIONS IN THE TELEVISION AGE

In the book, *Presidential Elections in the Television Age: 1960–1992*, I argue that mediated incumbency is superior to partisanship in explaining the outcomes of more recent national elections. By mediated incumbency, I refer to the relationships that now exist between the relative political strength of incumbent presidents and the manners in which television news media tend to understand and interpret that strength, are influenced by it, and subsequently respond by reporting it to its viewers in ways that are both recurring and predictable. These relationships, in turn, help define the contexts of elections and contribute to the creation and reinforcement of perceptions of political reality in the minds of many voters. With respect to definitions, in my previous work and in this one, I use the term television news media when referring to the organizations and reporters that produce television news programming.

The central theme that I raise is that the categories of partisanship that a generation of political scientists had used to describe the outcomes of presidential elections should be abandoned in favor of categories of incumbency. The earlier perspective saw elections as quadrennial power struggles between the Democratic and Republican parties where voters cast their ballots primarily on the basis of long-held partisanship. While certain short-term events unique to given elections would occasionally influence their choices, voters tended to give far more credence to their partisanship than to any other factor when making electoral choices. Moreover, voters' positions on issues and their assessments of the personal qualities of the candidates were frequently influenced by their partisanship to the extent that such influences could affect election outcomes. Through the use of this perspective, political scientists viewed national elections through categories of partisanship where they saw each election as being either maintaining, deviating, or realigning. Every election either maintained, deviated, or realigned from the stable underlying patterns of partisanship that operated in the nation at the time.

Rather than viewing elections as Democratic-Republican confrontations, I propose that we focus on them instead as efforts by incumbents to retain power in an age where candidate-centered campaigns dominate the political arena. The most important factor in deciding present-day outcomes is the strength of incumbency, as interpreted by television and other news media, while partisanship plays an important although secondary role. The strength of incumbency is not static and unchanging but varies widely among different presidents and can even change substantially within the same administration. With this perspective, I then identify the parties by where they stand in relation to incumbency and call them the presidential and opposition parties rather than the Democratic and Republican. As a consequence, each of the two existing parties will eventually occupy the role of both the presidential or opposition party over different elections. In addition, I introduce a new set of outcome categories for describing modern elections that is based upon the relative strength of incumbency. I argue that one should categorize all elections since 1960 as being either (1) elections with strong incumbents, (2) elections with weak incumbents, or (3) elections with surrogate incumbents.

In the first category, presidents and television news media together create contexts where the incumbents appear as successful and effective leaders deserving of reelection over the less qualified nominees of the opposition party. In the second category, the two create contexts where the incumbents appear more as failures undeserving of reelection while the opposition party nominees come across as qualified aspirants for the Presidency. In the third, the incumbents do not seek reelection but their vice presidents emerge as surrogates, win their parties' nominations, and then meet ambiguous fates as the Vice Presidency proves to be a valuable asset within a nomination campaign but seems of questionable importance and is perhaps even detrimental during a general election.

My purpose in this book is to apply the findings from my previous work to the presidential campaign of 1996 and to develop a more complete theory of the role of mediated incumbency in modern elections. In particular, I seek to demonstrate that the strength of presidential incumbency is the most important factor in explaining election outcomes and that television news media respond to variations in that strength in ways that are both recurring and predictable. I concluded my previous work with a forecast about 1996 by writing,

> It is far too early at this time [1993] to make any realistic forecasts about the outcome of the campaign and election of 1996, except to say that Bill Clinton will be the central personality in that quadrennial endeavor and that television news media will illustrate the events of that year in ways that are predictable today. The fate of Clinton will already be cast by the outset of the televised coverage of the campaign that will begin in January of 1996. Clinton will either have consolidated political power by that time and will have developed a widespread following as a result of a number of significant policy and personal successes, or he will have failed and thereby will be yet another ineffective and unpopular one-term president. If he has succeeded, television news media will treat him as the American equivalent of European royalty and will illustrate him performing favorably in the unifying role of statesman. They will also enhance his electoral prospects by directing considerable attention during the first half of the election year to the most divisive features and personalities of the Republican nomination campaign. If Clinton is a weak and embattled incumbent, however, television news media will illustrate his most important failures while depicting the front-running Republican contender as a highly qualified president-in-waiting. This pattern of coverage will enable that front-runner to unite his party quite early during the year and then win the election. Beware the Ides of March. We should know the name of the next president of the United States by that day. (Dover 1994, p. 173)

Indeed, we did. As we all know by now, his name was Bill Clinton and his victory in November 1996 was obvious to all by the middle of March of that same year. With this outcome in mind, I seek to demonstrate the validity of the various components of my 1993 forecast.

The initial chapter discusses why mediated incumbency has developed as the most important explanation of election outcomes and summarizes the findings and conclusions derived from my previous work that led me to make the assertions quoted above. I develop a framework to help better understand the events, personalities, results, and recurring patterns that now mark all elections of the television age. In the remaining chapters of the book, I apply that framework and explain how the variety of uniquely appearing events that characterized the 1996 campaign were not as unique as one might suspect but were more recent examples of the modern incumbency-media relationship that has defined television age elections over the past four decades.

In the first part of chapter 1, I explain the various changes in the institutional structures and public roles of the Presidency over the past few decades that have made the relationship between incumbency and media possible. I use the second part to review the patterns of presidential and media behavior characterizing the two categories of elections that occur when an incumbent seeks another term of office, that is, elections with strong or with weak incumbents. The contemporary Presidency has expanded from its nineteenth- and early twentieth-century counterpart in two ways: (1) in the policy development and administrative roles it plays as seen in the operations carried out by the Executive Office of the President, and (2) in the rhetorical role that serves as the basis for what a number of writers call the plebiscitary Presidency. The development of this latter rhetorical role has been influenced by two factors, the institutional power of the Executive Office of the President and the existence of television as the most significant medium of political communication in the nation. Television's news components have been particularly influential.

The emergence of television as this significant medium has affected election campaigns and even the operations of the Presidency itself. Incumbents often use television as a major component of their efforts to create imagery where they appear as tribunes of the people who are separate and distinct from the institutions and policies of government, as Clinton tried when he opposed the Republican majority in Congress over spending reductions in Medicare. In addition, television news media have been partners, perhaps somewhat unwilling, in the transformation of the Presidency from its earlier role as an institutional office into its present one where much of the American electorate views the incumbent as their personal leader. They have helped to personalize the office by focusing considerable attention on the words and actions of individual presidents while downplaying or even ignoring the words and actions of the other institutions and actors of government.

This relationship between incumbency and media leads to two very different categories of election contexts when an incumbent seeks another term of office. The elections with strong incumbents differ from those with weak incumbents in ways far more complex than simply the final outcomes.

The manners in which television news media treat incumbents and their challengers depends primarily upon how they perceive the strength of the incumbents. The 1996 election was, of course, one with a strong incumbent. Strong is a relative term, however, and is meaningful only when one considers it in relation to something that is less strong. In order to discuss the characteristics that mark elections with strong incumbents, and thereby explain the meaning of 1996, it is also necessary to delineate the more significant aspects of its antithesis, elections with weak incumbents. Any type of election is not deterministic, that is, it will not occur automatically only after the passage of a periodic interval of years. Instead, a combination of events must take place for an incumbent to either win or lose his bid for another term. The 1996 election could very well have involved a weak incumbent and instead might have resulted in Clinton's defeat. His prospects for a second term did not look promising after the stunning takeover of Congress by the Republican Party in November, 1994. A Gallup Poll survey of February 5, 1995, taken shortly after Clinton gave his State of the Union Address before the new Republican congressional majority, indicated that Senator Robert Dole (Kansas) would have defeated Clinton by 51 percent to 45 percent if the election had been held that day. Of course, Clinton would eventually transform these poll numbers into outcomes that were far more favorable to himself. With this in mind, I discuss the recurring patterns that take place in elections with strong incumbents and in elections with weak incumbents in the second part of chapter 1. My discussion summarizes findings from my previous work concerning the leading features of these two categories of elections. The reader is urged to consult that work for a more thorough review.

I follow this discussion by describing in chapter 2 the manner in which Clinton employed the institutional and rhetorical advantages of the modern Presidency during 1995 to become a strong incumbent by the beginning of 1996. He had a very erratic first term that was marked by wide sweeps in his personal popularity along with great policy successes and major strategic failures. His greatest early success came in 1993 when he won a budget battle with congressional Republicans over changes in the taxing and spending policies of the Reagan and Bush administrations. This victory was soon offset by his loss of the highly touted health care reform program in 1994, which eventually became the greatest policy setback of his first term. Clinton's prospects for a second term never appeared bleaker than after the Democrats lost control of both houses of Congress in the elections of 1994. This loss suggested that Clinton would be unable to set the national agenda any longer and would instead have to respond to the efforts of congressional Republicans such as House Speaker Newt Gingrich and Clinton's likely opponent in 1996, the new Senate Majority Leader Robert Dole. Clinton looked very much like a one-term President.

He would not become one, however. Clinton effectively used the powers of the modern Presidency and reversed his misfortunes. His reemergence began during several intense and highly televised battles with the Republicans during the latter months of 1995 over Medicare and the federal budget. Clinton opposed Republican efforts to increase the premiums that Medicare recipients had to pay for health insurance and to reduce the federal financial role in medical care. He rallied Democrats and senior citizens and then confronted the Republicans in a number of crucial showdowns. Clinton also fought the Republicans before television reporters who conveyed his side of the controversy to millions of their viewers. His use of the rhetorical powers of the Presidency induced television news media to define the issues at stake in a manner that implicitly advanced his political agenda. In addition, he supplemented this favorable news coverage with an expensive advertising campaign that depicted the Republican leaders as radicals bent on undermining Medicare. Clinton eventually won the Medicare battle in two measurable ways: the Republicans backed down, and his support increased as shown in public opinion surveys.

Clinton engaged the Republicans yet again, this time over the content of the federal budget. He vetoed several bills they advanced for reducing spending on a variety of educational, environmental, and health related programs. His vetoes, and the Republican responses to them, eventually resulted in two partial shutdowns of the federal government. Clinton employed his rhetorical and institutional powers once again and created imagery where he appeared as the defender of the public's interests against the efforts of a group of mean-spirited congressmen who sought to wreak havoc on the nation. As they had done before, television news media described the events of the shutdown periods in ways that supported Clinton's political goals. Clinton won these battles as the Republicans again backed down while he gained in the polls.

One of my purposes in chapter 2 is to demonstrate how television news media responded to the powers of the modern Presidency and defined the issues in these battles in ways that conformed to Clinton's wishes. Clinton relied upon the rhetorical powers of his office and his own personal skills to convince news reporters that his version of events was the correct one. They responded by broadcasting his version to their viewing audiences. I describe the highlights of these battles between Clinton and his Republican adversaries from the vantage point of voters who observed them primarily through the thirty minute evening news telecasts of the three major television networks: the American Broadcasting Company (ABC), the Columbia Broadcasting System (CBS), and the National Broadcasting Company (NBC). While many more news sources were available to television viewers, including 24 hour coverage by the Cable News Network (CNN) and the daily programs of hundreds of local stations, I concentrate on the three major networks because their evening telecasts were the most widely viewed news programs in the nation, and because they summarized the day's events into a few minutes of coverage that was not always available on the alternative sources mentioned above.

The televised component of the 1996 campaign began shortly after the conclusion of the budget fight and the second government shutdown. The one central fact that guided the actions of television news media and which eventually defined the context of the campaign was that Clinton had become a strong incumbent. He had united his own partisans behind his bid for reelection before the campaign had even begun and had taken a substantial lead in the polls over every Republican who might oppose him in the general election. In responding to Clinton's strength in their recurring and predictable ways, television news media concentrated their attention during the first months of the year on the most divisive events and personalities in the battle for the Republican nomination. While doing so, they depicted Clinton as a successful incumbent by illustrating him in a variety of scenes that created the appearance of statesmanlike behavior. This pattern of news coverage helped undermine the electoral prospects of all Republican candidates, and of Dole in particular, while increasing those of Clinton.

I describe and evaluate the battle for the Republican nomination in chapter 3. This was an unusual campaign for an opposition party in that it resulted in the selection of a major congressional leader as the standard-bearer, a rare outcome in the television age. Another unusual feature was its relatively early conclusion. Dole had secured the support of enough convention delegates by the end of March to claim victory. Dole's triumph became apparent as Pat Buchanan, the last remaining survivor of his ten original rivals, withdrew his candidacy. Despite this early ending, the campaign did not lack for intensity and animosity and television news media found many divisive themes to report. They covered the leading candidates extensively after the middle of January and stereotyped them into predefined roles, which they used as guides for future reporting. As with the battles over Medicare and the federal budget, I describe the events of this period from the vantage point of voters who observed them through the evening programming of the three networks. In particular, I focus attention on the leading events from the latter part of 1995 and from the caucuses and primaries of Iowa, New Hampshire, South Carolina, and California. My purpose is to demonstrate that television news media defined this campaign in the same recurring and predictable ways in which they respond to the opposition party in all elections with strong incumbents.

The general election campaign lasted for an astonishing seven months and was one of the longest in the nation's history. A unique and distinguishing feature that marked it was a pre-convention campaign of four months that occurred between the conclusions of the nomination battles and the convening of the national conventions. A pre-convention campaign of this nature rarely occurs because both parties usually do not resolve their nominations this early. One party may prolong its struggle until the convention. The nominations of 1996 were resolved by the beginning of April, however, but the first convention, that of the Republicans, did not start until August. In most years, at least one party holds its convention in July. The concluding of the nominations earlier than usual and the convening of the conventions later than normal created a unique period of time where the candidates and television news media defined the themes of their campaigns and news reporting long before the conventions even met. As a result, the election was effectively over by Labor Day, the traditional beginning of the general election campaign in most years. By that time, most voters had determined their choices and few changed their opinions. Few of the events and little of the reporting that followed in the weeks after the conventions differed from what had happened earlier. The candidates reemphasized the same issues while television news media reiterated the same themes that they had been reporting since mid-summer.

I use chapter 4 for describing the events of these seven months while once again drawing on the content of the evening news programming of the three networks. I focus attention on three chronological periods: the pre-convention time between April and August, the month of August with the national conventions, and the nine weeks after Labor Day which marked the concluding phases of the lengthy battle for power. Moreover, I direct attention to the news themes that resurfaced many times during these weeks and which share the central assumption that Clinton was a strong incumbent who deserved a second term in the nation's highest office.

I conclude this book in chapter 5 by evaluating the recurring features of this election while exploring the possibility that different outcomes of certain events might have led to the defeat of Bill Clinton. Clinton's actions account for the outcomes of those events, however, and for the eventual result of the election itself. While Clinton's victory made the events of 1996 into another television age election with a strong incumbent, those events could very well have unfolded in conformity with the recurring patterns of elections with weak incumbents. Clinton could have lost his battles with the congressional Republicans in 1995 and might have begun his quest for a second term as an embattled incumbent similar to the last two Democratic Presidents who sought reelection, Lyndon Johnson and Jimmy Carter. He did not share their fate, however. It is important to know why he did not, particularly in light of the fact that he came so close to doing so. I propose an alternative scenario of events and consider what might have happened if Clinton had failed in 1995 and had become a weak incumbent instead. In essence, this book assesses how an incumbent, in this case Clinton, successfully employed the vast array of rhetorical and institutional powers that define the modern Presidency as it operates in the highly televised world of national politics into a victorious reelection strategy. The 1996 election was decided by a combination of the powers of the Presidency, the recurring ways in which television news media respond to those powers, and the opportunities that an incumbent can exercise in manipulating them to bring about a predictable response from both television news media and millions of voters.

I wish to warn readers not to conclude that television news media are so powerful and pervasive they can dictate the outcomes of presidential elections. Instead, television news media are often victims of their own value systems and of efforts by incumbents and other aspiring candidates to manipulate them in order to advance their own self-serving agendas and contrived imagery. Television news media all too frequently help generate widespread political support for certain kinds of candidates while undermining support for others through their predictable responses to events over which they have little control. The incumbency-media relationships that operate during any particular election campaign derive from the strength of presidential incumbency as it exists at the outset of that election year and from the media interpretations of it rather than from any real or imagined media schemes for agenda setting. This is a theme I develop and reiterate throughout this book.

THE MODERN PRESIDENCY AND TELEVISION

The Executive Office of the President

One of the more significant but often unappreciated aspects of modern presidential election campaigns is the extensive political role played by a complex bureaucratic entity sometimes referred to as the presidential branch of government. Nelson Polsby writes that the emergence of this branch is perhaps the most interesting political development of the postwar period. He adds that it "sits across the table from the executive branch at budgetary hearings, and . . . imperfectly attempts to co-ordinate both the executive and legislative branches in its own behalf" (Polsby 1983, 20). The actual name of this entity is the Executive Office of the President (EOP). Since its creation in 1939, the EOP has evolved into one of the most significant players in the operations of the national government. Its existence has helped alter the distribution of powers within government by enhancing those of the President and weakening those of both Congress and the executive departments. Presently, the EOP contains eleven administrative divisions and employs over 1600 persons in a variety of policymaking and support roles. Its personnel are located in the Executive Office Building, which is part of the White House office complex, or within the White House itself.

For those readers unfamiliar with the organizational structure of the United States government, one should not confuse the Executive Office of the President with the executive branch of the national government. The latter contains the numerous departments, agencies, regulatory commissions, and public enterprises that exist in order to implement the vast array of programs and policies of the national government. It employs over three million civilian workers and about 1.6 million members of the Armed Services. In contrast, the Executive Office of the President is more akin to a personal staff for the nation's chief executive. It is, of course, a very large and politically powerful staff. It was started in an attempt to provide some greatly needed staff assistance to the President but it has grown considerably over the past six decades. Its role has become so significant that one writer, Ryan Barilleaux, depicts it as the President's general secretariat, "a central staff that enables the Chief Executive to direct and supervise the work of the Executive Branch." He adds that it is "a powerful, bureaucratic, and politicized extension of the President" (Barilleaux 1988, 17).

The EOP developed as a consequence of a controversial but presidentially solicited report from the Brownlow Commission in 1937 that declared the President needed administrative help. Franklin D. Roosevelt had created this commission in response to what he described as a problem of inadequate staff resources. Roosevelt intended to justify an expansion in the size of the presidential staff. At that time, the White House Office, the predecessor of today's EOP, consisted of only 37 persons (Hart 1995, 28) After nearly two years of intense partisan struggles and numerous political negotiations with Roosevelt, Congress passed Reorganization Act 1 which led to the creation of the EOP.

The most significant change that occurred at that time in the structure and operations of the federal government was the relocation of the Bureau of the Budget from the Treasury Department into the newly created EOP. Congress had created the Bureau of the Budget in 1921 as part of a comprehensive attempt to overhaul the processes of budget preparation and implementation by the national government. The Bureau was required to assemble the budgetary requests of each organizational component of the national government and to use that information for preparing a comprehensive report, that is, budget, for Congress that would explain all anticipated receipts and proposed expenditures of those components. The Bureau was also expected to propose more efficient means of operating the government.

This transfer of the Bureau of the Budget to the EOP gave the President far greater control over the planning, development, and administration of public policy than at any time previously. With this transfer, the President could now employ the Bureau as the institutional method for both developing and dominating the policies and actions of the various components of the executive branch. A practice known as central clearance began in which the Bureau would undertake a mandatory review of all proposals for new or amended laws that originated from these various components. These reviews considered such matters as the fiscal costs, benefits, and potential impacts of any and all proposed changes but also examined their compatibility with the President's programs. A lack of compatibility virtually guaranteed that the proposed changes would be rejected by the President and would not likely reach Congress or be enacted into law. The use of central clearance enables the EOP to serve as the primary source of the most important policy initiatives that actually reach Congress. Theodore Lowi writes that presidential initiatives now fill the agenda of Congress and most of its committees and dominate Congressional hearings and debates. The initiatives are personalized and are now frequently referred to as "the President's program, the President's budget, the President's administrative initiative" (Lowi 1985, 140). Finally, the Bureau provided the President with the institutional means of developing new policy proposals that reduced his reliance upon the executive branch. He could now develop a legislative program and submit it directly to Congress while bypassing the departments. In 1969, Richard Nixon expanded the role of the Bureau even further by including management of the executive branch among its tasks and renamed it the Office of Management and Budget (OMB).

The continuing expansion of the EOP over the past six decades has not been limited merely to increases in size, it has included the addition of significant new political and administrative responsibilities. Most of the current divisions of the EOP did not exist in 1939. The present divisions are: the White House Office, the Office of Management and Budget, the Council of Economic Advisors, the National Security Council, the Office of the U.S. Trade Representative, the Council on Environmental Quality, the Office of Science and Technology Policy, the Office of Administration, and the Office of National Drug Control Policy (Hart 1995, 5).

One cannot attribute the growth of the EOP exclusively to the efforts of various power-seeking presidents, however. Congress certainly deserves a share of the responsibility for the increase in its institutional and political powers. Two of the EOP's most important divisions were actually created by congressional initiatives during the immediate post-war period. The Council of Economic Advisors resulted from the Employment Act of 1946. Congress created the National Security Council in 1947 during a reordering of the nation's security institutions that combined the War and Navy Departments into the newly established Department of Defense.

The Employment Act of 1946, whose original purpose was to stabilize the national economy in the light of a post-war depression, also had the effect of turning the President into the nation's chief economist. This law requires the President to submit an annual economic report to Congress where he both reports on the condition of the economy and prescribes policies, some of which may be budgetary, that he believes are necessary for bringing about a politically acceptable balance between prices, growth, and employment. Congress created the Council of Economic Advisors to assist the President in preparing this report. Because of the passage of this law and its implementation over the past half century, the President, according to Thomas Cronin, is now recognized as the primary initiator of anti-unemployment and anti-inflation policies (Cronin 1980, 91).

The National Security Council has emerged in recent years as the dominant player in setting the nation's foreign and defense policies. The law which created the Council directed it to serve as a presidential advisory body and provided additional staff assistance for the President in order for the Council to carry out this mission. The staff is headed by the Special Assistant to the President for National Security Affairs. Henry Kissinger, who held the position during much of the Nixon administration, was among the most famous of Special Assistants. It was from this position that he played the role that led to his being the architect of many of the foreign and defense policies of the Nixon years. Today, the Council gives the

President the opportunity to oversee virtually all aspects of foreign and defense policy and enables him to promote a presidential perspective on security matters. He can and often does use the staff to manage, and sometimes to circumvent, the Departments of Defense and State (Barilleaux 1988, 19).

Congress had several motives for acting as it did in expanding the institutional powers of the Presidency with respect to budgetary, fiscal, security, and other policies, Cronin believes. The deliberative Congress, he writes, was so frequently overwhelmed or overtaken by events that it could not respond quickly enough. Congress could not set the broad policy goals or take the swift actions that the nation often indicated it preferred. Moreover, Congress usually was unable to manage any of these policies very effectively. It responded by delegating many of its responsibilities to the President and then chose to devote much of its time to overseeing, opposing, and sometimes even vetoing presidential government (Cronin 1980, 92). Lowi also writes that Congress freely chose to delegate the implementation of new programs to the executive branch. It deliberately wrote the laws that established new programs in broad and vague language in order to provide the largest amount of administrative discretion to both the agency responsible for implementing specific policies and to the President (Lowi 1985, 100–101).

In his evaluation of the rationale for this delegation of powers and the inevitable growth of the institutional Presidency that resulted from it, Lowi speaks of a gap in the constitutional structure of the federal government that the creation of the EOP alleviated. The constitution lacks any provisions for the existence of a cabinet or executive council that might assist the President in developing and implementing policies. The institutional Presidency, that is, the EOP, has risen in response to this gap, he writes. The nation now directs numerous demands to the President for governmental action and fully expects him to deliver on them. Presidents, of course, are frequently quite willing to accommodate these expectations. As an example of this pattern, the constitution requires that all revenue bills originate with the House of Representatives. This did not deter George Bush in 1988, however, as he told voters to "read my lips, no new taxes." He acted as if the President actually controls taxation rates and many voters apparently believed him. Lowi adds that the nation is also redefining democracy and increasingly associates it with delivery. This actually helps expand presidential powers as voters respond by placing many of their expectations for delivery directly upon the President. Finally, the steady decline of political parties as effective organizations for contesting elections and for organizing the government after achieving victories, and the rise of influential interest groups to fill the void left by this decline have also expanded the institutional powers of the Presidency. These developments have enabled the President to replace the party as a broker of interest demands. The President is now the nation's most important political broker in creating policy and governing coalitions (Lowi 1985, 100–101).

The institutional structure of the EOP was largely in place by the beginning of the 1960s although it underwent a number of revisions over the next few decades. Individual presidents now attempt to personalize the office even more than their predecessors while simultaneously seeking to expand its powers. One of the earliest and most effective leaders of this personalizing approach was John F. Kennedy through his interactions with television. Kennedy attempted to create a public image of himself where he appeared as the personal leader of the nation and as an individual who stood separate from the institutions of government. He was, in essence, attempting to appear as a charismatic tribune of the people rather than as the highest ranking official of the executive branch of the national government. Sidney Milkis and Michael Nelson believe that Lyndon Johnson and Richard Nixon also contributed to the personalizing of the presidential branch. Johnson did so by managing his two wars, the ones on poverty and communism, from the EOP. His efforts also concentrated even greater political and policy responsibility directly in the Presidency. Nixon attempted to use the administrative apparatus of the EOP to attain through other means what he was unable to attain through cooperation with either Congress or the executive branch. He sought to gain his objectives by having the OMB preempt the managerial roles of the departments and by then creating the Domestic Council in order to control the development of new policy (Milkis and Nelson 1994, 330–340). By the time Ronald Reagan became president in 1981, the EOP had expanded to the point where it was organized around what Cronin calls the three subpresidencies: foreign affairs and national security; aggregate economics; and domestic policy or quality of life issues. They are respectively concentrated in the National Security Council, the Council of Economic Advisors, and the Office of Management and Budget (Cronin 1980, 145).

John Hart writes that the EOP has changed its mission from its original purpose of assisting the President in his managerial and planning roles into a significant political entity instead that now effectively competes for powers with other institutions of the national government. He says that it has helped expand the capacity of the President to lead in three critical areas: management of the executive branch, formulation of public policy, and political outreach. The EOP can frustrate Congress by placing a significant amount of policymaking beyond the reach of congressional efforts at administrative oversight. In addition, the President can use the institutional powers provided by the EOP to more effectively organize public support for his policies and to bypass Congress while doing so (Hart 1995, 234–241). Two writers, Lester Seligman and Cary Covington, attribute this enhanced presidential political role to coalitions comprised of affected interests and blocs of congressional supporters who want the presidential branch to take on a more political role (Seligman and Covington 1989, 38).

Barilleaux adds that the modern presidential branch has given prerogative powers to the Chief Executive that he did not possess before. He says these new prerogatives range from the use of military force and arms control to budgeting and regulation. While prerogative powers do not necessarily guarantee the success of presidents in attaining their political goals, they often do provide them with additional leverage and autonomy in shaping and administering policy and in generating support for their efforts. Barilleaux writes that the EOP also facilitates legislative and administrative aggressiveness by the President. He attributes increases in the power of the EOP to two recent developments; the growing domination by the Office of Management and Budget over policymaking and implementation and the institutionalization of foreign and defense matters within the National Security Council (Barilleaux 1988, 14–17).

An important development relating to the expansion in presidential budgetary power occurred in 1974 when Congress passed the Budget and Impoundment Control Act. This law was designed to limit the President's exercise of budgetary power and discretion but had the unintended side effect of expanding his power instead. The law passed in response to Nixon's controversial attempts at impounding federal monies appropriated for social services, and to perceived declines in the abilities of Congress to compete effectively with the President in setting fiscal policy. The law established several new institutions including the Congressional Budget Office and two standing budget committees, one in the Senate and one in the House of Representatives. In addition, it required these committees to prepare budget resolutions to designate the maximum amounts of money that could be raised and spent each year and the total amounts of new debt that could be incurred. The resolutions were designed to enable Congress, for the first time in the nation's history, to determine aggregate levels of federal spending, taxation, and deficits through a single legislative act. Previously, Congress could view the entire budget only through an array of numerous and varied individual taxing and spending bills. The purpose of the law was to increase congressional powers over the setting of budget priorities.

Despite these intentions, the law actually enhanced the President's powers since it provided him with opportunities for gaining greater controls over legislative processes than he had previously, Louis Fisher writes. The President could use the annual budget resolutions as a means for expanding his influence and attaining greater control over the details of the various taxing and spending programs as they advanced through the budget committees. The committees helped expand presidential powers since they served as the primary locus of legislative action on the budget. There had been no such locus within Congress until 1974. Instead, budgetary action had been dispersed among about forty standing committees and an even greater number of subcommittees. Now, the President could focus his congressional lobbying efforts directly on these two new committees as they prepared annual budget resolutions and related measures. The President also became less responsible for budgetary estimates than he had been, but again, not in the way that Congress apparently intended. Previously, the President, assisted by the OMB, had prepared budgets that realistically estimated both expenditures and revenues. Congress had no comparable institutions capable of challenging the President's estimates, so it tended to accept them. The Congressional Budget Office now provided Congress with an alternative source of information, thereby giving it the institutional means to doubt the President's estimates and to then prepare its own alternative versions. Fisher writes that this law provided the President with the opportunities to submit unrealistic estimates and to then force confrontations with Congress when and if it rejected them. The President could make Congress appear as if it were the driving force behind governmental efforts to reduce spending on popular programs (Fisher 1993, 189–204).

Reductions in domestic spending and the corresponding expansions in defense appropriations actually enhanced the consolidation of presidential power over budgeting during the Reagan years, Barilleaux writes. In order to accomplish his political goals, Reagan found it essential to use the OMB as an institution for lobbying Congress and for managing spending because the existing Congressional budget process was unadaptable to any sudden and far reaching changes in priorities. Reagan used the reconciliation procedure to overrule the Democratic leadership in Congress during the early months of 1981 and then to enact his own taxing and spending changes. The political efforts for organizing the Congressional support that

Reagan needed for bringing about these changes was directed by OMB director David Stockman. Finally, Reagan started one additional but highly important practice that also expanded presidential budgetary powers. He required that all proposed agency rules be submitted to a cost/benefit analysis by the OMB before they were submitted to Congress. The use of cost/benefit analysis as such is an extension of central clearance, explained above (Barilleaux 1988, 12–19).

With respect to the major topic of this book, election campaigns, one of the more significant components of the EOP is the White House Office. Hart writes that the size of the Office, about 500 persons, is large enough that a president can use it as a place of employment for much of his campaign staff. This enables him to keep his staff intact between campaigns and to employ it in planning and directing either his bid for reelection or for the bid of his surrogate, the Vice President, if he is constitutionally ineligible for another term. The use of the White House Office in such a manner takes on even greater significance because today's candidate-centered campaigns often overshadow the importance of the party organizations. The White House Office serves as the management center for a personal effort aimed solely at reelecting the incumbent. There is another aspect to this practice, Hart finds, that also tends to increase the campaign powers of the EOP. The modern campaign requires the candidates to construct and maintain their own personal organizations, but it also tends to isolate them from party elites and effectively restricts their options relating to staff selection. As a consequence, the White House Office develops even more into a permanent campaign organization where virtually all presidential words and deeds are judged by their likely impacts on the upcoming election (Hart 1995, 128–129). Cronin adds that a president can benefit from this permanent campaign staff and its accompanying public relations efforts because it strives to show him as a man of action. The staff also helps him raise money and provides him with millions of dollars' worth of free publicity. A rival candidate has no such advantages. As a non-incumbent, the rival's motives often seem unclear, and he may very well appear to many observers more as a seeker of office than as a national leader (Cronin 1980, 43).

The Rhetorical Presidency

Related to the growth of presidential power through the development of the Executive Office is the expansion of the President's role as a political rhetorician. Rhetoric is defined here as the art of expressive speech. Some writers, among them James W. Ceaser and his co-authors, use the term rhetorical Presidency to depict the fulfillment of this new role of the chief executive. Ceaser attributes the rise of the rhetorical Presidency to three factors: (1) the doctrine of presidential leadership; (2) the modern presidential campaign; and (3) the mass media (Ceaser et al. 1981, 161).

Ceaser places the creation of the rhetorical Presidency and its doctrine of leadership squarely with Woodrow Wilson. He claims Wilson brought popular speech to the forefront of American politics through his dramatic appearances before Congress in support of his legislative agenda and in his speaking tour in 1919 on behalf of establishing the League of Nations. Ceaser writes that Wilson articulated the doctrinal foundation of the rhetorical Presidency and thereby provided a theoretical model of the office alternative to the one advanced by the founding fathers. According to Ceaser, Wilson believed that the greatest power in democratic regimes lay potentially with the popular leader who could sway or interpret the wishes of the people (Ceaser et al. 1981, 162–163).

Ceaser finds that the Wilsonian rhetorical Presidency consists of two interfused elements. First, the President employs oratory to create an active public opinion that he hopes will pressure Congress into accepting his goals. The deliberative rhetoric that often characterizes congressional debate gives way to popular rhetoric that the President advances through his public addresses. Second, in order for the President to actually reach and move the public, the rhetoric must tap the public's feelings and articulate its wishes. Rhetoric, according to Ceaser, does not instill old and established principles as much as it seeks to infuse a sense of vision into the President's program. It also places considerable emphasis on personal leadership. The doctrine of leadership inherent within the rhetorical Presidency exhorts in the name of a common purpose and a spirit of idealism (Ceaser et al. 1981, 163).

Jeffrey Tulis, a co-author with Ceaser who has written subsequently about the rhetorical Presidency, says that the presidential office is buffeted by two constitutions which both constrain and shape its actions. One is the written constitution that creates the system of separation of powers and checks and balances. The second is the rhetorical, one that he claims emphasizes active and continuous presidential leadership of popular opinion. This second constitution is buttressed by such extra-constitutional factors as the mass media and the primary elections that now serve as the modern method of choosing a president (Tulis 1987, 17–18).

A second factor that Ceaser believes accounts for the rhetorical Presidency is the modern campaign. The campaign is important, he writes, both for the inflated expectations it raises and for the effect it has on governing. The campaign so thoroughly defines both oratory and the expectations of leadership that we have now come to expect that the actual process of governing imitates the campaign itself. The campaigns, according to Ceaser, set the tone for governing rather than governing setting the tone for campaigning. Mass rhetoric now serves as a principal tool that presidents use in governing. Presidents now consider it appropriate to move the public by speeches that exhort and set forth grand and ennobling views. Candidates are now obliged to demonstrate their leadership capacity through an ever growing number of rhetorical performances, with the impact of their words on governing being one of their least concerns. The pressure to say things continues well after the conclusion of the election, Ceaser adds. The President is continually expected to speak out on perceived crises and to minister the moods and emotions of the people (Ceaser et al. 1981, 161).

Tulis adds that the Presidency is more energetic now than it was in the nineteenth century and that it is now far more capable of leading comprehensive social change than it was earlier. An important aspect of this transformation is the emergence of rhetorical power. Tulis calls rhetorical power a special case of executive power. Not only is it used to justify presidential actions, it provides the people to whom it is addressed with much of the equipment they need to assess its use: the metaphors, categories, and the concepts of political discourse (Tulis 1987, 203).

Lowi considers the modern campaign to be a continuation of a personal relationship that is initially forged between the candidates and their popular bases of support. He adds that the legal powers and responsibilities of the Presidency actually contribute to myths about the ability of presidents to meet those responsibilities. The rhetoric that flows from the presidential office encourages myths about the capacity of presidential government because it magnifies the President's personal responsibility and surrounds his power with mystique (Lowi 1985, 151).

Ceaser's third factor is mass media. The media did not create the rhetorical Presidency, he says, doctrine did. Instead, media facilitated its development and gave it some of its special characteristics. Media have changed the mode by which the President now communicates with the public by replacing the written message with the spoken word that is delivered in visible and dramatic performances. Presidents understand, he says, that it is the visible performance, not the actual text, that creates the lasting public impression (Ceaser et al. 1981, 164).

Tulis claims that mass media have facilitated the development of this rhetorical role by giving the President the means to communicate directly and instantaneously to a large national audience and by reinforcing the shift from written messages to verbal dramatic performances as the leading means of presidential communication. He finds the phrases of presidential speeches to be significant in that they are primarily designed to accommodate television news and to create the contexts for the President's dramatic performances. Presidential messages tend to be filled with short one-sentence paragraphs that are consciously designed to accommodate television news. Tulis believes that such sentences are unlikely to be quoted out of context since little context exists for them. They are themselves the context for which the speeches are delivered (Tulis 1987, 186–188).

Television news media are important components in the functioning of the rhetorical Presidency, particularly with respect to the values they often bring to their coverage. Cronin claims that a personalized Presidency is the central feature of contemporary political journalism. Reporters often view the President more as an individual than as the institutional leader of the national government and see his actions primarily as those of a solitary actor. Cronin attributes much of this pattern of belief and reporting to Theodore H. White and his series of books on the making of the President. White concentrated on describing the styles and personalities of the candidates and promoted what Cronin calls a benevolent orientation toward the Presidency in the minds of both readers and other practicing journalists. The writing style that White used when describing the details of the power struggles during the elections of the 1960s and 1970s helped promote suspense and encouraged reverence for the eventual victor. Cronin writes that in White's dramas the victor in this drawn-out ritual appears to deserve the nation's respect and approval. The individual who assumes the Presidency after such an election, has, by undergoing this ritual as White described it, changed both physically and spiritually (Cronin 1980, 83).

Cronin finds that significant changes in the patterns of television news reporting have helped expand the apparent power of the Presidency. Television has downgraded local news while elevating the importance of the national, he says. Presidential travels and addresses are accentuated with the national networks invariably committed to what is an almost mindless superficiality in their coverage of the Presidency. Cronin sees a problem in that symbolic actions carried out via videopolitics by shrewd presidents often seem as effective as concrete action itself. In addition, television places enormous power in the President's hands that is not provided for by the constitution. This power enables the President to influence public perceptions and one's sense of reality and to dominate the range of issues discussed by the nation. Presidents can maintain a near monopoly over political communication by using television in shaping the issues considered in the political arena. Moreover, a president's words and actions receive far more television coverage than the efforts of other political actors. The President's access to the consciousness of the average citizen is unmatched, Cronin adds. Presidents can use television to focus national attention on what they want and to shape the televised activities of other leaders and governmental institutions in such ways as to preserve their own superior visibility and public preeminence.

Cronin continues by saying that the American public has become so conditioned by both mass media and by presidential manipulation of it that people do not believe in the reality of a public act until it has actually been transformed into a dramatic performance by the President before television cameras. The actions of the President in contexts that are either symbolic, priority-setting, or crisis related often convey images of strength, vigor, and rigor, Cronin writes. Presidents often appear to be virile and effective in these areas of their job performance (Cronin 1980, 96–99).

One of the foremost writers on presidential power and performance is Richard Neustadt. In his most recent work, Neustadt reiterated the arguments that he raised in 1960 but added observations about the importance of television in the functioning of the modern Presidency. Presidents have three sources of influence, he writes; their formal powers as found in the constitution and laws, their professional reputations, and their prestige. He defined reputation as the collective impressions of the Washington community regarding the President's skill and political will. Prestige assesses being the President's public standing—the impressions held by the country about how well or badly he is doing as President (Neustadt 1990, 185).

Neustadt acknowledges that television has modified the nature of the relationship between reputation and prestige. Today, a president's ability to attract and motivate a television audience is as interesting to Washington insiders as his ability to use his actual powers. Neustadt writes that a president must use the popular connection in framing policy and shaping coalitions since party organizations and congressional party discipline, traditional sources of presidential power, have declined while interest groups and issue networks have grown (Neustadt 1990, 264).

The Presidency and Television News

Lowi and other writers use the term plebiscitary to describe the modern Presidency. By this, they mean that a direct relationship exists between the

President and the American public that is unmediated by institutions such as Congress or the political parties. The President makes his own personal appeals to and derives his political support exclusively from the public. In an electoral context where the President acts in this plebiscitary role, television news media serve as significant players for two reasons. First, television is now the leading source of political information for most voters, and in a great number of instances, it is the only source. Second, the manner in which television news media define and report politically related news helps create and then perpetuate the version of political reality that guides the voting behavior of many members of their viewing audiences.

A significant aspect of this reality creation derives from the television news media practice of employing visual images as components of coverage. Reporters may supplement their narratives with action- or emotion-related imagery. The explicit and implicit messages conveyed through this imagery sometimes tell a story that may differ from the one that reporters describe in the narrative. The manipulation of visual images by the Reagan administration in order to present a favorable view of the chief executive is a well known fact today. The reliance on visual images provide television news media with the capacity to enhance events and personalities in ways that are often unavailable to other media, particularly those media that rely exclusively on the printed word. Visual images enable television news media to direct attention to specific individuals and highlight their unique personal characteristics. An example of this pattern is the televised emphasis directed to the face and body of a speaker rather than to the audience.

Moreover, the visual nature of television allows news reporters and producers many opportunities to personalize events through the behavior of specific actors. Television news media do so by identifying events with actors rather than with impersonal governmental institutions or widespread social movements. This pattern of personifying events with the behavior of particular actors often encourages voter perceptions that the actual occurrence of the events in question would not and could not happen without the unique efforts of specific and identifiable people.

This personalizing feature also enables television news media to convey the message, intended or not, that the actor is separate from any institutional or political contexts that may be related to the reported events. By directing attention to the behavior of actors, television news media detach events from the contextual settings in which those events occur by making the events appear primarily as the actions of solitary individuals. With this pattern of news reporting, candidates appear more as solitary aspirants for office than as leaders of governmental institutions or as spokesmen for political parties.

The value system that guides news reporting dictates that particular events must differ from the usual course of events in order to be newsworthy. The routine happenings of government rarely meet this criteria because government operates more as a continuing pattern of interrelated activities than as a collection of random and discrete events. The consolidation of political power by strong incumbent presidents, a topic considered later in this book, occurs through a pattern of interrelated activities and thus fails to meet this media criteria of newsworthiness. As a general practice, television news media rarely report about an actual consolidation of power while it is occurring but almost always reflect its existence in their subsequent reporting.

In order to be newsworthy, events must also be of fairly recent origin and must be undergoing a variety of rapid changes. For example, a candidate must change the content of his standard campaign speech almost daily if he wants his actions to be reported. Moreover, events that generate news interest often involve economic, social, or foreign policy problems that can be personalized through the actions of specific government officials or are about a variety of personal scandals or controversies associated with well-known public figures.

This personalized imagery and focus on the unusual can encourage audiences to see government and politics as primarily a series of never-ending, fast-breaking stories about solitary and isolated individuals who are preoccupied with one new crisis after another to the exclusion of all else. It can encourage the creation of a version of reality where viewers see government as incompetent and leaders as flawed individuals undeserving of public trust or respect.

Television news media can also influence the course of events. This occurs because television news media are not separate and distinct from the events of their observation but are instead very much a part of them. Their presence alone can affect the development, sometimes even the actual existence, of events. The presence of the television camera can encourage certain outcomes while discouraging others. This is because human actions are not deterministic, that is, with only one possible outcome, but probabilistic where a variety of outcomes are likely. Some outcomes are more probable than others, but there is often uncertainty about how events may actually unfold. Television news media can affect the course of events by altering the probabilities that certain ones will occur.

Television news media are important players in current presidential elections because of their ability to influence the unfolding of events and the meanings that participants and observers give to the contexts in which those events occur. They can affect elections by enhancing the personal characteristics of those individuals who are the subjects of their attention. This pattern of reporting, including the personalizing of events, often diminishes the importance of partisanship upon voters' electoral choices while enhancing the short-term forces of personality and imagery.

One should not place the blame for these developments solely on television news media however, for the candidates must bear some of the blame. Many candidates attempt to create their own personalized imagery where they appear as solitary individuals separate from government and party. They seek to convey this imagery through news coverage while reinforcing it through their own paid advertising. Often, news reports may simply reflect these manufactured images of political candidates.

Television news media have been influenced by the manipulative efforts of recent presidents and have responded by making the Presidency the central feature in their coverage of government and politics. They often personalize their coverage by directing their attention to the actions of the individual president. Moreover, they measure the importance of political actors and evaluate the significance of domestic and international events through the relation those actors and events have with the President and of how they might affect his choices. Finally, they exaggerate the importance of the Presidency by illustrating and narrating the actions of the incumbent as if they are indeed the most important events in government.

Through this pattern of reporting, television news media contribute to voter perceptions that the President is a solitary leader separate from governmental and political institutions, including, in some instances, even other components of his own administration. They illustrate him as an outsider who fights against entrenched institutions of government. In a sense, they show him as a "Lone Ranger." In contrast, they all too often depict other governmental institutions as little more than personal obstacles the President must overcome in order to govern the nation and lead the world. Such reporting encourages viewers of televised news to see the President as the personal leader of the nation who governs through the strength of his individual character rather than through the management of governmental institutions.

The leading electoral results of these personalizing practices, deriving from the efforts of both television news media and office-seekers, is to encourage the existence and perpetuation of candidate-centered campaigns, as modern elections have come to be known. These elections occur when candidates strive to gain office as individuals rather than as spokesmen for political parties and where voters rely more on the personal characteristics of candidates than on partisanship when making electoral choices. Televised candidate-centered campaigns are especially useful for incumbents today because of the extensive news coverage of the Presidency. This media focus helps to undermine the electoral prospects of congressional leaders who run for president by making them appear as the leading defenders of an unpopular governmental institution than as solitary tribunes of the people. The popular dislike of Congress is reflected in public opinion surveys where some people place its members among their most despised occupations, sometimes comparable to that of organized crime leaders. Ironically, these same people usually approve of their own congressman and constantly reelect him. Even in 1994, when Republicans gained 52 seats in the House of Representatives and seven in the Senate, about 92 percent of the incumbents who sought reelection were successful.

This contradiction, where people dislike Congress but approve of their own congressman, appears glaring but makes sense if one considers that individual members of Congress, like presidents, also seek to develop public images where they appear as solitary champions of justice from outside of government. Many are often quite successful. It is the institution of Congress, not the individual members, that voters tend to dislike.

Television news media sharpen this distinction between personalized leadership and impersonal institutions in the ways in which they depict the President and Congress. They depict the President as an individual person and Congress as an impersonal institution. When reporting about today's Presidency, they almost always illustrate Clinton engaging in some activities. When reporting about Congress, however, they usually include an image of the Capitol Building. When television news media juxtapose an impersonal institution such as Congress against a solitary, personalized, and perhaps well-liked president, they implicitly encourage their viewers to regard Congress as an obstacle standing in the way of the President in his efforts to solve national problems. Many voters do not understand the complexities of Congress and are often unaware of the roles played by its standing committees, procedural rules, behavioral norms, and party caucuses. They often do not appreciate the different roles that Congress and the President play in the separation of powers constitutional order.

Congressional leaders who seek the Presidency encounter not only the popular dislike of Congress but often discover that both their institutional powers and the personal characteristics that enabled them to acquire those powers are not readily translated into voter support. In order to become an effective congressional leader, one must possess such skills as conciliation, compromise, reciprocity, and deference, and be able to build coalitions and master procedural rules and strategy. These are not the skills of a political "Lone Ranger." Moreover, possession of them may clash with popular images conveyed through television news that preferred political leaders are solitary tribunes of the people who fight against corrupt institutions, such as Congress.

Television News Coverage of Nomination Campaigns

Television news media are particularly influential at affecting voter choice in nomination campaigns, perhaps even more so than they are during general elections. This is because the effects of partisanship, which play a major role in general elections, are usually absent from nomination campaigns. A strong Republican voter who casts a ballot in a primary election, for example, would not be faced with a choice between one Republican candidate and one Democrat as in a general election, but would need to choose from perhaps as many as ten Republican contenders. The ideological and policy differences that distinguish these ten from one another are unlikely to be as sharp as those that separate the major party nominees in a general election. Moreover, this hypothetical Republican voter will probably have very limited knowledge about many of the contenders and should be very susceptible to televised news reports that focus on them.

The influence of television news media is quite evident during the winnowing period. Winnowing is the reduction in the number of candidates from a large number of aspirants to a smaller number of actual contenders. It usually occurs after the conclusion of the initial primaries and caucuses, that is, during late February and early March. Television news media are integral components of winnowing in that they actively seek to restructure the campaign into a struggle between two role-playing "semi-finalists." They attempt to do this by limiting their coverage to a maximum of two candidates, and in some instances, to only one. They also stereotype these candidates into predefined roles which they then use as guides for future reporting. Finally, they depict the remaining candidates as losers and virtually cease reporting about any of them.

The more important of the two stereotypical roles is "front-runner." Television news media assign this role to the candidate who appears to have the greatest chance of winning the nomination. Sometimes, an actual front-runner is obvious as one candidate leads his rivals in public opinion surveys and defeats them in the earliest primaries and caucuses. Ronald Reagan in 1980 is one such example. In other instances, there is no obvious front-runner, so television news media help create one by focusing attention on the one candidate who initially attains the most votes or the highest poll standings, even though the differences between this candidate's accomplishments and those of his rivals may be quite small. Jimmy Carter in 1976 is an example. After designating a front-runner, television news media use him as the central actor in their reporting and evaluation of campaign events. They attribute meaning to future events only with respect to the relation those events have to the efforts of the front-runner.

Television news media create and perpetuate a theme in which the predominant story of the campaign is the personal quest of the front-runner for the Presidency. Their model is Theodore White's depiction of John F. Kennedy in *The Making of the President 1960*. White used Kennedy as the central actor in his description of the 1960 campaign and examined political events through their relation with him. He depicted the other candidates as obstacles that Kennedy needed to overcome in order to advance to the White House. Kennedy struggled and overcame them; an experience White found ennobling. Television news media employ White's style when reporting about contested nomination campaigns. They define a front-runner as early as possible and stereotype him into the role White defined for Kennedy. They depict this front-runner as the central actor of the campaign who is engaged in an unending struggle to overcome a vast array of personal and political obstacles that stand between him and the Presidency. If this front-runner overcomes the obstacles, as Kennedy did, he proves his virility and demonstrates his qualifications for holding office. If the obstacles overpower him, he fails the test and is thereby unqualified to lead the nation.

The second role is "leading adversary." Television news media depict this candidate as the antithesis of the front-runner and as a personification of the obstacles the front-runner must overcome. They rarely depict him as a candidate in his own right. The actions of the leading adversary take on meaning only through their relation to the continuing story of the front-runner seeking the Presidency. Leading adversaries develop in some campaigns without the need for media intervention. In other instances, television news media enhance this development by focusing attention on one of the front-runner's rivals and then stereotyping him in this role. Gary Hart's emergence as the leading adversary of Walter Mondale after the 1984 Iowa caucuses is an example of this approach.

Television news media create self-fulfilling prophecies when they stereotype candidates into these predefined roles. By depicting campaigns as two-candidate battles, they help turn them into two-candidate battles. Their coverage often creates a catch-22 dilemma for the candidates who fail to attain either of these two roles and encourages their rapid departure from the campaign. Candidates who trail their rivals in money, poll standings, or actual votes acquired in primary elections during the early stages of nomination campaigns can rarely reverse their fortunes and win the nomination unless they attain extensive televised news coverage of their efforts. They cannot attain that coverage if they are trailing their rivals, however. Candidates disappear from campaigns about as quickly as they disappear from televised news. They also depart from the campaign before many voters become aware that they are even in it.

After the winnowing period, television news media attempt to reduce the number of major candidates for the nominations of the two parties to only three. These are the two "semi-finalists" for the nomination of one party, the front-runner and leading adversary, and the one candidate who has emerged as the front-runner within the other party. They accomplish this goal by directing more attention to one party's campaign while downplaying that of the other. News coverage of this nature helps perpetuate a battle between two role-playing candidates in one party while encouraging the rapid resolution of the nomination within the other party behind the candidacy of the front-runner. Television news media do not need to have a leading adversary in both parties in order to create a newsworthy campaign, one is sufficient. A campaign involving two front-runners and two leading adversaries competing in two separate "races" of two candidates each is more difficult to report than a campaign that has only one contested nomination.

In all but one television age election, 1960, only three contenders attained any substantial televised news coverage after the conclusion of the earliest caucuses and primaries. In the elections with strong incumbents, two semi-finalists emerged, or were encouraged to emerge by television news media, for the nomination of the opposition party, while the incumbents were unchallenged for renomination. In the elections with weak incumbents, each President engaged in an intense battle for renomination with one adversary, while the nominees of the opposition party emerged early during the campaign seasons. This television-enhanced winnowing and stereotyping of candidates affected the outcomes of these elections. Since 1964, the party that had the misfortune to become involved in a two-candidate battle for its nomination, complete with a front-runner and one leading adversary, lost the ensuing general election.

CATEGORIES OF TELEVISION AGE ELECTIONS

Elections with Strong Incumbents

In addition to Bill Clinton in 1996, three incumbents have won presidential elections during the television age. Moreover, each of the three incumbents previous to Clinton won his campaign by a popular and electoral vote margin that ranks among the largest ever attained in the history of the Presidency. In the first such election, 1964, the Democratic incumbent Lyndon B. Johnson overwhelmed his Republican challenger, Arizona Senator Barry Goldwater, by a popular vote margin of 61.1 percent of the vote to 38.5 percent. Johnson also carried the electoral votes of 44 states and the District of Columbia. In the second election, 1972, the Republican incumbent Richard M. Nixon attained 60.7 percent of the popular vote compared to the 37.5 percent achieved by his Democratic challenger, South Dakota Senator George McGovern. Nixon carried 49 states in his bid for a second term. Finally, in 1984, Republican incumbent Ronald Reagan recorded a victory comparable to the earlier ones of Johnson and Nixon when he acquired 58.8 percent of the popular vote against 40.6 for his Democratic challenger, former Vice President Walter Mondale. Reagan also carried the electoral votes of 49 states. While the victory of Bill Clinton in 1996 also involved a strong incumbent, I limit my discussion in this section to the three elections mentioned above.

These three elections share a number of characteristics that appear likely to occur again in the foreseeable future. Consequently, I place them in the category "elections with strong incumbents." The first characteristic is the highly personal nature but corresponding short-term duration of the incumbents' triumphs. They appear to be more personal than partisan. Each incumbent achieved a level of voter support that vastly exceeded the backing his party could attain in elections for offices other than the Presidency. Moreover, the presidential party was unable to acquire that same level of support in the next election. The Democrats lost the election of 1968 while the Republicans failed in their bid for a third consecutive term in 1976. While the Republicans won in 1988 with Reagan's vice president, George Bush, Bush's margin of victory was considerably smaller and much more difficult to come by than Reagan's. In addition, each of the presidential parties suffered widespread losses in the congressional elections that occurred two years after their landslide victories. The Democrats lost more than forty seats in the House of Representatives in 1966 while the Republicans suffered a comparable loss in 1974. The Republicans lost eight seats in the Senate in 1986 and forfeited the control they had acquired six years earlier when Reagan won his first term as president.

The three incumbents recorded their electoral triumphs after first consolidating political power within their own parties prior to the outset of their election years. As a result, all three were virtually unopposed for renomination. Johnson and Nixon attracted some minor challengers, but their adversaries fared poorly and disappeared from the campaigns shortly after the end of the earliest primaries. Reagan was unopposed throughout his renomination effort.

While the incumbents encountered few difficulties in securing their nominations, one cannot say the same about their general election challengers from the opposition party. All of the opposing nominees were forced to engage in very prolonged and divisive struggles in order to attain their party endorsements. Not one—Goldwater, McGovern, or Mondale— could escape from months of bitter competition that left his partisans divided and his public image shattered beyond any realistic chances of revival.

Television news media responded to these circumstances by defining the roles and reporting about the actions and words of the incumbents and challengers quite differently. These variations in response, in turn, affected the manners in which many voters perceived the context of the campaigns, interpreted political events, evaluated the personalities and qualifications of the candidates, and eventually cast votes. In all three campaigns, the voters considered the incumbents to be more qualified than their opposition party challengers and responded by granting them additional terms of office by popular and electoral vote margins that are among the largest in the nation's history.

Reagan's victory is particularly interesting in that it discredited an explanation frequently raised to account for Johnson's and Nixon's earlier triumphs. This explanation postulated that voters rejected Goldwater and McGovern because they saw them as ideological extremists whose views were far removed from the political mainstream. Voters instead supported candidates more attuned to the political center, such as the moderate to liberal Johnson and the moderate to conservative Nixon.

An ideologically related explanation of this nature fails to take the significance of presidential incumbency into account. This shortcoming did not seem particularly important until after 1984, but the Reagan victory raised doubts about its validity. Reagan was more ideologically distinct than Mondale. Instead of being referendums on ideological extremism, these three elections were actually referendums on incumbents. In each election, a first-term incumbent president won an additional term of office after consolidating political power within his own party and by using televised news coverage of both presidential election campaigns and of the Presidency itself as a means of generating a widespread personal and political consensus in support of his reelection.

While television news media implicitly provided each incumbent with innumerable opportunities for developing such a consensus, they also enhanced the dissension within the opposition party. They helped bring about both conditions by the means in which they defined and reported politically related news. They devoted the first half of each election year, that is, when the campaigns for the party nominations occurred, by depicting the incumbents and their challengers quite differently. They directed far more attention to the Presidency than to any other political institution: they concentrated more on personalities than policies and they illustrated campaign events that allowed for plenty of action, pictures, competition, and controversy. While doing so, they often downplayed or even ignored topics related to the more subtle and far less picturesque consolidation of power by incumbents and of the institutional limitations of American parties in selecting leaders who can effectively oppose those incumbents. They often depicted incumbents as performing in a statesman-like manner, that is, as competent leaders guiding the nation and advancing American interests throughout the world, while directing considerable attention to the most divisive features of the nomination campaigns of the opposition party. Finally, they depicted the contenders of the opposition party as unqualified aspirants for power rather than as experienced leaders qualified for the Presidency. The juxtapositions of contrasting imagery of statesmanlike appearing incumbents against poorly qualified challengers helped set the stage for what eventually became three personal triumphs by strong incumbent presidents.

The most significant political fact in these elections, and what set the stage for all that followed, was that the incumbents had consolidated political power among their own partisans well before the outset of their campaigns for reelection. The lack of opposition to their renominations reflected the extent of the incumbents' political strength. All three had effectively convinced the leading political actors of their own parties that they were quite simply unbeatable for renomination. Moreover, the fact that each incumbent began his renomination campaign without opposition demonstrated the existence of a united core constituency that supported his reelection bid. While the numerical magnitudes and emotional depths of these popular followings were uncertain at the time, the images that other political actors had of the incumbents possessing widespread and unequivocal support eventually became the realities of these election years and ultimately affected the actions of candidates and news reporters accordingly.

A major factor that contributed to the partisan unity within the presidential party was that the party had only recently acquired power and had not yet developed any factional differences among its activists that might have jeopardized that unity. In each strong incumbent election prior to 1996, the presidential party had attained power four years earlier by either beating the incumbent of the other party (1980) or by defeating the Vice President and surrogate of a retiring incumbent (1960, 1968). Four years in office quite simply had not provided this party with enough time to implement its program or develop disputes among its members that would lead to dissension during a nomination campaign. Moreover, the party had attained power in the previous election because its members had united behind a leader who held out the promise of victory. John F. Kennedy (1960), Richard M. Nixon (1968), and Ronald Reagan (1980) led united opposition parties that had been defeated in the previous election and which had exhibited substantial disunity while doing so. These presidents may have had detractors throughout the nation, but their own partisans remained united behind them during the initial years of their administrations. The Democratic support for Kennedy eventually extended to his successor, Lyndon B. Johnson.

The three incumbents supplemented their strength with several policy initiatives that activists of their parties viewed as successful. Johnson's efforts at advancing Kennedy's domestic program, Nixon's attempts to conclude the Vietnam War, and Reagan's taxing and spending policies united their own partisans behind their reelection drives. This unity was the most valuable political asset of these incumbents and it influenced the manner in which television news media understood and illustrated the events of their campaigns.

During the early months of an election year, television news media often focus their attention on the personalities, competition, action, and controversies within the campaigns for the party nominations. A multicandidate campaign within the opposition party all too frequently provides the media with innumerable opportunities for extensive coverage of these themes. An uncontested campaign within the presidential party does not, however. Television news media encounter difficulties with the nomination campaigns of unopposed incumbents since they rarely find much competition, action, or controversy to report. The values they employ in determining the newsworthiness of events encourage them to disregard or downplay routine exercises of political power. They cannot depict through action-related pictures what may have already occurred through much more subtle means, the consolidation of political power by an incumbent president prior to the outset of the election. Since they prefer to judge the newsworthiness of events by the opportunities those events provide for action-related pictures and related narratives, television news media often find the contrived appearances of unopposed incumbents at emotionally upbeat rallies as the most newsworthy events in the presidential party.

Television news media cannot illustrate this subtle and continual acquisition of political power actually happening, but they can depict its aftermath. They do so by showing an unopposed incumbent in the act of governing rather than in the act of seeking office. By responding to an incumbent's consolidation of power in this manner, by illustrating the aftermath of power rather than its acquisition, television news media implicitly become integral parts of the consensus building efforts in support of an incumbent's reelection bid. Their coverage often makes the incumbent appear as a statesman governing the nation rather than as a politician seeking votes. This prior consolidation of power is a necessary precondition for an uncontested renomination campaign within the presidential party and for television news media to respond by performing in a consensus-building communicative and persuasive role.

American presidents perform two roles: head of state and head of government. They often project statesmanlike appearing imagery while performing in the head of state role but seem more divisive when they act as head of government. If an incumbent unites his party before the outset of the nomination campaign, he can act in the head of state role while the opposition party spends its time struggling to designate its standard-bearer. Strong incumbents frequently employ the "Rose Garden Strategy" while doing this. They use the rhetorical and institutional powers of their office and create statesmanlike appearing imagery that television news media readily transmit to their audiences. Incumbents skilled in the use of television can use the preoccupation that news reporters have with the Presidency and create imagery where they appear to be alleviating serious foreign and domestic problems. Television news media all too willingly broadcast this contrived imagery while failing to be sufficiently critical of the incumbents who generate it.

The unchallenged renomination candidacies of incumbent presidents create a serious and often insurmountable dilemma for the opposition party. Its candidates often fall so far behind the incumbents in public esteem, as estimated through surveys, that they eventually lose any chances whatsoever of winning the election. The problem originates even before the beginning of the campaign. The party lacks a standout leader who can immediately provide unity and focus attention on the incumbent. This problem exists because there are no structural means by which an American opposition party can designate an undisputed leader before the year of a presidential election. As a consequence, the party must devote the first half of an election year to selecting its leader. Moreover, the party may have to undergo a highly divisive and highly televised battle among its own activists in order to determine the identity of that individual. The candidates who triumph in such battles often pay a very high price for their success, they become unelectable. They may very well have been discredited as potential presidents by the divisive nature of the same campaigns that led to their nominations. By the time the opposition parties concluded their nominations in these three elections and finally took the field to face the incumbents, the opposition's best opportunities for victory had passed.

An important contributing factor in the divisiveness of the opposition party's campaign, and which occurred in the three elections discussed here, is that the party may not have resolved the internal divisions that contributed to its defeat in the preceeding election. The opposition party had fallen from power four years earlier because it had failed to alleviate some of the more pressing problems the nation faced at the time. This fall was accompanied by a bitter power struggle among the party's activists that developed as a consequence of those policy failures. Two antagonistic factions fought one another for control of the party and eventually extended their disputes into the next election.

Historically, American parties have been broad-based coalitions of diverse and sometimes contradictory interests whose primary goal has been to seek control of government. They are not well suited to emulate European parliamentary democracy where ideologically distinct parties advance policy agendas and exert sufficient discipline over their elected officeholders to implement those agendas. The constitutional doctrines of federalism and separation of powers, including state control of election laws, divide the institutions of American government among so many centers of power and create so many political subdivisions that no one party can realistically hope to take complete control of and enact its agenda among the many governments within the nation.

American parties specialize in contesting elections and in staffing and organizing government. In fulfilling these roles, parties appeal to a wide variety of voters from many different constituencies in the hope of winning as many elections as possible. Their appeals vary across political subdivisions and contribute to the creation of diverse and contradictory coalitions whose members may disagree with one another about a wide variety of issues. Public officials elected by such coalitions may reflect those disagreements. While these coalition-building strategies are often useful for contesting elections, they can create problems when a victorious party attempts to govern. The party may not always have the necessary unity among its officeholders to enact parts of its program or even to convince all of its constituency to support the program.

Intra-party factional fights tend to originate when a party controls the Presidency and erupt when the party is no longer dominated by a powerful leader. They frequently are grounded in the contradictions that exist within the diverse electoral majorities that had made past victories possible. These fights expand those contradictions to the point where unity and victory are no longer possible. Such fights are usually of limited duration since the prolonged absence of a party from power often helps diminish the intensity of its conflicts or even resolve them. The unity that makes future victories possible may not occur immediately after the party ceases to occupy the Presidency, however. The party may need some time, perhaps as long as one or more elections, to resolve its internal disputes. These fights may contribute to the political strength of incumbent presidents by making those incumbents appear more qualified than the leaders of the opposition party.

A nomination campaign involves the interplay of certain events that originate from the political context of the time with other events that derive from the needs and choices of participating actors. The context includes those influences that derive from environmental and institutional factors such as domestic or foreign conflicts or from the interests of political parties, the Presidency, and television news media. Within such contexts, individual candidates pursue those actions which they believe will enhance their chances of victory. For a divisive campaign to occur, the demands that arise from the political context and the demands that derive from the needs of the individual candidates must complement one another.

With few exceptions, most aspirants for the nomination of the opposition party are not prominent national leaders at the outset of a campaign. Many lack a constituency and must devote much of their time and resources to finding or creating one. They often seek to gain electoral advantages over their rivals by appealing to the party's antagonistic factions. Television news media respond by personifying factional fights in the speech and action of the individual candidates. This pattern of reporting makes the candidates appear mostly as divisive partisans rather than as statesmen qualified for the Presidency.

Previously, I described how television news media seek to illustrate contested nomination campaigns as struggles between two major aspirants, the front-runner and his one leading adversary. This characterization is particularly applicable within the opposition party in elections with strong incumbents. The front-runner is usually the major spokesman for one party faction while the leading adversary performs this same role for a competing group. For example, while Goldwater, McGovern, and Mondale fulfilled the roles of front-runner and leading spokesman for conservative Republicans, anti–Vietnam War activists, and establishment Democrats respectively, their leading adversaries; Nelson Rockefeller, Hubert H. Humphrey, and Gary Hart, served as the major spokesmen for such antagonistic party factions as moderate Republicans, Cold War supporters, and New Ideas Democrats. This personification of faction with candidate also helps to lengthen campaigns. In each of the three elections, the front-runners spent months fighting against the faction represented by his leading adversary. Despite the fact that each front-runner defeated his adversary in several critical primaries while clinching the nomination, he could not drive that adversary from the race until the conclusion of the national convention in July.

The incumbents used these same months as an opportunity for generating the statesmanlike imagery that contributed to their reelections. Johnson signed the historic Civil Rights law and responded, in what seemed at the time to have been a reasonable and cautious move, to difficulties in the Gulf of Tonkin. Nixon made his breakthrough trip to China in early 1972 and later signed the first Strategic Arms Limitation Treaty with the Soviet Union. Reagan dominated the agenda of television news for months with many contrived actions, with his appearances at the fortieth anniversary of D-Day in France and at the Olympic Games in Los Angeles being among his most successful endeavors.

For all intents and purposes, these three campaigns were concluded by the ends of the national conventions. Despite the vast quantities of speeches, rallies, and reporting that occurred in September, October, and the first days of November, the general election campaigns hardly seemed necessary. By mid-summer, most voters had already decided to support the incumbents for second terms. Each incumbent had developed an approximate twenty percentage point survey lead over his challenger by Labor Day and never relinquished it.

The incumbents continued using the "Rose Garden Strategy" during these final months with television news media showing much of the upbeat imagery that resulted. This reinforced the supportive attitudes that many voters had previously developed about the incumbents. Contrastively, the challengers could not escape from the disastrous imagery of their nomination campaigns. They also encountered a new problem. Television news media focused increasing attention on the horserace and emphasized the dual themes that the incumbents were ahead and winning while the challengers were trailing far behind and gaining little ground. Reporters accompanied their narratives by juxtaposing imagery of the incumbents as successful statesmen and their rivals as political failures.

Television news media employed Theodore White's formula by telling their viewers that the incumbents had passed the test of political virility and were deserving of reelection while the challengers had failed at this same endeavor and were therefore undeserving of office. Television news media served as integral parts of the efforts of strong incumbents to generate consensus in support of their reelections.

Elections with Weak Incumbents

There is a second category of television age elections in which the incumbent seeks another term of office. It includes those instances when the incumbent fails in his endeavor and is denied a second term. I name this category "elections with weak incumbents." It is comprised of three recent campaigns with the first being 1976 when Republican Gerald Ford lost to Democrat Jimmy Carter. Ford had served as President for nearly two and one-half years, a majority of the second term to which Richard Nixon had been elected. Four years later, in 1980, Carter failed to extend his own tenure beyond one term and was replaced in the Oval Office by Republican Ronald Reagan. Most recently, in 1992, Republican George Bush was denied a second term when he lost to his Democratic rival, Arkansas Governor Bill Clinton. A fourth television age election, 1968, initially involved a weak incumbent, but the embattled Democrat Lyndon B. Johnson announced in late March that he would not seek another term. Johnson's withdrawal helped turn that election into one with a surrogate incumbent, part of a category beyond the scope of this book. Nonetheless, several features of the early part of the 1968 campaign corresponded to recurring patterns usually exhibited in elections with weak incumbents. I include those features in my discussion.

As with strong incumbent elections, those with weak incumbents have a number of similarities that appear likely to recur in future years. In particular, the weak incumbent presidents, Johnson included, encountered circumstances that were virtually the mirror opposites of those faced by the strong incumbents. Each had significant political troubles at the outset of his reelection effort. None of them had effectively consolidated political power within his own party prior to the beginning of the campaign. Johnson had lost the consolidation of power that had characterized his successful reelection bid of 1964. As a consequence, all four were unable to manipulate the televised news coverage of the Presidency and of presidential election campaigns and project imagery where they appeared as statesmanlike leaders deserving of reelection. The magnitude of their troubles was reflected in the fact that each was eventually opposed for renomination by a prominent member of his own party.

Television news media responded to the challenges of these four incumbents by directing much of their attention during the nomination season to three major candidates: the incumbent, his leading adversary for the nomination, and the one aspirant who emerged, or whom they helped to emerge, as the front-runner for the nomination of the opposition party. Their reporting helped weaken the reelection prospects of the incumbents while enhancing those of the nominees of the opposition party. They directed more attention to campaign events within the presidential party than to those within the opposition and used the incumbents as the central actors for reporting and interpreting those events. This practice derived from two factors: the importance that television news media give to the Presidency as the most significant source of politically related news, and the emphasis they place upon competition and controversy when reporting about election campaigns.

Their depiction of the reelection efforts of these weak incumbents differed from their treatment of the efforts of the strong incumbents. Television news media illustrated the incumbents as embattled politicians struggling for power rather than as statesmen leading the nation. Con-trastively, their reporting of the opposition enhanced that party's electoral prospects. They directed much of their attention to the efforts of the opposing party's front-runners rather than to issues or causes that might have proven more divisive. They downplayed or even ignored the other candidates and used the front-runners as the central actors in defining and evaluating these campaigns. They also illustrated the front-runners as presidential appearing alternatives to the beleaguered incumbents. Report-ing practices such as these affected how viewers of televised politics interpreted the events of the time, evaluated the personal abilities and campaign promises of the candidates, and eventually cast votes.

The opposition party nominees who eventually defeated the weak incumbents relied on two factors in winning the Presidency. One was the apparent willingness of their own partisans to set aside past differences and unite behind candidates who held out the promise of victory. The three nominees—Carter, Reagan, and Clinton—were selected at unified na-tional conventions that occurred after what had proven to be relatively harmonious nomination campaigns. The second was that televised news coverage of the campaigns enhanced the generation of consensus within the opposition party. The candidates who initially emerged as the front-runners eventually won the nominations and went on to win the general elections.

The combination of these two factors enabled the front-runners to clinch their nominations quite early during the primary election season. Their emergence as the new leaders of their respective parties by such an early date, about the end of April if not sooner, allowed them sufficient time to generate even broader followings from among voters other than their own committed partisans. These nominees opened up substantial leads over the incumbents by the conclusions of their national conventions and did not relinquish them during the remainder of their campaigns.

The nomination campaigns within the presidential party in these three elections were the types of clear-cut and continuing struggles that televi-sion news media prefer to report. Each was a two-candidate affair from the beginning that involved a troubled and beleaguered incumbent who was challenged by a prominent spokesman from one of the party's ideological factions. Television news media encountered no difficulty in finding an available front-runner to serve as the central actor for their daily coverage and in locating his one leading adversary whom they could then depict as the antithesis of that front-runner and as the personification of his political obstacles. Of course, the incumbent easily fit into the role of front-runner and central actor for news coverage and evaluation. The one leading adversary was just as easy to identify. In each election, only one major rival opposed the incumbent for the nomination.

While the reasons for the political weaknesses of these incumbents were extensive, the factor that stands out was the lack of unity that existed within their own parties at the beginnings of these campaign years. They had been unable to consolidate power among their partisans in ways comparable to those of the strong incumbents. All three had failed to successfully employ the rhetorical and institutional powers of the modern Presidency in ways that would have united their partisans in support of their continuance in office. Instead, the presidential party of each year was bitterly divided into ideological factions that were ready for a struggle over control. Each incumbent was the leader and primary spokesman for one of the factions. As mentioned earlier, American parties are broad-based coalitions of contradictory interests. They may win the Presidency when their factions temporarily set aside their differences and unite behind a candidate who holds out the promise of victory. This unity may be super-ficial, but it is often strong enough to enable the party to win an election and to form a governing coalition. This unity sometimes fails and the party coalitions devolve into factional fighting. The factions also originate out of issues that develop when the party controls the Presidency and intensify when the incumbent can no longer unite them behind some common cause. The reasons for an incumbent's defeat do not necessarily originate during his campaign or even during his final year in office. Instead, they are often symptomatic of problems that exist at the beginning of the election year. The weak incumbent has often generated substantial oppo-sition from the general population, as seen in his low public approval ratings, and from many of his own partisans.

There is a strong chance that he will face a challenge to his nomination from a political actor of some prominence within his own party. This challenger might well be one of the most important party leaders who does not hold an office in the executive branch of the national government. He may also garner, possibly very quickly, the support of a significant block of partisans who are disenchanted with the incumbent. The challenge may be of such magnitude that the incumbent will be unable to dispense with it easily or even before the conclusion of the national convention.

Each of the three weak incumbents faced a challenge that eventually divided his party. Ronald Reagan opposed Ford for the Republican nomi-nation in 1976, Senator Edward Kennedy (Massachusetts) challenged Carter for the Democratic bid in 1980, while Pat Buchanan ran against Bush in several early primaries in 1992. Senators Robert Kennedy (New York) and Eugene McCarthy (Minnesota) opposed Johnson in the early months of 1968 before Johnson announced he would not be a candidate.

Despite the fact that these incumbents faced some very difficult political troubles, the chances they would fail to win renomination were slight. It is a monumental, perhaps impossible, task to defeat a modern incumbent president for renomination. Except perhaps for an unusual period, such as during the last weeks of the Watergate scandal, the majority of a President's own partisans rarely abandon him. This is particularly true during a renomination campaign. The public relations opportunities of televised incumbency can prove so overwhelming that any President, almost as a matter of course, enjoys significant electoral advantages over his intra-party rivals. Moreover, an incumbent's most intensive detractors rarely are his own partisans. They are usually members of the opposition party. While there may be some exceptions to this when an incumbent is in trouble, his own partisans are among the most supportive of all voters for his renomination effort. They may very well support him because they agree with his views on the issues dividing the party or because they believe he is the strongest candidate the party can advance in the general election.

Even though the obstacles were powerful and the chances of failure strong, the weak incumbents attracted important challengers. A personal justification for such a challenge is that it might prove to be the best opportunity available for the rival to become President. A weak incumbent may be a strong contender for his own party's nomination, but his chances of winning the general election are often far more questionable. If the presidential party were to nominate the incumbent, it might lose the election and thereby create a context for the next election where the Presidency would be held by a strong incumbent of the other party. If an intra-party rival did not step forward now and challenge the weak incumbent, his chances of ever winning the Presidency might well disappear. Robert Kennedy faced such a dilemma in 1967. Significant numbers of Democrats were opposed to the renomination of Lyndon Johnson and many wanted Kennedy instead. Kennedy decided against opposing Johnson because he believed his candidacy would divide the Democrats and help elect Richard Nixon. Kennedy learned that events were about to pass him by, however. Many of Johnson's detractors soon joined McCarthy's campaign. Moreover, Nixon had become the front-running Republican and potential election victor. Kennedy decided to enter the race when it became clear to him that the Johnson Presidency was over. Ronald Reagan, Edward Kennedy, and Pat Buchanan faced similar circumstances in the years of their respective challenges. It seemed apparent to them that the presidencies of Ford, Carter, and Bush were finished and that their best chances of winning the office were in the present election rather than in a future one.

The decisions by party leaders of the stature of Ronald Reagan, Edward Kennedy, and Pat Buchanan to actively oppose the incumbents virtually assured that television news media would direct much of their attention to the presidential party during the first halves of these election years. The prolonged and divisive campaigns that developed were the leading political news events of this time. Correspondents looked upon the incumbents as the central actors in these unfolding dramas. They often described the campaigns from the vantage point of an incumbent fighting for renomination against a formidable challenger who could not defeat him but whom the incumbent could not drive from the race. Moreover, they depicted the challengers as the antitheses of the incumbents and as the personifications of the obstacles the incumbent had to overcome rather than as candidates in their own right. This news emphasis on the challengers reinforced popular images about the limitations of the incumbents.

Television news media encounter the same difficulties in showing weak incumbents failing to consolidate power as they do in showing strong incumbents succeeding. Similarly, they show the aftermaths of these failures by depicting the incumbents as embattled politicians fighting for their political lives. They treat the actions, words, and travels of weak incumbents as campaign gimmicks designed for gaining competitive advantages over rivals rather than as efforts related to governing. Reporting themes of this nature deny the weak incumbents the opportunities enjoyed by their stronger counterparts for projecting statesmanlike appearing imagery. While strong incumbents frequently succeed at manipulating presidentially centered televised news into an invaluable reelection asset, weak incumbents all too often find that this same news coverage is an immense political liability. Occasionally, these incumbents generate imagery where they seem to be performing well in the statesman role, but it is usually far too inadequate for overcoming their troubles. Television news media have already stereotyped them as embattled politicians incapable of vanquishing their rivals.

After months of bitter struggle, the incumbents triumph over their challengers and secure their nominations. They have lost the battle for the general election, however. Not only are many of their partisans still opposed to them, so are most of the nation's voters. Televised news coverage of their prolonged struggles has encouraged many people to see them as ordinary politicians rather than as statesmen. They have spent so much time fighting to retain control of their own parties that they have lost the one feature of televised incumbency that is so valuable in winning second terms, the ability to project imagery where they appear as the personal leader of much of the nation.

Each of the nomination campaigns within the opposition party between 1960 and 1992 began with many contenders, and with the eventual winners not self-evident. This occurred whether the incumbent was challenged or unchallenged for renomination or if he was constitutionally ineligible for another term. Despite this similarity, the campaigns in the weak incumbent years were unusually brief. The opposition party encountered relatively little trouble in uniting behind one candidate and did so relatively early during the primary election season. The successful candidate emerged as the front-runner during the winnowing period.

Two reasons account for this early unity. First, the party had been out of power for a long enough period of time that many of the conflicts that had divided it earlier had receded or concluded. In addition, the party attracted a number of little-known candidates who avoided controversial issues in their individual quests for the nomination.

Television news media implicitly aided the party in its efforts to unite under new leaders by treating the campaigns as personal battles among individual candidates who pursued votes and convention delegates rather than the leadership of ideological factions. Most correspondents emphasized White's formula when they viewed the candidates' abilities to win primaries as political virtues qualifying them for the Presidency, while their inabilities to win were identified as political vices and personal shortcomings. They depicted the early front-runners as the candidates who possessed the requisite abilities for leading the nation and portrayed the other candidates as losing politicians unqualified for office. When public perceptions of campaigns actually develop in this manner, the constituency of the opposition party finds few reasons for supporting the losing candidates and responds by uniting behind the front-runners. These front-runners monopolized television news coverage and emerged as the inspiring new leaders who promised to take their parties directly to the White House.

Regardless of whether an incumbent is challenged for renomination, television news media begin their coverage of the opposition party's campaign by identifying the front-runner. They use this front-runner as the central actor in reporting of campaign events. The emphasis they place on the rivals of the front-runner is dependent on the existence of a challenge to the incumbent, however. In years when the incumbent is strong, television news media direct most of their primary election coverage to the campaign within the opposition party. If the incumbent is weak, they reduce their coverage of that party significantly by disregarding the front-runner's rivals or by failing to distinguish any one of them as his leading adversary. Moreover, they rarely depict any candidate as the antithesis of the front-runner and the personification of the obstacles that stand between him and the Presidency. Reporting of this nature increases voter familiarity with the front-runner while undermining the chances of his rivals. It enhances the front-runner's electoral prospects by encouraging the early departure of his rivals from the campaign and by providing him with an opportunity to project statesmanlike imagery where he appears as a qualified alternative to the troubled incumbent.

The number of aspirants who compete for a nomination influences the actions of individual candidates. In most years, nearly all candidates within the opposition party are unknown to most voters at the beginning of the campaign. Essentially, they are candidates without constituencies. They must devote a considerable amount of their time and resources to those activities that television news media like to use in depicting campaigns as horseraces; raising money, building organizations, generating name familiarity through personal appearances and media advertising, and attacking their opponents in many places and upon a wide variety of issues. Success or failure in these activities often serves as guideposts that television news media use in reporting about the campaigns and indicate the changing prospects of individual candidates. Television news media help define political realities by depicting the successes of the front-runner in the above-mentioned activities as the important tests of political leadership. Moreover, they measure the performances of the other candidates by comparing them with those of the front-runner. In response, partisan voters rarely can find any compelling reasons for supporting the failing candidates and quickly abandon them.

The post-convention campaigns in these three elections were quite similar. The incumbents trailed the challengers in public opinion surveys throughout the entire period and eventually lost. The incumbents were virtually assured of defeat because of the divisiveness of their nominations and the relative harmony of those of the opposition. They had appeared as embattled politicians rather than as statesmen through much of the year and would continue as such in the months ahead. They had already lost so much esteem with voters that their chances of victory had been severely compromised. In contrast, the challengers had used their opportunities quite effectively for projecting imagery where they appeared as qualified replacements for the incumbents. The juxtaposing of imagery of the candidates was just as vivid and far reaching in these elections as it was in those with strong incumbents, but the incumbents were the losers.

The incumbents began their post-convention quests for second terms while facing significant political divisions among their own partisans that they had not alleviated during the primary election season or even at their national conventions. In addition, a majority of the nation's voters did not want them reelected. They had only one remaining option, to convince hostile voters that their challengers would make far poorer presidents than themselves. The use of such a strategy would hopefully induce uncertain voters to oppose the challengers and reelect the incumbents. All three incumbents gained on their rivals in public opinion polls during the final weeks of their respective campaigns, but they could not discredit those challengers enough to win the election.

The challengers had problems of their own, however, and had to address them or face the distinct possibility of losing. Skeptical voters increasingly became doubtful of their promises and uncertain of their abilities as the campaigns intensified. Each challenger had begun his quest for the Presidency as simply one of many candidates in a year when a weak incumbent dominated the political news. All three emerged as the front-runners for the nominations early in the year and then projected vague imagery where they appeared to have the personal and political skills that voters expect of a President. The optimism that followed their nominations was illusory in that it was based on the euphoria that developed over the prospects of defeating a weak incumbent. The challengers had to alleviate these image problems as their standings in the polls diminished.

While many voters were skeptical about the challengers, they were still quite disenchanted with the incumbents. They were supportive enough of change that they were willing to vote for these unproven candidates if the challengers could reassure them they were at least the equals of the incumbents they sought to replace. Carter, Reagan, and Clinton made those reassurances and ended the tenure of the three weak incumbents after only one term in office.

CHAPTER 2

CLINTON BECOMES A STRONG INCUMBENT

The most important fact about the presidential election of 1996 is that Bill Clinton was a strong incumbent who won a second term by a substantial margin of votes. Moreover, Clinton led Robert Dole and all other Republican challengers in every national survey taken throughout the year. His leads were often substantial, sometimes larger than twenty percentage points, and rarely less than ten. Every major political development of the campaign—including Clinton's uncontested renomination within the Democratic Party, the conduct of the struggle for the Republican nomination, the foreign events that appeared to affect the interests of the United States, the actions and statements of the two major candidates during the seven month general election campaign, and the means by which television news media interpreted these developments and eventually reported them to their viewers—derived from this one central fact of Clinton being a strong incumbent. The election followed the script described in the previous chapter: Clinton began the campaign as a strong incumbent and then won his second term accordingly. His reelection was never in doubt during any part of 1996. It was not always that way, however. During much of 1995, and even in some parts of 1993 and 1994, many political observers found reasons to believe that Clinton would fail in his bid for a second term. His emergence as a strong incumbent by the beginning of 1996 was a phenomenon that resulted primarily from his responses to a number of political events in 1995, particularly his televised battles with congressional Republicans over Medicare and the two government shutdowns.

My purpose in this chapter is to discuss the means by which Clinton became that strong incumbent. In doing so, I review several of the leading developments that contributed to the political strength that Clinton appeared to have at the beginning of 1996. This review is not limited to a mere description of events, however. I link Clinton's political revival with the institutional and rhetorical features that characterize the modern Presidency and which now provide the television age incumbent with substantial opportunities for developing the personal and political follow-ings that make second terms possible. Television news media were affected by Clinton's strong incumbency and illustrated it to their viewers through-out the campaign. They depicted Clinton as a qualified and statesmanlike leader who deserved another term while they looked upon his rivals as little more than role-playing politicians who lacked the personal attributes of leadership that voters expect from their presidents. The campaign of 1996 was defined by three interrelated themes: (1) Clinton became a strong incumbent before the beginning of 1996, (2) television news media re-sponded to that fact in ways that were recurring and predictable, and (3) Clinton won reelection as the patterns of televised news coverage helped to generate a consensus in support of his candidacy.

This chapter contains seven sections, the first of which is this introduc-tary discussion. I begin the inquiry into the rise of Clinton's strong incum-bency with the second section which is an overview of Clinton's initial election victory and of the problems it posed for him. Clinton won the Presidency in 1992 by defeating George Bush and Ross Perot. Bush had failed in his efforts at using the opportunities of the modern Presidency in ways that would have secured his reelection. As a consequence, he entered the campaign of 1992 as a weak incumbent. Television news media re-sponded accordingly by depicting Bush as a troubled incumbent who was spending his time struggling for reelection rather than acting as a statesman leading the nation. While this was happening, they also directed much of their attention within the Democratic nomination campaign to the efforts of front-runner Bill Clinton and depicted him as a unifying leader and qualified replacement for Bush. These complementary patterns of televised news coverage provided Clinton with opportunities both for developing an insurmountable lead over Bush by the conclusion of the national conventions and for eventually winning the general election.

Clinton's victory was not particularly sweeping, as he attained only 43 percent of the popular vote in a campaign that involved three major candidates. He ran better in the Electoral College where he won 32 states and the District of Columbia and 370 votes compared to 168 votes for Bush. His popular vote showing was actually less than the 46 percent Michael Dukakis had attained in 1988.

Clinton began his Presidency with an ambitious agenda but with a very limited base of popular support. Moreover, many Republicans believed him to be an accidental President. The Republican Party had controlled the Presidency for much of the preceding quarter century and had become accustomed to viewing it as their office. The period of Republican control began with the election of Richard Nixon in 1968 and initially extended for eight years until Jimmy Carter won in 1976. It resumed in 1980 with the victory of Ronald Reagan and lasted for twelve more years until Clinton's triumph in 1992. This longevity, coupled with Clinton's 43 percent of the popular vote, convinced many Republicans that they could regain the Presidency in 1996. They were not intimidated by Clinton.

I direct attention in the third section to the first two years of Clinton's Presidency and focus on some of the difficulties that helped make him appear to be a weak incumbent by the beginning of 1995. These two years were marked by a number of controversial political struggles between Clinton and the congressional Republicans that ended with very mixed results for both Clinton and the Democrats. Clinton attained his greatest victory during these two years in August 1993 when Congress approved his budget plan that called for a substantial decline in the size of the annual deficit through tax increases and spending reductions. He attained this triumph only after months of infighting with Republican congressional leaders, and with Robert Dole in particular. His political gains from this victory did not seem apparent at the time; in fact, he was often attacked by Republicans for raising taxes. The payoff came in 1995 and 1996 when the changes that Clinton's first budget had made in federal fiscal policy contributed to strong improvements in the performance of the national economy. This improved economic performance provided the underlying foundation of support for Clinton's strong incumbency in 1996.

Clinton's greatest failure during his first term of office in 1994 was his inability to gain acceptance of an extensive health care reform program. He had proposed a massive set of changes in the nation's health care system at the beginning of 1994 and had even placed his wife Hillary at the head of the effort. Unfortunately for him, he had to spend much of the year engaging in what eventually proved to be a losing battle both with Congress and with much of the American public. By autumn, the Clinton proposal was headed toward certain defeat. He withdrew it rather than allowing it to be brought before Congress for a vote.

Clinton's first two years were also marked by a number of scandals that would not end despite the lack of evidence that directly proves Clinton's involvement in any of them. The most notorious was the failed land deal that eventually came to be known as Whitewater. Republicans believed they had finally found a scandal that could bring down a Democratic president, if not by forced resignation, at least by the political defamation of his character. The story was newsworthy at various times over several years and eventually included the appointment of a special prosecutor. In addition, Clinton had an unusual amount of difficulty in attaining Senate approval of a number of his appointments to federal administrative positions. These failed fights often undermined his popularity. Finally, the first two years of the Clinton Administration was the time when conservative talk radio hosts such as Rush Limbaugh were at their zenith in terms of influence. The daily attacks by Limbaugh and others contributed to a belief on the part of many voters that Clinton was the devious and incompetent leader of a corrupt national government.

The congressional elections of 1994 were a disaster for Clinton. The Democratic Party lost 52 seats in the House of Representatives, seven in the Senate, and majority control of both chambers. The Republicans had controlled the Senate for the first six years of Reagan's Presidency and had even reduced the Democratic majorities to only a small number of seats on several other occasions. Despite this, permanent Democratic control of the House seemed to be a fact of life in American national government. The loss of both chambers of Congress, coupled with the fact that the nation had 31 Republican governors after the elections of 1994, reduced the political holdings of the Democratic Party to little more than Clinton's Presidency. At the beginning of 1995, the Republican Congress, dominated by its leaders, Speaker Newt Gingrich and Senate Majority Leader Robert Dole, seemed poised to enact its newly proclaimed Contract With America while ignoring Clinton's goals. Clinton seemed a mere bystander in a Republican government that appeared likely to expand its control to the Presidency at its next available chance.

This election was more devastating for the Democrats than a mere change of seats would indicate. The Republican gains actually helped bring the House into line with voting trends that had been developing for a number of years and which made the partisan distribution of seats conform to national electoral patterns. The hopes by some Democrats that the Republican victory was an electoral fluke that could be undone in the next election was far too optimistic. The Republican majority in the House gave many indications that it would remain in power for years to come. I use the chapter's fourth section to discuss this Republican House victory and to show how it indicated why the Democrats may have been relegated to minority status for many years.

Clinton began 1995 by trailing Dole in several national surveys. Moreover, he had also lost control of the nation's political agenda to the Republicans and even faced the very real prospect of a bitter struggle for renomination by the Democratic Party. He managed to reverse all of this within one year, however. By the beginning of 1996 he had taken the agenda from the Republicans while successfully depicting them as mean-spirited ideological radicals who were bent on destroying the most successful features of government. In addition, he had united Democrats behind his reelection bid while the Republicans, increasingly unpopular by now, seemed likely to destroy their electoral chances during their own bitter nomination campaign. The turning points for Clinton were his battles with the congressional Republicans over Medicare and the budget. By winning these battles he entered the campaign in a much stronger political position than he appeared to have been in one year earlier. The nature of these battles, and particularly how Clinton combined the vast resources of the Presidency with televised imagery where he appeared as a solitary "tribune of the people" who stood against the Republican excesses is my theme for the fifth and sixth sections of this chapter. I direct attention in the fifth section to the battles that Clinton chose to fight with the Republicans over Medicare and other health-related issues. These battles provided Clinton with opportunities for generating imagery where he appeared as the defender of popular health care programs against the efforts to decimate them by a radical group of Republicans. Television news media were implicit allies of Clinton as they willingly transmitted his imagery to their viewers. Clinton's political recovery began at this time.

I focus the sixth section on the leading events of the two government shutdowns that occurred during the final two months of 1995 and which pitted Clinton directly against the man who would become his election adversary, Robert Dole. These events helped define the issues at stake and provided television news media with a context from which to report about the actions of Clinton and the Republicans. By the conclusion of the second shutdown in early January, television news media had developed a set of stereotypes of the principal players that they would use throughout the election year. They would depict Clinton as the strong incumbent who was qualified for a second term and Dole as the troubled Republican who stood in his way. Clinton used the shutdown period for strengthening the public support that he had attained previously during the Medicare battles.

In the final section, I raise the question of what might have occurred in 1996 if Clinton had failed in his struggles with the congressional Republicans and had become a weak and embattled incumbent instead. Here, I advance an alternative scenario of how the campaigns for the party nominations and the general election might have developed if Clinton had failed to reverse his political misfortunes. A discussion of an alternative scenario, when contrasted with the actual one, should encourage the reader to appreciate the significance of the opportunities that the institutional and rhetorical features of the modern Presidency now offer to incumbents, and to better understand how the successful use of these features by an incumbent contributed so much to the actual outcome of the election of 1996.

THE FIRST CLINTON ELECTION OF 1992

Clinton won his first term in 1992 in an election involving a weak incumbent. While the most significant historical and political fact of that election was Clinton's triumph—a fact that would eventually define the context of national leadership for the remainder of the decade—by far the most important political actor during the course of the campaign was George Bush, not Bill Clinton. The incumbent, even if he fails in his quest for another term, is always the most important actor in any television age presidential election. This is true because of the central role that the Presidency plays in setting the nation's political agenda and because of the tendency of television news media to direct much of their politically related reporting toward the actions and statements of the incumbent.

The reasons for the fall of the Bush Presidency are far beyond the scope of this book. Instead, I direct attention to how that fall affected the context of the 1992 campaign and the Clinton victory that marked it. One symptom of Bush's weaknesses was the strong challenge he encountered from conservative commentator Pat Buchanan in five primary elections, including New Hampshire. Buchanan was unable to defeat Bush in any of those primaries, but he did expose the very significant fact that large numbers of Republicans were unhappy with Bush's performance. Bush won in New Hampshire but he attained only 53 percent of the vote compared to the 37 percent acquired by Buchanan. One can see the critical nature of Bush's showing by comparing it with that of Lyndon Johnson in 1968. Johnson won the New Hampshire primary by defeating anti-war candidate

Eugene McCarthy by a margin of 49 percent to 42, but that outcome encouraged Robert Kennedy to announce his own candidacy and quickly convinced Johnson to decline another term. Bush had done little better than Johnson. Following this promising showing in the initial primary of the year, Buchanan acquired between 30 and 36 percent of the vote in the four primaries that followed, those in South Dakota, Maryland, Colorado, and Georgia. While Buchanan had not won in any state, he had averaged about one-third of the vote in those where he had competed. Moreover, the states were not concentrated in one locale but were instead distributed throughout the nation and included places in New England, the Great Plains, the Mid-Atlantic, the Southeast, and the Rocky Mountains. These results indicated that a large number of Republicans wanted someone other than George Bush as their nominee. This message was not lost on Ross Perot who thereafter entered the campaign, although as a third-party candidate rather than Republican.

The Buchanan challenge to Bush did not last much longer than the five primaries mentioned above. In fact, Buchanan soon withdrew from the campaign entirely and endorsed Bush, although he managed to inflict some fairly heavy damage on Bush's effort with his divisive convention speech about the existence of a cultural war within the nation. Despite his withdrawal, Buchanan attained more than twenty percent of the vote in several of the remaining primaries. Television news media responded to Buchanan's candidacy by focusing their attention on his efforts and by defining the battle for the Republican nomination as a two-man struggle with both candidates performing in stereotypical roles. Bush was the embattled incumbent and Buchanan was his leading, or in this case only, adversary. The news coverage was often vivid and contrasting with Buchanan often shown directing his comments at alleged failures by Bush, including the poor condition of the New Hampshire economy. The campaign drew televised news attention to the major shortcomings of the Bush Presidency.

While the Buchanan effort actually ended after only a few primaries, television news media did not respond to that development by suddenly depicting Bush as a unifying leader or even as the eventual Republican nominee. They were not yet ready to focus on the general election phase of campaign 1992. Instead, they continued treating Bush as if he was a candidate in pursuit of a contested nomination. Perot soon replaced Buchanan in the televised role of leading adversary of the front-runner. For several weeks during the latter primaries and early weeks of summer, television news media downplayed the Democratic campaign and its candidates and focused on an imagined battle between Bush and Perot. They reported about the troubles of the Bush Presidency and then followed by illustrating Perot as Bush's leading critic. This pattern ended during the first days of July, which was shortly before the Democratic National Convention. At that time television news media altered their coverage and began depicting all of the remaining candidates as involved in the general election part of the campaign. Bush was finally the candidate of the Republican Party and actually seemed to be facing a Democratic challenger as his major rival.

The news emphasis on Bush, Buchanan, and Perot affected the campaign for the Democratic nomination. Television news media are fairly consistent over a number of elections in the amount of broadcast time they devote to campaign events. Their coverage differs between elections in the themes they use and in their distributions of time between the campaigns of the presidential and opposition parties. The opposition party attains less televised news coverage in the years when an incumbent is opposed for renomination than in those years when he is not. While this may appear unfortunate, it often proves to be a valuable political asset for the party and its nominee for the reasons discussed previously in chapter 1. This was the nature of Clinton's nomination campaign in 1992.

Clinton was one of six candidates for the nomination of a party that had lost three consecutive elections and five of the past six. The campaign started slowly and had very little activity until the latter months of 1991. There were two reasons for this slow beginning, one being the apparent popularity of Bush after the Persian Gulf War. The second was that several leading Democrats, particularly Richard Gephardt, Albert Gore, Mario Cuomo, and Jesse Jackson, did not run. Bush registered an approval rating of 88 percent in the Gallup Poll in March, 1991, the highest figure for any President since the Poll was established in the 1930's. This standing led many Democrats to hesitate about opposing him since they wondered if he was unbeatable. In addition, candidates like the four mentioned above would probably have overshadowed others and would have left few opportunities for them to even compete. By late summer, 1991, Bush's popularity had declined substantially as voters started focusing their attention on economic issues. The decisions by well-known Democrats against running made the nomination seem far more inviting. The candidates who finally emerged were Clinton, who was the governor of Arkansas, Senators Tom Harkin (Iowa) and Robert Kerrey (Nebraska), former Senator Paul Tsongas (Massachusetts), former governor Jerry Brown (California), and Governor

Douglas Wilder (Virginia). Wilder's campaign failed and he withdrew from the race in early January 1992.

There was no obvious front-runner for the Democratic nomination at the outset of the campaign, so television news media attempted to create one. The objective indicators of fundraising or poll standings were not particularly helpful. No candidate had raised significantly more money than any of the others nor had any taken command in the polls. With the exception of Brown, most were generally unknown to much of the American public. Television news media found a front-runner nevertheless, and it was Bill Clinton. While Clinton had not actually assumed the lead in any of the indicators mentioned above, he had suggested in other ways that he had a better chance of winning than his rivals. He had attained the endorsements of more governors than any other candidate, a result related to the fact that he had recently chaired the National Governors Conference. Moreover, he described himself as a moderate, "new" Democrat and was a leader of the Democratic Leadership Council. This organization was comprised of officeholders, often Southern, who believed the national Democratic Party was far too liberal and needed to become less so in order to win the Presidency. They wanted an ideological moderate and believed they had found such a candidate in Clinton. The combination of these factors soon encouraged a number of political observers from mass media to conclude that Clinton was the "most likely to succeed" of the Democratic aspirants.

The campaign expanded in both intensity and televised news coverage at the beginning of January. Television news media began focusing far more attention on Clinton at this time as he contested the New Hampshire primary. The first electoral test of recent election campaigns has been the Iowa caucuses, but they were irrelevant in 1992 because of Harkin's candidacy. Since none of the candidates had any desire to compete with Harkin in his home state, the New Hampshire primary became the first electoral prize of the year. Hardly had Clinton emerged in the media-defined role of front-runner, and this designation occurred before any votes had actually been cast, than he found himself in a scandal that threatened to destroy his candidacy before it even started. A supermarket tabloid, the Star, carried a story where a Little Rock nightclub entertainer, Gennifer Flowers, claimed she had engaged in a twelve-year sexual affair with Clinton. This affair had occurred when Clinton was Governor of Arkansas, Flowers claimed.

Whether an alleged scandal such as this could destroy the prospects of a presidential candidate is problematic. However, Clinton was particularly vulnerable because most voters knew very little about him. Sometimes voters support candidates who may be involved in scandals but they need to have some good reasons for doing so, such as strong records compiled by the candidates through many years in office. As a newcomer to national politics, Clinton had no such record. In a response to the charges, Clinton and his wife Hillary appeared on a special telecast of the CBS newsmagazine 60 Minutes. Their interview took place immediately after the conclusion of the Super Bowl football game of January 26, which had been shown on CBS that year. Since the Super Bowl is the most watched television program of any given year, the Clintons had an excellent audience for their interview.

The appearance was an immediate success. Not only had Clinton assured viewers that he had done nothing wrong, he also gained public respect by the strong personal backing provided by Mrs. Clinton. Television news media soon lost interest in the scandal, but continued depicting Clinton as the central actor in the nomination drama. There is another aspect to the story, however, for Clinton did far more than simply deny improper behavior. He had effectively used this opportunity to present himself, and his wife, favorably to the nation. For all intents and purposes, 60 Minutes served as the introduction of the Clintons to America. Many people saw and heard them for the first time that evening and were impressed. By way of an anecdote, sometimes I ask students in my classes if any of them had watched the interview. The majority say yes. I then inquire if they had seen or heard of the Clintons before that evening. Very few answer yes.

With respect to its effect on the final outcome of the election, Clinton's 60 Minutes appearance was equivalent to Richard Nixon's "Checkers" speech of 1952. Nixon had hardly been nominated for Vice President when a scandal developed regarding a "slush fund" that wealthy California businessmen had allegedly provided him. The existence of the fund suggested that Nixon had been accepting bribes. There were calls for Eisenhower to drop him from the Republican ticket. In what turned out to be an effective and fitting response, Nixon denied the charges in a nationally televised address and persuaded his audience that he had done nothing wrong. The outpouring of support for Nixon was extensive and convinced Eisenhower to keep him on the ticket. Moreover, Nixon also used this opportunity to reintroduce himself to the nation. While he had gained substantial notoriety at the Republican convention, he had also been overshadowed by Eisenhower. Nixon now had an unusual opportunity of his own to appeal directly to the nation's voters without sharing the stage with Eisenhower. Without his effective use of television, Nixon quite likely would have been politically finished at that time. The same appears true for Clinton.

Clinton attained 25 percent of the vote in the February 18 New Hampshire primary and finished second to Tsongas who had 33 percent. Clinton labeled himself as the "Comeback Kid" with this performance. The struggle for the nomination lasted less than two months after this initial vote and was frequently overshadowed by the events within the Republican Party. The various candidates divided the victories in the next four prima-ries among themselves with no one gaining a particular advantage. The outcomes often depended on the amount of time and money that a given candidate devoted to a particular state. Clinton won Georgia, Tsongas took Maryland, Kerrey and Harkin finished first and second in South Dakota, while Clinton, Tsongas, and Brown divided the Colorado vote and that state's delegates about evenly among themselves. The outcomes changed rapidly after this, however, as Clinton won the primaries of the major states by fairly substantial margins. He captured the primaries in Texas and Florida on March 9 and won Michigan and Illinois one week later, all by majority votes. Within days of the latest victories, all of his rivals except Brown had withdrawn. Clinton ended any hopes that Brown might have had on April 6 when he won the New York primary, also with a majority vote. While Brown continued his candidacy until the national convention met in mid-July, his chances were over. Television news media responded accordingly by generally ignoring him after the New York vote.

The televised news coverage of this Democratic campaign conformed with those that characterize elections when a weak incumbent is chal-lenged within his own party. Television news media began their reporting by declaring Clinton as the front-runner and then focused much of their attention on him as the central actor in the ongoing battle. They assigned the remaining candidates to stereotypical roles where those candidates appeared as little more than obstacles that stood between Clinton and the nomination. Since each candidate was losing the horserace to Clinton, television news media kept emphasizing Clinton as the front-runner; consequently, not one of the candidates was able to advance any strong arguments to Democratic voters of why they should support them instead of Clinton. As a result, Clinton soon united his partisans around the general theme that he was the one candidate who could return them to the White House, a goal that had eluded them for twelve years.

The national convention was one of unusual harmony for the Demo-crats, a consequence of their optimistic prospects for an election victory.

Clinton was the overwhelming winner of the nomination, attaining nearly 4,000 delegate votes on the first and only ballot with only a few hundred cast for Brown. His choice of Gore for Vice President was well received by Democratic and Independent voters alike as was the highly publicized bus trip from New York to St. Louis that the Clintons and Gores took shortly afterwards. By now, Clinton was projecting a public image where he appeared as a qualified and capable alternative to the weak incumbent Bush. He also looked like a winner during these latter days of July as he led Bush in the Gallup Poll by a margin of 54 percent to 39 percent.

There was a major problem for Clinton as he began the campaign against Bush, however, and it was one that could well have led to his eventual defeat. His unification of the Democrats had been impressive, but there had been a distinct shallowness to it. As discussed in the previous chapter, the nominee of an opposition party that has not held the Presidency for several terms tends to unite his diverse partisans on general and contradictory themes that mostly hold out the promise of victory. While many voters may be euphoric about this new leader in July, they often become apprehensive about him as the campaign advances and start doubting whether he is worthy of their support. Unless Clinton could address those doubts, he ran the risk of losing. Such had been the fate of Michael Dukakis in 1988. Dukakis emerged as a new and unifying leader of the Democrats during the primary election campaign and held a substantial lead over Bush in the July polls. He proclaimed his campaign was about competence, not ideology. Aggressive advertising efforts by Bush, including a number of charges that Dukakis failed to address, convinced many people that the Dukakis campaign was about ideology, not competence. The Dukakis lead was gone by September and did not return. Clinton needed to avoid this fate.

Clinton devoted most of the last weeks of the campaign to various efforts aimed at avoiding a repeat of the Dukakis disaster. He promptly answered any charges that Bush threw at him and continued emphasizing the theme of change during his strong performances in the nationally televised debates. In addition, he gained some support because of voter unease over the vitriolic attitudes toward cultural differences that Buchanan and Marilyn Quayle had expressed in speeches at the Republican convention. Bush was also hurt by Perot who often attacked him rather than Clinton and who acquired the support of more conservatives and Republicans than of liberals and Democrats. Despite all of this, Clinton's July poll lead of fifteen points diminished to less than six by election day. Nonetheless, he led Bush through the entirety of the last five months of the campaign and won with

43 percent of the vote compared to the 37 percent for Bush. His promises were still quite general at the conclusion of the campaign, however, with an often undefined call for change being foremost among them. Clinton's vague promises would raise some significant problems for him during the next two years and would contribute to his low popularity at the beginning of 1995.

CLINTON'S FIRST TWO YEARS

Clinton engaged congressional Republicans in a number of significant political battles during his first two years in office while relying on the Democratic majorities in both chambers of Congress. The most important battle of 1993 involved the budget while the leading one of 1994 was over health care reform. Robert Dole served as Clinton's major Republican adversary each time.

The budget was by far the most contentious issue that Clinton and the Republicans clashed over during the first Clinton term and it was the one issue that contributed the most to Clinton's subsequent reelection. Budgetary battles between the President and Congress are not new for they have occurred since the beginnings of American government. They have been far more intense since 1973, however. For several decades after the end of the Second World War, budgeting was usually an incremental activity that included almost none of the points of contention that became so pervasive during the 1980s and 1990s. The United States underwent a period of sustained economic growth that stretched from approximately 1947 until 1973. Government revenues also increased sharply during this time and provided a foundation by which the various departments could enjoy and expect annual increases in their appropriations. Quite frequently, the budgetary process involved a practice where the participants would assume the legitimacy of a "base" and then make some slight, or incremental, additions to it. A base is "the expectation that the expenditure will continue, that it is accepted as part of what will be done, and, therefore, that it will normally not be subjected to intensive scrutiny" (Wildavsky and Caiden 1997, 46). The oil embargos of 1973 and the extensive debt that the Johnson and Nixon administrations had incurred in fighting the Vietnam War contributed to some far-reaching changes in the American economy during the 1970s and in the decades that followed. These changes also helped undermine the incremental budgetary processes that had dominated the national government and moved the battles over the levels of federal taxing and spending into the forefront of national politics.

In 1974 Congress passed a new law known as the Budget and Impound-ment Control Act. This law, amended since that time, designates the various steps and procedures that now occur in the annual budget process. It is important for the reader to understand the major points in this law in order to better comprehend and appreciate the significance of the budget-ary battles that occurred between 1993 and 1996 and which contributed to Clinton's reelection. With this in mind, I briefly digress from presidential politics in order to summarize those major points.

The first step in budgeting that involves either of the two major institutions of the national government, that is, the President and Con-gress, is preparation. Preparation is the legal responsibility of the President and is carried out by the Office of Management and Budget (OMB). As the reader may remember from chapter 1, the OMB is a significant part of the institutional apparatus that has contributed to the expansion of presi-dential power over the past few decades. In today's budget process, each organizational entity within the federal government receives instructions from the OMB relating to budgetary preparation. These instructions take such matters as the current levels of spending, new legal requirements that must take effect, the changing conditions of the economy, and the Presi-dent's political agenda into consideration. The organizations, that is, the many departments, agencies, commissions and so forth, that comprise the executive branch of the government then prepare their requests for funding and submit them to the OMB. The OMB holds hearings with these organizations in order to arrive at final requests that correspond to the President's fiscal and political goals. In addition to helping reduce the costs of government, this examining process also serves to enhance the power of the President over the management of the executive branch. No govern-mental organization can make independent requests for funding directly to Congress and none can seek changes in existing laws without prior approval, or central clearance as it is called, from the OMB. The OMB, as we know, is not a politically neutral entity that objectively reviews plans for taxing and spending but is instead an integral component of the modern presidency. It seeks to advance the political goals of the President and attempts to force the rest of the executive branch to conform to those goals.

With the assistance of the OMB, the President prepares and then finally sends a proposed budget to Congress during the first week of February of each year. The President's budget estimates the levels of governmental revenue and required spending for programs such as Social Security and requests funding for other more discretionary programs. The estimates and requests within this budget are for the following fiscal year but include projections for the next five years. The fiscal, that is, budgetary, year differs from the calendar year in that it begins on October 1 rather than on January 1. Moreover, the correct dating for any fiscal year is its ending. The budget that Clinton submitted to Congress in early 1993 was to take effect on October 1, 1993 and was for fiscal 1994.

The Congress assigns the President's budget to two new committees that were established by the 1974 law, the House and the Senate Budget Committees. These committees have the responsibility to write the Congressional Budget Resolution and to then submit it for debate, amendment, and eventual adoption by the House and Senate. The Resolution does not actually raise or spend any money, it merely estimates the amounts that might be raised and sets limits on what can be spent. It establishes annual spending limits for twenty different individual categories of public policy including national defense, Medicare, administration of justice, transportation, interest on the debt, etc., and sets a grand total for all federal spending. Once passed, the Resolution is supposed to bind the budgetary actions of Congress but it is not a law since it is not sent to the President for his signature. Since the Resolution is also a political matter, it is subjected to significant political debate. Usually, the President and his supporters have their version while the leaders of the opposition party have theirs. This leads to partisan and institutional battles with neither side able to impose its version. The Budget Resolution that finally passes is often the version preferred by the congressional majority party. This majority was the Democratic Party in 1993 and 1994 and the Republican Party during 1995 and 1996.

After the completion of work on the Budget Resolution, Congress moves into the committee stage of its activities. Each of the approximately forty standing committees of Congress focuses on certain assigned parts of the budget and writes the legislation that governs taxing or spending within those parts. The final legislation of each committee must not exceed the maximum numbers of the Budget Resolution. As an example of how this works, the Resolution for fiscal 1996 set $261.424 billion as the maximum spending for national defense. The committees with jurisdiction over the defense budget had to develop legislation that would not allow spending beyond that predetermined amount. Since the sum of all proposals for defense spending was greater than that number, the committees had to propose some reductions in order to conform to the totals of the Budget Resolution. Of course, any changes are political and lead to yet more disputes between the participants.

The final stage of the budget process, reconciliation, is a new one that was created in 1974. In this stage, the two budget committees advance several changes in existing laws that force the taxing and spending allowed by those laws to conform, that is, reconcile, with the maximum totals of the Budget Resolution. Sometimes, a Reconciliation Act can make hundreds of changes in existing laws and can require some important compromises from the various participants. The Reconciliation Act that was finally adopted in late 1990 required George Bush to agree to several increases in taxes, and to thereby violate his 1988 campaign statement of "read my lips, no new taxes," while the Democrats, led by House Budget chairman Leon Panetta, agreed to some reductions in spending. This agreement was a contributing factor in the disenchantment that many Republicans had with Bush when he sought reelection two years later. The most significant budgetary fight that Clinton would have with the Republicans in Congress, and with Dole, was over reconciliation in 1993.

Clinton began his first term with an immediate need to respond to the difficult problems of massive annual deficits and the increasing national debt. To some extent, both of these problems derived from the fiscal policies implemented by the Reagan administration. In 1981, Reagan secured the congressional approval of some taxing and spending measures that eventually contributed to a significant increase in the size of the deficit. One important measure, the Kemp-Roth Bill, enacted the concept of "supply-side economics." The advocates of this concept sought to expand economic growth by stimulating the producer side with large tax cuts for higher income people and with a reduction in the costs and demands of federal regulation. These higher income people, in turn, would respond by investing their additional monies in new business enterprises which would lead to the creation of more jobs and opportunities. This concept differed from that of "demand side economics" which had been the policy of recent Democratic administrations. In this latter approach, government stimulated growth by creating more demand through expanded governmental purchases and social welfare spending.

While these tax changes did stimulate growth, they also reduced the revenue of the federal government by several hundred billion dollars over the remaining years of Reagan's Presidency. This latter consequence, when coupled with the spending policies of the Reagan Administration, created some significant problems for Reagan's two immediate successors, Bush and Clinton. Reagan was unwilling to bring about any reductions in government spending proportionate to the reductions in revenue. He managed to enact some fairly widespread spending reductions concerning social services, transportation, education, and a number of other domestic matters, but state and local governments absorbed most of these reductions with increased spending of their own. With respect to the federal budget, however, the reductions in domestic spending were offset by significant increases in defense spending. Reagan wanted to expand the size and readiness of the armed forces and both develop and procure high technology weapons and communications systems. Moreover, he was unwilling to support spending reductions on entitlement programs such as Social Security, Medicare, and Medicaid. The costs of these programs were increasing at rates far greater than the corresponding growth of inflation or population and were giving few signs of slowing in the immediate future.

While the shift from domestic to military spending was substantial, the overall spending by the federal government did not decline during the Reagan years. It was revenue that declined. Reagan's taxing and spending policies eventually brought about large annual deficits and rapidly increasing interest payments. One can see an indication of the size of the problem in the growth of the federal debt during the Reagan and Bush years. This debt, the total of all accumulated annual deficits, was slightly less than $1 trillion at the end of the Carter Administration but had increased to approximately $4 trillion by the conclusion of the Bush Presidency. A debt of this magnitude also meant that a larger portion of the budget of each succeeding year would be used for interest payments, thus reducing available funding for other policies. With this in mind, the deficit had already become a significant political issue even before Reagan left the White House. Adherents of the two leading American ideologies, liberalism and conservatism, opposed the large deficits and wanted them reduced but for different reasons. Liberals were angry because large deficits meant fewer available funds for new initiatives or expansions in existing government programs. Conservatives were dismayed because the higher interest rates that came from a growing deficit weakened private sector economic growth.

The Gramm-Rudman-Hollings Act of 1986 was one of the first congressional attempts to address the deficit problem. It was designed to bring about automatic spending cuts if the deficit during any particular year was larger than a predetermined figure. Two different versions of this law were eventually enacted, but neither proved effective at reducing the deficit, primarily because they exempted so much of the budget from the cuts. A different approach occurred in 1990 and resulted in the tax increases that George Bush had promised to oppose. This did not work either as the deficit increased to $291 billion by the time Clinton became President. There were some forecasts that it might become even larger.

Clinton made the deficit problem his major priority during his first year in office. With the assistance of the OMB, he developed a proposal for deficit reduction that would include some reductions in spending but which also included substantial increases in the taxes of higher income people. This proposal contradicted Reagan's tax cutting strategy and thereby generated substantial opposition from congressional Republicans. Clinton's proposal would reduce the deficit by approximately $500 billion over five years and was the central component of his economic plan. The showdown came in August, 1993, in the reconciliation part of the budget process. Clinton sought to enact his program through the statutory changes that accompany reconciliation rather than by relying on specific legislation addressed to tax codes and the authorizations of government programs.

The Republicans opposed Clinton's initiatives, partly because of their ideology, and partly in the hopes that his failure to enact them would force Clinton into negotiations with their party's leaders. The Democrats had majorities in both chambers of Congress, 256 to 178 in the House and 56 to 44 in the Senate. Straight party line votes would assure the passage of the Clinton program. There was a problem with this assumption, however. The Democratic Party was not very cohesive since a substantial minority of its elected officials did not agree with Clinton. While they had united in order to elect Clinton, Democrats could not necessarily unite in order to pass a budget. If the Republican leaders could unite their partisans in opposing Clinton's proposals, they could, with the help of enough Democrats, defeat them. After losing, Clinton would then have little choice but to develop a new budget far more acceptable to Republicans and which would weaken or eliminate his proposed tax increases. The Republican strategy almost worked. Even though every Republican voted no, Clinton found enough Democratic support to win. The House acted first and passed the proposal by a thin margin of 218 to 216. The Senate action that followed was even closer, with Gore breaking a 50–50 tie.

While there are many factors that encourage economic growth and deficit reduction, one important political fact stands out. The Clinton program helped reduce the deficit to only $109 billion in 1996, far below its levels during the latter Bush years. Moreover, the economy was growing rapidly during 1996 and this was a contributing factor in Clinton's reelection. The first battle of the election of 1996 had been fought in August, 1993, with Bill Clinton the clear winner and with Robert Dole the definite loser.

The most important confrontation between Clinton and the Republicans in 1994 involved health care. In early 1993 Clinton announced his intentions of seeking fundamental changes in the nation's health care payment structure. He created a commission, chaired by Hillary Clinton, to draft the administration's proposal. Afterwards, he used part of his 1994 State of the Union Address to place health care at the center of the national political agenda. The rapidly escalating costs of Medicare and Medicaid was the heart of the problem. Medicare, a major part of Social Security, is paid through a federal payroll tax and is used by the elderly. Medicaid, administered by the states, is paid for by the federal and state governments with the federal share coming from income taxes and the states' shares from varieties of taxes: it is designed for low income people. Today, its major use is for nursing homes for the elderly and for people on public assistance. Some of the major factors that account for the cost increases is that life expectancy is longer than it was when the two programs were created, new medical technology is expensive to develop and operate, and governments and insurance companies directly pay most health care costs. This last practice discourages price containment efforts. Medicare cost about $178 billion and Medicaid $96 billion in 1996.

A related problem is the approximately 35 million people without health insurance. These people often obtain their medical care in hospital emergency rooms with providers then passing the costs on to the general public in the form of higher fees. The public often carries the financial burdens for the uninsured through higher insurance costs.

While Clinton's plan provided one means of addressing these problems, it eventually failed. Opposition was so powerful that Clinton finally abandoned his efforts without even seeking a congressional vote. The plan was massive in both size and complexity and was not well understood by much of the public. Its most prominent opponent, the insurance industry, also feared the loss of its influence over health care. After several months of televised attack advertising, unfavorable political commentary, and poor performances by the news media in reporting the nature of the proposals (Fallows 1997, 205–234), much of the public opposed Clinton's ideas. Many people were now convinced they would have to pay higher taxes or would have fewer health care choices.

Dole defeated Clinton in this confrontation. He often attacked the actual or perceived weaknesses of the Clinton plan without necessarily offering an alternative. He also manipulated the public fear that often accompanies proposed changes in the status quo. Unlike the budget battle of the previous year, this time the united Republican opposition worked in

Dole's favor. Clinton could not convince enough of his majority Democrats to provide him with yet another narrow victory. His extensive losses among Democrats doomed his plan to certain defeat. The Republican payoff came just a few weeks later when they won control of both chambers of Congress for the first time since 1954. Their electoral triumph encouraged them to believe that Clinton would be limited to only one term. There was another aspect to the strategy of manipulating voter fears over health care, however. It was not the exclusive property of Dole and the Republicans. Clinton would use it against them the next year, and he would do so with an equally devastating effect.

THE REPUBLICAN VICTORY OF 1994

Clinton's worst political setback during his first term was the Democratic loss of Congress in 1994. It effectively ended any chance that he could enact an agenda. Instead, he was reduced to the role of fighting against the initiatives of the Republican congressional majority. The House version of that majority began 1995 by advancing a ten point plan it called the Contract With America. At its heart, this plan advocated a major reduction in the activities of the federal government to be accomplished by significant reductions in taxing, spending, and regulations.

I attribute the Democratic loss to a combination of two factors that came together at the same time, the low opinion that the public held of Clinton during the last months of 1994, and the steady development of the Republican Party into a national majority over a period of several decades. With respect to the first, Clinton must bear some of the responsibility for the Democratic disaster. He had begun his Presidency with the strong public support that usually greets a new chief executive. The initial Gallup Poll measurement of his approval, taken one week after his inauguration, indicated that 58 percent of respondents approved of his performance as President while only 20 percent disapproved. While these numbers were probably inflated because of the tendency of many voters to give a new President a "honeymoon" for several months, Clinton did garner strong approval ratings throughout most of his first eighteen months in office. He eventually suffered some setbacks during 1993 and his approval declined to only 39 percent, with 50 percent disapproving, by June 21. Clinton's setbacks derived from his unsuccessful battle relating to gays in the armed forces and to a number of failed nomination battles with Congress. However, he regained his earlier levels of support after his August budget victory and his subsequent triumph with NAFTA, the North American Free Trade

Agreement. The Gallup Poll of October 10th indicated that 50 percent approved of his performance while 42 percent disapproved. These numbers remained consistent for about one year, as they totaled 51 percent approval, 42 percent disapproval, on May 22, 1994. Clinton could no longer sustain them after that time.

Clinton's declining popularity was apparent in the Gallup Poll of September 7, as only 39 percent approved of his performance while 54 percent did not. This was the worst showing that Clinton recorded in this poll during his entire first term, and it occurred only two months before the 1994 elections. Clinton recovered no support during the remainder of the year as his approval was only 40 percent, with 52 percent disapproving, on December 30. Throughout the twentieth century, every congressional election in a non-presidential year, except for 1934, resulted in a loss of seats in the House of Representatives by the presidential party. The forecast for 1994 was the same, the Democrats could expect to lose some seats. The Democrats had the additional political misfortune in 1994 of contesting the elections with an unpopular national leader, however, and they would pay the price.

The Republican Party attempted to make the elections a referendum on Clinton's performance, including that of his ill-fated health care plan. They also used it to affirm their "contract" in which they sought to reduce the size and scope of government. It is a rare circumstance when congressional elections actually assume national significance, for the outcomes of most seats are decided by local issues and actors. This view, perhaps best expressed by former House Speaker Tip O'Neill as "all politics is local," does not seem to have applied in 1994 as the Republicans recorded one of the most one-sided victories of the twentieth century. The Republicans gained control of the Senate by winning seven seats, thereby increasing their numbers from 44 to 51 seats. This was not a particularly unusual result if one considers the trend within the Senate over the past two decades, however. Previously, the Republicans gained twelve seats in 1980 when Reagan won his first term. Those gains expanded the Republican seats from 41 to 53 and began what would eventually become six years of Republican control of that chamber. The Democrats rebounded in 1986, gained eight seats, and acquired control for what proved to be an eight year period. The Republican Senate gains of 1994 were smaller than those of either of these two earlier elections.

The great electoral change of 1994 occurred in the House, and this change is the topic to which we now turn. The distinguishing characteristic of American government during the quarter century between 1968 and

1992 was the consistent division of institutional control between the two political parties. The Republicans were the presidential party during much of this time as they won five of six elections. Their only setback was in 1976 in an election influenced by the Watergate scandal. The Democrats were the party of the House as they constantly controlled that chamber, often by overwhelming majorities, despite occasional election years such as 1980 that favored Republicans. The Democrats won control of the House in 1930 and maintained it until 1946. They regained their majority in 1948, held it until 1952, and reinstated it in 1954 for forty consecutive years. The Democrats had maintained their majorities in the House for sixty of the sixty-four years preceding 1994. It was indeed their chamber.

The House was the scene of some of the most significant budget battles between Republican Presidents Nixon, Ford, Reagan, and Bush and the Democratic Congress. This fact was a consequence of the Republican domination of the Presidency and Democratic control of the House. In contrast, the Senate frequently served as the mediator between these two institutions since it was less likely to be dominated by one party. Reagan scored his most significant budgetary victory in 1981 when the House enacted the Gramm-Latta Bill, a Republican version of the Budget Resolution which contained reconciliation language. The Democrats' greatest budgetary victory before Clinton's Presidency came in the House in 1990 when they forced Bush to accept several tax increases in order to reduce the size of the deficit. The Democratic control of both the House and the Presidency in 1993 was a major factor in explaining Clinton's successes in attaining the enactment of his economic and budget proposals during his first year in office. It was this recent history as the institutional foundation of Democratic Party power that made the Republican takeover of the House in 1994 so significant.

It is my contention that the outcome of the 1994 House elections was more than simply a short-term reaction to the presidential performance of Bill Clinton, although that was certainly a strong contributing factor. Some important long-term trends also affected the results. The Democratic power in the House had been based on voting patterns that were unusual from those of other elections. A substantial number of Democratic House members had represented districts that often voted Republican for other political offices. A number of explanations have been raised for this phenomenon, including the argument that incumbents now possess so many electoral advantages that personnel changes in the House are likely to be infrequent regardless of the outcomes of other elections. House members often strengthen their electoral prospects by using redistricting as a means of creating favorable boundaries; by commanding greater media attention and special interest contributions than their challengers; and by acquiring choice committee assignments and leadership positions which give them vast opportunities for building personal followings that extend far beyond those of their fellow partisans. The combination of these advantages often makes House incumbents difficult to defeat. Since the House had been Democratic for so many years already, these advantages of incumbency may well have helped to perpetuate that Democratic control during an age of candidate-centered campaigns.

One can see an indication of the unusual strength of House Democrats before the election of 1994 in the data exhibited in Table 2.1. This table divided the 435 districts into three categories based on the voting patterns of those districts in the presidential elections of 1988 and 1992. The district boundaries used are those that were in effect in 1994. Republican districts supported George Bush in the elections of 1988 and 1992 while Democratic districts voted for the two Democratic candidates, Michael Dukakis and Bill Clinton, in those same elections. Mixed districts voted for a Republican in one election and a Democrat in the other. With the exception of one Iowa district that voted for Dukakis in 1988 and Bush in 1992, all mixed districts voted for Bush in 1988 and Clinton in 1992.

This table indicates that a strong relationship existed in the presidential voting preferences of most districts. A total of 314 districts, or 72 percent, supported the same party in the elections of 1988 and 1992. In addition, the table indicates that each party dominated the seats in the districts where its presidential candidates ran strongest. Democrats were particu-

Table 2.1

Partisan Distribution of Congressional Districts prior to the 1994 Election by Presidential Election Results

	Republican Held Seats	Democratic Held Seats	Total
Republican Districts	127	50	177
Mixed Districts	38	82	121*
Democratic Districts	13	124	137
Total	178	256	

Gamma = .79

*Note: The one seat from Vermont, mixed in presidential voting, was held by an Independent.

Republican districts voted Republican for President in the elections of 1988 and 1992. Democratic districts voted Democratic for President in the elections of 1988 and 1992. Mixed districts voted Republican once and Democratic once in the elections of 1988 and 1992.

larly strong as they held 91 percent of the seats from Democratic districts. Republicans were not as successful, although they were strong nonetheless, as they held 72 percent of the seats in Republican districts. The third category, mixed districts, was the source of Democratic control of the House. The Democrats held 68 percent of the seats in the mixed districts prior to the election of 1994. It was here that the Republicans were to gain their new House majority.

The extent and long term significance of the Republican victory is apparent from the data displayed in Table 2.2. This table shows the distribution of House seats by the presidential voting classification scheme employed in Table 2.1. It indicates that the outcome of the House elections was not exclusively a rejection of Bill Clinton, but was partly a consequence of House electoral patterns finally conforming to those of the Presidency.

These results virtually wiped out the advantages that Democrats held among the various categories and created a division of House seats where the strength of each party corresponded to the support that it had attained in recent presidential elections. After 1994, the Democrats held 88 percent of the seats in Democratic districts, which was nearly the same as they had held before the election. The Republicans had virtually equaled them as they held 86 percent of the seats in Republican districts. Moreover, the Republicans had completely eliminated the advantages enjoyed by the Democrats as each party held 60 seats from the mixed districts. The partisan distribution of seats across the three categories is so symmetrical now that the election of 1994 appears to have brought an end to the abnormal control of the House by Democrats and replaced it with a partisan distribution closer to underlying national divisions. The political significance

Table 2.2

Partisan Distribution of Congressional Districts after the 1994 Election by Presidential Election Results

	Republican Held Seats	Democratic Held Seats	Total
Republican Districts	153	24	177
Mixed Districts	60	60	121*
Democratic Districts	17	120	137
Total	230	204	

Gamma = .85

*Note: The one seat from Vermont, mixed in presidential voting, was held by an Independent.

Republican districts voted Republican for President in the elections of 1988 and 1992. Democratic districts voted Democratic for President in the elections of 1988 and 1992. Mixed districts voted Republican once and Democratic once in the elections of 1988 and 1992.

of this outcome is that the Democratic Party is unlikely to regain its control of the House in the foreseeable future by the numbers that it had become accustomed to enjoying. Moreover, no party seems likely to be a permanent majority in the House. The size of the Republican majority is slight and could be altered by the shift of only a few seats. With respect to the outcome of the election of 1996, the Republicans prefaced that year by gaining six seats in 1995 as five conservative Democrats switched parties and the party won a Democratic seat in a special election. This brought the Republican numbers to 236 House seats. The party then lost nine seats in 1996 and ended the year with 227 seats, only three less than what it had held after the takeover of 1994. The Democrats held 207 seats after the election. The Republicans expanded their seats to 228 after they won a special election for a former Democratic position in early 1997.

An important component of the Republican gains has been the Southeast. The Southeast is a region of thirteen states comprised of five from the South Atlantic—Virginia, North and South Carolina, Georgia, and Florida—and eight from the South Central—Kentucky, Tennessee, Alabama, Mississippi, Arkansas, Louisiana, Oklahoma, and Texas. Historically, it has been a stronghold of the Democratic Party, particularly with respect to congressional voting. While individual states have been straying from the Democratic ticket in presidential elections regularly since 1948, those same states have supported the Democrats in most congressional elections until recently. Today, the Southeast has become a region of significant Republican strength at virtually all levels of national voting. It is now the most Republican part of the nation with respect to both presidential and congressional electoral patterns. The Republicans currently hold eighteen Senate seats in the Southeast compared to only eight for the Democrats. Since the partisan division of the Senate is now 55 to 45 in favor of the Republicans, the rest of the nation divides its seats equally by a margin of 37 to 37. This means that the entire ten vote Republican margin comes from the Southeast. The House division is even more revealing about the extent of Southeastern power within the Republican Party. This party now holds 82 Southeastern seats compared to 55 for the Democrats. The other 37 states divide their seats in favor of the Democrats by a margin of 152 to 145. The top leadership of Congress also provides an indication of the importance of the Southeast to the Republican Party. The Senate Majority Leader, Trent Lott, is from Mississippi while House Speaker Newt Gingrich comes from Georgia. Texas provides the nation with three major House leaders: Majority Leader Dick Armey, Whip Tom DeLay, and the chairman of the Ways and Means committee Bill Archer.

There is some hope for the Democrats in these regional losses, however. With the Republican Party increasingly coming under the control of the nation's most conservative region, the Democrats have an unusual opportunity to seize the political center and construct a new national majority. This became quite obvious in the early months of 1995 when the agenda of the House Republicans seemed far more radical in both style and substance than most voters preferred. In response, Clinton managed to revive his weakened Presidency and eventually win reelection by creating a new public image where he appeared as the popular defender of the nation from the excesses of a radical Republican congressional majority.

CLINTON SETS THE STAGE WITH MEDICARE

Clinton began his third year in office with unusually bleak prospects for reelection. Very few presidents of the twentieth century had encountered a political reversal of the magnitude that Clinton received in the 1994 elections. Even those who suffered significant defeats at such early dates in their tenure, such as Hoover (1930) and Ford (1974), were less unfortunate than Clinton. In 1930, the Republicans lost control of the House but retained the Senate by a one vote margin. They had less to lose in 1974 since both houses of Congress were already under Democratic control before the elections. The Democrats increased the sizes of their majorities that year. The circumstances that Clinton faced were different, however. He had initiated an ambitious program upon becoming President, and appeared to have the support of the Democratic Congress for enacting it. While some of his proposals failed, Clinton attained some successes, as mentioned earlier. The congressional losses brought an end to any possibilities that Clinton would dominate the legislative agenda for at least two years. The Republicans had their own political contract to implement and one of their top goals was to supplement their control of Congress by winning the presidency in 1996. When he faced the Republican Congress in late January 1995, while delivering his State of the Union Address, Clinton seemed like yet another of the ineffective one term presidents that have become so commonplace during the last few decades. He would not be one, however. Much to the disappointment and surprise of the Republicans, Clinton successfully used the institutional and rhetorical features that define the modern presidency and created imagery where he soon appeared as a "tribune of the people" who stood in the way of the efforts of congressional Republicans to bring about a reorganization of American life. My purpose in this section is to explain how he did it.

The crucial events of 1995 that helped turn Clinton into a strong incumbent and that kept other Democrats from challenging him for the nomination occurred during the final four months of the year. The events of the first eight months of 1995 were important in that they helped set the stage for what was to come, but the important changes in public attitudes that eventually marked Clinton's reelection were not visible during those months. The Gallup Poll of August 30 indicated that voters were still dividing their presidential preferences about evenly between Clinton and Dole. Each candidate attained the support of 48 percent of the voters in this survey, identical to the results of the Gallup Poll of May 14 (Table 2.3).

Clinton spent these first eight months developing his strategy for opposing the budgetary plans of congressional Republicans. In particular, he depicted his adversaries as heartless radicals whose efforts to reduce federal spending would cause severe damage to the nation's most vulnerable

Table 2.3

Gallup Poll Recorded Support for Clinton and Dole in 1995

Date of Poll	Clinton	Dole
A. First Eight Months of 1995—January through August.		
1. Feb. 5	45	51
2. Apr. 19	48	49
3. May 14	48	48
4. June 6	46	51
5. July 9	47	48
6. July 23	49	45
7. Aug. 7	46	48
8. Aug. 30	48	48
B. Pre-Shutdown Period—September and October.		
1. Sep. 24	50	45
2. Oct. 5	49	45
C. Government Shutdown Period—November and December.		
1. Nov. 8	53	43
2. Nov. 17	55	39
3. Dec. 18	54	43

Source: The Gallup Poll.

citizens. He then confronted the Republicans over Medicare in mid-September. This date is important because Congress considers budget-related legislation during the final weeks of the fiscal year, that is, in September. While the battle over Medicare had already lasted for several months and would continue even after the election, what most influenced voting behavior was the confrontation that occurred before television cameras during the latter months of 1995. It had two components: the daily story as reported by television news media, and the version told by the Clinton campaign through its massive advertising efforts. These two stories were similar and often complemented one another. With respect to the news story, the controversy first surfaced on September 14 when the Republicans announced their plans for changing the funding of Medicare. Dan Rather hinted at the media response when he introduced the CBS *Evening News* broadcast of that day by saying, "Republicans in Congress announced their long delayed proposal to lop more than $250 billion from Medicare spending for thirty million older Americans. There was no delay in the nasty partisan and political exchanges that followed."

Television news media often focus more attention on the visual and dramatic aspects of a controversy relating to an issue than on the issue itself. Politicians also contribute to this practice by engaging in visual and dramatic actions of their own in order to attain news coverage. A politician and media relationship of this nature was apparent in the Medicare battle from the beginning. Rather's quote told viewers that his network was focusing on two themes: the attempts by Republicans to cut spending, and the efforts of Democrats to oppose them. Although Rather did not say it directly, these themes complemented Clinton's electoral strategy. The term "cut," or "lop" as Rather described it, is particularly interesting. A cut refers to efforts aimed at reducing the rate of growth of future government spending. The President's executive budget and the budget resolutions of Congress now project spending and revenue for five years with the fiscal totals of every program and organizational entity usually increasing each year. Republicans claimed their changes would reduce the probable spending on Medicare in future years from current projections but added that the actual monies spent would be larger. They wanted to call their changes "savings." Clinton and his supporters instead labeled them "cuts" and appear to have convinced television news media to adopt that term. The "cuts" over five years would have been about $250 billion.

The battle over Medicare involved more than a simple dispute between Clinton and congressional Republicans over the direction of future spending. Both sides agreed that Medicare faced some significant financial troubles that seemed to defy solution. The costs of the program have been increasing at rates significantly greater than inflation. In addition, the payroll taxes that support Medicare are inadequate to continue this level of funding without some changes taking place in either costs incurred or services delivered. A number of forecasts from a variety of sources indicate that without some financial changes Medicare will become bankrupt shortly after the turn of the century. The major question that political leaders have to answer is how to save Medicare from that imminent fate. The alternatives by themselves are not particularly complicated, one must either increase revenues, reduce expenditures, or pursue a strategy that combines both. The overheated political environment of recent years relating to taxes makes this option unlikely, if not impossible. Moreover, a fundamental restructuring of health care financing along the lines of a single-payer plan comparable to the Canadian and European systems also appears unlikely in that far too many Americans are unwilling to trade lower costs for less convenience. In light of this, the cost-cutting alternative seems to be most feasible. One of the contributing factors in the Republican takeover of Congress in 1994 was voter fear about the expansion of federal power and taxes that might accompany the enactment of Clinton's health care plan. The fact that such increases would also have reduced the need for private health insurance coverage seems to have been lost in the debate. The congressional Republicans soon learned, however, that they could not enact their campaign promises of reducing federal spending and taxes without also reducing the costs of Medicare. This stubborn fact turned out to be the Achilles heel of their Contract With America. In order to accomplish their taxing and spending goals, the Republicans needed to bring about a significant reduction in the amounts of federal monies spent on health care programs, and on Medicare in particular. Clinton used this fact to his political advantage during the debate while Republicans seemed to have little to say in response.

Television news media demonstrated, in the reports that followed Rather's opening remarks of September 14, the manner in which they would define the Medicare story over the next few weeks. They directed far more attention to the controversy between Clinton and the congressional Republicans than to the conditions of Medicare and the fiscal options available for addressing them. Linda Douglass started the CBS coverage this day by telling viewers, "The great Medicare debate opened with vitriol and venom." She included scenes of Gingrich speaking before a group of Republicans where he said, "You know what you're going to get, lie after lie designed to frighten people." Douglass then focused her attention on Richard Gephardt, the House Democratic Minority Leader, who commented, "This is the best program that's ever been put forth for our people and they're going to decimate it," and next on Dole who spoke before the same audience as Gingrich and told them Medicare would soon go bankrupt. Douglass then provided some information to viewers about the relevant financial issues but continued emphasizing the political controversy by explaining, "Republicans want to cut $270 billion from the growth of spending over seven years," and adding, "It is such a politically perilous plan that they are reluctant to release details. Democrats call it the stealth plan." Her report then included a scene of Democratic Congressman Sam Gibbons (Florida) demanding, "When are they going to let the American people know what they are going to do?" Douglass continued explaining the contents of the Republican plan, adding that it included higher monthly premiums, caps on hospital and doctor fees, and incentives for people to join Health Maintenance Organizations (HMOs). Douglass returned to the controversy by summarizing other comments, "Democrats say the plan will force seniors into substandard care. That makes Gingrich boil." Gingrich appeared again and said the Democrats were morally bankrupt. However, Clinton managed to get the final word and perhaps even the best imagery of the day when he spoke from his White House desk and said, "Republicans are not being honest. . . . They know that not one red cent will go to the Medicare trust fund. It will go to fund a tax cut that is too big." The other networks had similar coverage of the day's events.

The events of September 15 provided television news media with far fewer opportunities for juxtaposing imagery of the major players as Clinton and the Democrats started their counterattack. Clinton was particularly influential as he promised to veto the Republican plan and called it "extreme, radical, and unacceptable." He also created his own upbeat imagery by appearing before a group of elderly citizens and remarking, "If these health care cuts come to my desk with this size, I will have no choice but to veto." The Democratic attacks also included statements by Gephardt who compared the Republican plan, with its vague references to premium increases, to Nixon's secret plan for ending the Vietnam War. Finally, Bob Schieffer's report (CBS) had scenes of elderly citizens demonstrating against Gingrich.

Since September 15 was Friday and Congress was not in session over the weekend, actions and comments relating to Medicare diminished for several days. They resumed on the following Wednesday, September 20. Clinton raised the stakes by traveling to Denver where he spoke and then created some of the most effective televised imagery of the Medicare and budget battles. He attacked the Republicans on the related issue of Medicaid and emphasized the strong relation between that program and nursing home care. Clinton used a nursing home for the imagery where he spoke to a group of elderly patients and their health care providers about his plans to fight the Republican proposals relating to Medicaid. Rita Braver (CBS) began her report by saying, "President Clinton and the Republicans in Congress are on a collision course about Medicaid. Clinton says that Republican plans would deny nursing home care to the neediest and stick middle class people with bills for aging parents." She said that Clinton had blasted the Republican plan that would cut $182 billion from the projected growth in Medicaid and added that Clinton's appearance at the nursing home was designed to make the point that two-thirds of Medicaid recipients are disabled or impoverished elderly. "Over 300,000 American senior citizens who are eligible for nursing homes will be ineligible in just a few years," Braver said while outlining the major themes of Clinton's speech. Clinton created a photo opportunity with one of the residents of the nursing home, Helen Cooper, who told reporters after she had been photographed with Clinton that she would have been destitute without Medicaid.

In what most certainly appeared to be a triumph of the visual scene over the spoken word, Clinton provided the imagery that advanced his cause while concluding this news report. He walked through the nursing home courtyard while flanked by several nuns and patients, some of whom were in wheelchairs. In a juxtaposition of imagery that made the President seem human and Congress impersonal, CBS had scenes of Virginia congressman Thomas Bliley speaking at a press conference in the Capitol newsroom where he accused Clinton of opposing some of the same proposals that he had advanced previously as Governor of Arkansas. While there may have been a point to his remarks, Bliley lost the image battle with Clinton. A picture of the Capitol building was on the wall directly behind him as he spoke and was available for all television viewers to see. The emotion associated with Bliley's comments and imagery was hardly a match for the scenes of Clinton walking through the courtyard in the presence of the elderly. Once again, the visual contrast was between a personal-appearing President against an impersonal building and the President won.

Clinton's media triumph was not limited to the imagery from his Denver speech. Bob Schieffer (CBS) reported from the Capitol about the leading events relating to Medicare this same day and included scenes and remarks that certainly helped Clinton triumph in the rhetorical battle. One of the more important scenes was of Sam Gibbons angrily walking out of a committee meeting and objecting, in strongly emotional language, about the efforts of Republicans to "railroad" their plan through without benefit of hearings. Schieffer then remarked, "Democrats have been seething about Republican efforts to ram through major changes in Medicare without extensive hearings." In addition to reporting this same story, ABC included imagery of several congressmen arguing with one another in the hallways about the ethics of the Republican actions and then included remarks by Gibbons, Gephardt, and Senate Minority Leader Tom Daschle denouncing the actions and proposals of the Republicans. This network concluded its Medicare-related coverage by interviewing three senior citizens who spoke about why they supported Medicare and about how they would be hurt by the Republican proposals.

The televised story of the Medicare battle continued to attract network interest for approximately six more weeks, but it finally disappeared in late October. Correspondents focused much of their daily coverage on comments by the principal players; congressional leaders of both parties and a variety of White House spokesmen, including Clinton. The coverage of September 21 is typical of the manner in which television news media reported the continuing controversy. Network correspondents began their Medicare-related coverage this day by reviewing the contents of the Republican plan and by including combative remarks by Gingrich and Gephardt (CBS). The remarks are not significant by themselves but are important when considered in the context of the themes that television news media employed during these six weeks. The imagery of two major House leaders appearing opposite from one another while delivering short "sound-bites" about the Medicare controversy told viewers of televised politics that the fundamental issue at stake was one of "cuts" versus "no cuts" rather than about alternative methods of financing the nation's most expensive health care program. This news theme implicitly supported Clinton's attempts at depicting the congressional Republicans as mean-spirited radicals bent on depriving people of needed health care.

Television news media continued focusing attention on the combative remarks of the principal players for several more days, and as before, showed far more interest in the controversy associated with proposed changes than with the rationale for the changes themselves. On September 22, Gephardt and Panetta, now serving as the White House chief of staff, attacked the Republican proposal with Panetta hinting at a possible presidential veto. Three days later, the Democrats held a mock Medicare hearing on the Capitol lawn (ABC) and Hillary Clinton referred to the Medicare controversy while delivering an unrelated speech (CBS). When Gingrich was interviewed by ABC on October 1 he attacked Clinton. The next day, several Democrats angrily walked out of a congressional hearing (NBC).

Gephardt denounced the Republicans on October 6 while speaking before a group of Medicare recipients (ABC) and attacked the American Medical Association (AMA) on October 11 for their support of the Republican plan (NBC). In addition, Panetta and John Kasich, chairman of the House Budget Committee, commented on the AMA's actions on October 11 (NBC). The related issue of Medicaid resurfaced on October 6 when NBC reported on Republican plans to replace the program with block grants to the states. Two days later CBS examined the possible impact of this change and concluded that states would lose money. These Medicaid changes appeared to be more "cuts."

A second front soon opened in the Medicare battle. The Democrats began a television advertising campaign aimed at depicting Clinton as the protector of the program from the excesses of congressional Republicans and their two most visible leaders, Dole and Gingrich. The initial news references to this campaign appeared on October 12 when CBS re-aired the Clinton campaign's most recent commercial. There were two scenes in this commercial with the initial one including an image of Dole and Gingrich appearing behind a caption that said "Cut Medicare." The second had Clinton working in the White House office with an announcer adding, "Republicans are wrong to want to cut Medicare benefits and President Clinton is right to protect Medicare." The cost of this Democratic National Committee effort would finally total nearly $65 million.

October 12 was a newsworthy day in the battle for yet another reason. Clinton used the rhetorical powers of his office and created some White House imagery where he looked statesmanlike, as described by Rita Braver (CBS). Clinton appeared in a scene with a group of small children and then participated in a conference call discussion with several hospital administrators. He used these moments as opportunities for restating his opposition to the Republican plans. Clinton also demonstrated how a president can dominate news during a controversy when he upstaged House Republicans on October 19. The House passed the Republican plan that day but Clinton responded by threatening to veto those actions. The House vote placed the Medicare controversy at the center of this day's network news. While network correspondents reported about the vote, they actually placed far more emphasis on Clinton's remarks when he said, "That is not the right way to balance the budget. It is not fair and it will not happen."

The final day of significant network reporting about Medicare was October 26, when House Republicans passed their budget plan. The measure was the reconciliation language described earlier that concludes the congressional phase of the budget process. The plan that passed the

House this day contained the Medicare cuts but was not limited to them. It also contained much of the language that would serve as the foundation for the political battles of the next two months over the role of the federal government and which would finally result in the two government shutdowns. Despite this, the political news involved Medicare. Network telecasts included remarks by a variety of the principal players, among them Gingrich, Gephardt, Kasich, Gibbons, Panetta, Armey, White House press secretary Mike McCurry, and of course, Clinton and Dole. Television news media continued reporting about Medicare during the days that followed and included even more comments by these same players. The controversy disappeared shortly afterwards, however, as the more significant issues contained in the vote of October 26 moved to the head of the political and news agenda.

Clinton eventually accepted some minor increases in the size of Medicare premiums paid by program recipients when he reached a budget agreement with the Republicans and their new Senate leader Trent Lott in early 1997. He was quite unwilling to do this in 1995 when Dole led the Senate and was his likely election opponent, however. Instead, Clinton used Medicare against the Republicans for his own short-term political gain. He defined their financing plan as a direct attack on senior citizens and positioned himself to appear as their defender. It is important to understand this strategy in order to more fully appreciate the pro-Clinton response of many voters during the budget battles and the government shutdowns. Clinton successfully placed Medicare in the forefront of the budget debate and television news media responded accordingly by reporting the controversy as if it was the most important issue facing the nation. Even after the Republicans passed their version of reconciliation with its emphasis on the entirety of the federal budget, Clinton attacked them over Medicare. When the Republicans attempted to introduce other matters, such as a tax cut, they found their ideas trapped in the Medicare debate. Clinton placed the Republicans and their leading spokesmen, Newt Gingrich and Robert Dole, on the defensive.

Clinton's strategy, the television news media response, the supportive actions of leading Democrats, particularly Richard Gephardt, and the reactions of Gingrich and Dole kept Medicare at the center of the political and media agenda for weeks and defined the issues for the upcoming budget battles. Clinton used the Medicare funding issue as an effective first step for reversing his political fortunes and becoming a strong incumbent in time for the election. Moreover, television news media fulfilled their role in the modern world of mediated incumbency. They were on their way to helping generate a consensus in support of the reelection of a strong incumbent.

CLINTON WINS THE BUDGET BATTLE

The Medicare issue virtually disappeared from network news after the end of October as the battle over the budget grew in intensity. The shift in news attention occurred on November 9. This particular day was significant because it marked the expiration of the most recent continuing resolution. Each year, Congress passes thirteen individual appropriations bills to fund the various components of the national government. These bills expire on September 30. Consequently, any changes in spending after that time must await the enactment of new appropriations bills. Since it is unusual for all thirteen bills to be finished by this date, Congress normally responds by passing one or more short-term spending bills known as continuing resolutions. These resolutions permit temporary spending for a designated period of time and usually at the same rate as in the preceding fiscal year. Congress used this approach earlier in 1995 and allowed spending to continue until November 14. The Republican majority was now refusing to pass any more resolutions and instead sought to enact some of its legislative program through the appropriations bills rather than through statutes. Clinton opposed these efforts and refused to sign any new resolutions or appropriations bills that would enact the Republican program in this manner. By November 14, the new resolutions had to be in effect or the appropriations bills had to be completed. Without one of those measures the government would lack authority to spend money. As he had done earlier with the Medicare fight, Clinton used the institutional and rhetorical powers of the Presidency and dominated both the debate over the budget and the agenda of television news media.

Television news media expressed a distinct pattern in their daily reporting of the events associated with the first shutdown. They began each telecast by reporting about the leading event of the day. More often than not, Clinton created the event. He either announced or implemented some executive action, such as vetoing a Republican sponsored spending bill or ordering emergency measures to cope with the shutdown. He then placed the blame directly on the Republicans. After illustrating Clinton's deeds and words in ways that usually advanced his reelection strategy, television news media turned their attention to the comments of other participants in the crisis, particularly Gingrich and Dole. These Republican spokesmen usually stood adjacent to one another in some congressional setting at the Capitol Building, or in some setting such as the pressroom where a picture of the Capitol was displayed, and attacked Clinton. Television news media also included comments by other major participants, both Republican and Democratic. Finally, one or more correspondents reported about the problems ordinary people encountered as a result of the shutdown, with those people often expressing anger at Congress for having caused the problems.

Dan Rather's opening comments on the CBS *Evening News* of November 9 reflected the themes that television news used during the budget show-down. Rather remarked, "Clinton says he would rather have that (the shutdown) than sign what he considers to be a radical Republican spending bill loaded with conditions he will not accept." The leading news story of the day was a cabinet meeting where Clinton and his aides reviewed the emergency measures they might have to implement in the case of an actual shutdown. Since television news media could not show the cabinet meet-ing actually occurring, they broadcasted scenes of administration officials arriving at the White House instead. Clinton, although not shown, seemed to be directing a significant government response to an emergency. Perhaps the nation was threatened by an enemy attack, or a major hurricane, or even an act of Congress. Gingrich, Dole, Panetta, and Daschle commented this day about the impending crisis. In addition, Rita Braver (CBS) supplemented her narrative about the problems associated with a shutdown with images of buildings and people. She included an unnamed govern-ment building, the front door of the Department of Agriculture, a major lobby within another federal building, the Pentagon, an air traffic control-ler at work, the office of the Securities and Exchange Commission, several uniformed soldiers marching, and numerous veterans' checks being pro-cessed. She had referred to each of these in her report.

Clinton created the leading news event of November 10 when he announced he would veto the latest Republican resolutions because they would raise Medicare premiums, cut spending for education, and reduce three decades of environmental regulation. Gingrich, Dole, Panetta, Gib-bons, McCurry, and Robert Livingston, chairman of the House Appropria-tions Committee that had prepared the resolutions, each had their fifteen seconds or so of commentary this day (ABC and NBC). Finally, Dan Rather said that 800,000 federal workers might be furloughed, the processing of new veterans' claims could be suspended, national parks and monuments might be closed, and higher interest rates, including those for variable home mortgages and payments, could result (CBS).

There were no new events on November 11 or 12 since these days comprised a weekend, so correspondents focused their attention on the other two themes while reiterating much of the same information they had reported earlier. Several participants, including Dole, Gingrich, and Panetta, appeared on various Sunday talk shows, such as "This Week with David Brinkley" (ABC) while directing most of their remarks to Clinton's previous actions. Even without new actions, Clinton continued dominating the political agenda. Two events defined the news agenda of Monday, November 13. Treasury Secretary Robert Rubin planned emergency actions for avoiding a government default on required interest payments, while the second event was Clinton's vetoing of the two resolutions that Congress had recently passed. The network news programs included images of Gingrich signing the resolutions while saying Republicans were committed to a balanced budget without spending increases. Clinton, speaking from the White House and referring to the battle, said he would "fight it next week and next month. I will fight it until we get a budget that is fair to all Americans" (CBS).

The shutdown began on November 14 and served as the major news story of the day. Clinton attained more news coverage than any other participant when he attacked the Republicans while speaking from the White House press office. He sought to depict them as radicals when he said, "Republican leaders in Washington have put ideology ahead of common sense and shared values in their pursuit of a budget plan" (CBS). He added that the budget could be balanced without the cuts the Republicans were advancing (ABC). Gingrich, Dole, Panetta, Kasich, and Pete Domenici, chairman of the Senate Budget Committee, commented about Clinton's statements. Finally, Linda Douglass (CBS) supplemented her narrative about the problems of the shutdown with imagery of the Capitol Building, a highway, the Lincoln Memorial, the front door of the Social Security Administration building, the Washington Monument, a lockup of an unnamed gate, government workers leaving the Department of Education, an interview with a leading executive of the Center for Disease Control, the space shuttle, a national park entry gate, the Liberty Bell, and tourists at the Statue of Liberty. She included some angry comments from a German tourist who was visiting the Statue of Liberty.

Television news media started their coverage on the following day with this same three-part formula. Each network began its daily telecast from the White House and concentrated on Clinton's announcement of his intention to veto the latest continuing resolution. The Republicans had removed their Medicare changes from this resolution but had substituted a provision requiring a balanced budget in seven years (ABC and NBC). Clinton, in an interview with Rather, said he favored balancing the budget but not if it was going to undermine the nation's basic values and the strength of the economy. The budget should take care of obligations, the elderly, children, health care, education, and technology, he added. In a more confrontational tone, Clinton described Republican efforts to bring about a government shutdown in order to force him to accept their proposals as an exercise in raw, naked power. He said the controlling element in Congress believed it should undermine and break the role of the federal government in all areas of America's life except national defense. In addition, television news media also carried Gingrich's and Dole's comments about Clinton's veto plans while several correspondents looked at the problems of individual people rather than directing attention to the impersonal imagery of buildings and monuments. Their reports included scenes of angry people failing to obtain passports or the processing of new veterans' claims.

There was a new feature in the news this day—the horserace question of who was winning and who was losing. Several correspondents assessed which side had done the better job of persuading the American public and concluded that the preponderance of the evidence supported Clinton. Bob Schieffer (CBS) indicated as much when he remarked, "Republicans are very aware that the public perceives their position as being more to blame for the current budget stalemate." He included scenes of Gingrich and Dole and said the Republicans knew many Americans blamed them for shutting down the government. Schieffer concluded by adding that Republicans were trying to shift the blame to Clinton.

Clinton seized the headlines one day later on November 16 when he announced he would recall 50,000 workers to process Social Security, Medicare, and veterans' benefits claims. Following reports relating to this announcement, television news media once again included scenes of Dole and Gingrich standing adjacent to one another in the Capitol Building while commenting about Clinton's latest actions. Finally, the day's news reports about the problems of the shutdown concerned an announcement by the National Park Service that it planned to close the Grand Canyon for the first time in history (NBC).

There was a second major story on November 16 and it very rapidly turned into an embarrassment for Gingrich. The *New York Daily News* reported on its front page about Gingrich's reaction to a "snub" from Clinton which allegedly occurred when the two had returned from Israel on Air Force One after the funeral of Yitzhak Rabin. Clinton required Gingrich, and others as well, to board the airplane through the back door rather than with him at the front. The *Daily News* described Gingrich as angry over this incident and used the caption "Cry Baby" as its headline while accusing him of taking a hard line on the budget in retaliation. Several Democrats held signs on the House floor this day referring to "Newt's Tantrum." Congresswoman Patricia Schroeder (Colorado) held a mock Oscar she said should be awarded to Gingrich for the best performance by a child actor (CBS). Clinton, grinning, said he would say he was sorry if that would get the government to reopen.

The battle continued on November 17 when House Republicans passed another temporary spending bill that also called for a balanced budget in seven years. In the words of ABC, it would also "cut" $270 billion from Medicare, shift the cost of Medicaid to the states, and reduce taxes by $245 billion. Clinton quickly announced he would veto it just as he had done with the previous resolutions. Gingrich, Dole, and Domenici advanced the usual critiques of Clinton's actions (NBC).

The final day of the first shutdown was Monday, November 20, when the two sides reached an agreement on a temporary spending resolution. This agreement would last for only one month, would expire on December 15, and would lead to yet another confrontation and shutdown. The battle was over for now, however, and 800,000 furloughed workers returned to their jobs (CBS).

Clinton won both the rhetorical and political battles of the budget. He dominated the news most days with his initiatives and partisan attacks and eventually forced his adversaries into the position where they could do little more than comment about his actions. He also convinced television news media to define the crisis in the language he was using to advance his own reelection. The Gallup Poll surveys of September 20 and October 5 indicated just how successful Clinton had been. He had now overtaken Dole in the presidential race. Clinton led his Republican rival by 50 percent to 45 percent in the first survey and by 49 percent to 45 percent in the second (Table 2.3). Clinton's lead grew even larger as the November 8 survey showed him ten points ahead of Dole, 53 percent to 43 percent. The timing of these surveys is significant. Gallup conducted the first two during the Medicare battle and the third several days before television news media began their intense daily reporting about the events of the shutdown period. Clinton had actually taken the lead over Dole during the Medicare fight. While he would also fare better than Dole during the budget battle, he would not register any significant gains in voter support during that time. Instead, the shutdown period events strengthened the lead that Clinton had previously attained. Clinton would retain this support during the second shutdown in December and would solidify it during the most intense part of the Republican primary election campaign between January and March.

Clinton was not idle during the three weeks between the two shutdowns; he dominated political news with his overseas travels. He started his foreign activities on November 21 by announcing that the Bosnian negotiations taking place in Dayton, Ohio, had just produced an agreement. Clinton said he would travel to Paris to sign the resulting accords. He followed this announcement by addressing the nation on November 27 regarding future American efforts at implementation. He was in London on November 28 and appeared in several highly photographed scenes with Queen Elizabeth II, Prime Minister John Major, and members of Parliament. The imagery was upbeat and statesmanlike. Clinton generated similar imagery in Belfast and Dublin, where he was greeted by large and enthusiastic crowds, and in Germany when he spoke to some American troops soon departing for Bosnia. He traveled to Madrid for a meeting of the European Union and then returned to the White House on December 6, just in time to veto the latest Republican budget proposal and set the stage for the next showdown with Gingrich and Dole. He returned to Europe on December 14 and signed the peace accords. This was the major news story of the day. In fact, ABC had six reports about it, including a Peter Jennings interview of Clinton.

The coverage of the second shutdown was less pervasive than that of the first, particularly since there was little new to report. The same adversaries said and did the same things as they had said and done earlier. Clinton used his institutional and rhetorical powers on December 15 and vetoed the latest Republican appropriations bill. He surrounded himself with children while speaking from the Oval Office and said that ten million children would have to live by toxic waste dumps if the bill became law. In contrast, Dole was only one of several participants who commented this day about Clinton's actions. He had to share available airtime with Gingrich, Gephardt, Domenici, and Kasich. One network, ABC, even had a background scene of him while referring to "Republicans."

The imagery that accompanied televised news during this shutdown was far more interesting than the actual words of the participants. Clinton hosted daily White House meetings with Dole and Gingrich in search of possible resolutions. The imagery included scenes of the two Republicans entering the White House or talking with Clinton. The three would usually comment briefly before their meetings, although the content was rarely important. The imagery was significant in that it personified the gamut of ideological and partisan differences in the identities of these three participants. Since television news media were also proclaiming Dole as the front-runner for the Republican nomination, this imagery had strong implications for the upcoming campaign. The President and his probable challenger from the opposition party were meeting for the express purpose of negotiating an end to a monumental battle over the future direction of the nation. They were not meeting on equal terms, however. Not only did Clinton have a greater public following than Dole and the trappings of White House power at his disposal, he was also the only spokesman for his side of the controversy. Other leading Democrats, including Gephardt, Daschle, and Gibbons, had disappeared from network news by this time. Dole, in contrast, had to share his leadership role with Gingrich who was by now one of the most despised political actors in the nation. Many voters were associating Dole with Gingrich since the two had appeared together on so many occasions during the Medicare and budget fights. Democrats would continue speaking of a Gingrich-Dole Congress during much of the campaign and quite a number of voters would believe them. Finally, television news media divided their political coverage of the next two weeks between the budget battle and the rapidly expanding campaign for the Republican nomination. Their interest in the budget declined sharply after the end of the year and stopped entirely in the middle of January.

Clinton accomplished his most important political goal of 1995, he became a strong incumbent by opposing the taxing and spending plans of congressional Republicans. He had a double-digit lead in the polls and would maintain it through the entire campaign. As a consequence of his victories, he would attain the highly favorable televised news coverage that regularly accompanies strong incumbents. While he would occasionally attain unflattering news, particularly in relation to Whitewater and Democratic Party fundraising, Clinton would appear far more frequently in the desirable role of a statesman leading the nation. Television news media would also focus even more attention on the divisive aspects and personalities of the campaign for the nomination of the Republican Party and help undermine that party's prospects. The outcome of the election of 1996 was decided before the year even began. Clinton had used the vast array of institutional and rhetorical powers that now define the modern Presidency and had returned from the political dead, that is, the electoral disaster of 1994. He was now poised to demonstrate his new political virility by vanquishing his partisan adversaries once again.

AN ALTERNATIVE SCENARIO

One may well wonder about what might have occurred in 1996 if the outcomes of 1995 had been different. With this in mind, I sketch an alternative scenario while working from the assumption that Clinton lost the Medicare and budget battles. In this scenario, Clinton began 1995 in much the same political condition as he actually did and faced the same challenges from congressional Republicans. After the Republicans advanced their plan for Medicare funding in this scenario, Clinton failed to confront them or did so in a way that was far less effective than what he actually did. In addition, he failed to mobilize senior citizens and his own partisans behind his efforts. Clinton's political weaknesses emboldened his adversaries while convincing many news correspondents that he was failing as President. The Republicans dominated the Medicare debate and persuaded most voters their approach was essential for saving the program from certain bankruptcy. With Clinton offering no viable alternative, the Republican plan carried the day.

Clinton then encounters a significant rival from within the Democratic Party, for many of his partisans no longer believe he can win another term. While the identity of such a rival can never be known with certainty, I use Richard Gephardt in this scenario. Gephardt is a likely choice because of his major leadership role among House Democrats during the Medicare and budget controversies, and because he has also expressed an interest in running for President in 2000. By early 1997, Gephardt had emerged as the principal rival of Albert Gore for the next Democratic nomination. Moreover, he had openly opposed some of Clinton's policies by that time, including the budget agreement with Trent Lott and various trade and human rights policies with China.

If we assume that Gephardt is a rational political actor who wishes to become President, we should also assume he will seek the office in the most advantageous years while avoiding it during less promising ones. Reagan's retirement made 1988 an advantageous year. Gephardt quickly responded by seeking the Democratic nomination, but failed. His next opportunity came in 1992, but he declined to run because Bush's widespread popularity following the Persian Gulf War suggested that year would not be particularly promising for Democrats. Gephardt, and perhaps even Gore, may well have regretted bypassing that election after Clinton's victory. With Clinton's triumph, Gephardt's next opportunities would come in either 1996 or 2000. His possible effort in 1996 would require a weak incumbent while he would have to oppose a sitting Vice President for the 2000 nomination, assuming that Clinton would win in 1996. Gephardt demonstrated the extent of Clinton's political strength when he decided to delay his candidacy until after Clinton's second term.

Clinton begins this alternative campaign seeking the support of his fellow partisans. As a weak and struggling incumbent, Clinton finds few opportunities for creating statesmanlike imagery. Television news media treat his State of the Union Address as a confrontation with Gephardt rather than Dole. Moreover, they have already prefaced this coverage by directing more attention to Gephardt during the budget fights than they actually did. In the real scenario, they quoted Gephardt extensively during the initial phases of the Medicare battle in September and October, but stopped after Clinton began dominating his confrontations with Dole and Gingrich. In this alternative scenario, television news media direct their attention to four participants: Clinton, Dole, Gingrich, and Gephardt, rather than to just the first three. Clinton then confronts Gephardt in the primaries. He eventually defeats him, but he does not yet unite his partisans. Many Democrats continue to oppose his candidacy until the national convention meets in late August. Their efforts deny Clinton the opportunity to use that conclave as a televised infomercial as he did in the actual scenario.

The campaigns for the Republican nomination and general election are also different. Television news media focus much of their attention during the early months of 1996 on the Democratic nomination battle and reduce their coverage of the Republican race accordingly. Dole is not affected by this change, however, for he continues to fulfill the role of central actor in the news drama through his front-runner status. Pat Buchanan, Steve Forbes, and Lamar Alexander pay the price for Clinton's weaknesses and Gephardt's insurgent candidacy as they attain far less news coverage than in the real scenario. This accelerates the conclusions of their failed efforts. None last much beyond the New Hampshire primary. Dole clinches the nomination by no later than the Ides of March and uses this as an opportunity for projecting imagery where he appears as a statesmanlike leader of a very productive Republican congressional majority. The election ends much like those of 1976, 1980, and 1992 as Dole attains a substantial and insurmountable lead over Clinton by mid-summer. Television news media spend the final months of the campaign telling their viewers how poorly Clinton is running and implicitly help generate a consensus in support of the nominee of the opposition party, soon to be President Robert Dole.

CHAPTER 3

THE BATTLE FOR THE REPUBLICAN NOMINATION

The campaign for the Republican nomination in 1996 was, as is certainly true of all other campaigns, unique in a number of ways. First, it was a relatively brief endeavor when compared with campaigns of previous, and perhaps of even future years. Senator Robert Dole was the overwhelming front-runner and probable nominee from the outset and ended his efforts in late March with a one-sided victory in the California primary. His last opponent, Pat Buchanan, ended his bid at that time. These actions allowed Dole to clinch what would eventually become a unanimous nomination at the August national convention. This early Republican decision, when coupled with the fact that Bill Clinton was unopposed among Democrats, resulted in a lengthy seven month general election campaign that stretched from April until November. This general election campaign became one of the longest in modern history.

A second unique feature of 1996, although contributing very greatly to the occurrence of the first, was the fact that many states had advanced the dates of their primary elections or nominating caucuses to either the latter part of February or to some day during the month of March. Over thirty states had completed their primaries or caucuses by the time of the California primary on March 26. This practice, sometimes referred to as front-loading, helped bring about the earliest conclusion of the primary election season in history. While not new—it had been an important factor in such recent years as 1988 and 1992—front-loading occurred far more extensively in 1996 than ever before. For example, California held its primary during June in 1988 and 1992. Moreover, there are some strong indications that many states are planning to conduct their primaries for election year 2000 at much later dates, thus making the scheduling of the primaries of 1996 into a one-time phenomenon.

Finally, a third unique feature was the fact that the opposition party nominated a major congressional leader for President. As I mentioned in chapter 1, the opposition party rarely nominates such candidates because the personal attributes that enable an individual to become a leader in Congress are not the ones often required for victory in a presidential election. The party nominates junior members of the Senate, current or former governors, or past Vice Presidents instead. The selection of the Majority Leader, in this instance Dole, as the nominee of the opposition party, is an unusual event for the television age and will probably not occur again anytime soon.

Despite these features, the context, related patterns of televised news coverage, and even the final outcome that marked the Republican nomination campaign were quite similar to those of other television age elections. The election of 1996, including both the final and convincing victory of Bill Clinton and the nomination battle within the Republican Party, conformed to the consistent and recurring patterns of mediated incumbency outlined earlier that distinguish elections with strong incumbents. I intend to demonstrate the validity of this contention as it relates to the nominations throughout this chapter.

There are eight sections in this chapter, with this introduction being the first. The second provides a general overview of the campaign as it developed during 1995. I direct initial attention to the context of the campaign and discuss the political actors who became candidates and those who declined to enter the fray. I then review the early stages of the campaign and examine the events before January 1, 1996. This period of time, the year preceding the election, is often called the invisible primary. Here, candidates are far more oriented toward generating support from political activists and financial contributors than they are at directly attaining the backing of voters. The more important events include the successes and failures of candidates in raising money and attaining measurable support in public opinion surveys.

The events of the invisible primary are rarely major topics of television news, but the themes of news reporting during this time often help set the stage for what will be reported when the campaign moves into its more public phase. That public phase occurs when the candidates actively seek votes in caucuses and primaries. Consequently, I review the major themes that television news media raised in reporting about the Republican candidates during 1995.

The third section focuses on the early phases of actual campaigning by the candidates in the initial caucus and primary states of Iowa and New Hampshire. This period of time was marked by a greatly expanded media interest in the campaign, including virtually daily coverage by all networks. This change occurred shortly after the beginning of the new year. Television news media began defining and stereotyping the candidates and interpreted and highlighted events by how those events conformed to the definitions and stereotypes. As expected, television news media identified Dole as the front-runner and focused on Steve Forbes as his leading adversary. They divided the other candidates into two groups: those who seemed to be fighting for third place in Iowa and New Hampshire, and those who had by now failed. The news coverage followed this script as Dole and Forbes received the lion's share of attention while the others struggled for the limited coverage that remained. This period of time lasted for about five weeks, through January and the first few days of February.

The first significant electoral tests of the year were the Iowa precinct caucuses on Monday, February 12, and the New Hampshire primary eight days later on Tuesday, February 20. The fourth and fifth sections focus attention directly on the campaigns in each of these states respectively during the week immediately preceding the actual votes. Some of the most intense media coverage of the year occurred during this time. This coverage also provided virtually the only linkage that existed between the campaign and the candidates on one hand and the millions of voters who did not reside in either of these two small states on the other. This was also when many voters, including Republicans who would vote in subsequent primaries and the non-partisans and Democrats who would cast their ballots in the general election, first learned about the campaign and the candidates. It was also when many of these people made the judgments and formed the opinions that would guide their later choices.

These first two electoral tests form the heart of what political observers call the winnowing process, that part of a campaign when a large number of candidates are reduced in number to a smaller number of actual contenders. One of the more significant participants in the winnowing process, as explained earlier, is television news media. The manner in which television news media contributed to the winnowing of the candidates of 1996 is a major theme of these sections.

The Republican campaign lasted only five weeks after New Hampshire and concluded with Dole's California victory. For all intents and purposes, it ended with the primary in South Carolina on Saturday, March 2 and in eight other states on the following Tuesday, March 5. Three candidates— Dole, Forbes, and Buchanan—won primaries during February, but every electoral contest from South Carolina onward belonged to Dole. These early March primaries were significant in that they eliminated virtually all doubts that Dole would be the nominee. Previously, four of his opponents had given some indications that they might have succeeded. Their hopes finally disappeared after Dole won nine primaries in less than a week. The campaign events and related televised news coverage from the conclusion of the New Hampshire primary to the Dole victories of the first week of March are the topics of the sixth section. In addition, I also link the news coverage of this period to the definitions and stereotyping that television news media developed during the winnowing period.

With Dole's conclusive victories, the campaign advanced to its next stage, when Dole needed to unite his partisans and focus his efforts on the upcoming battle with Clinton. Television news media responded as they usually do during the concluding stages of nomination battles: they helped to generate a consensus of support in favor of the apparent winner. They depicted Dole as the obvious nominee and then restructured their reporting in ways that enhanced the rapid termination of the candidacies of his remaining rivals. This stage ended with the California primary. The seventh section is about the campaign events and related news coverage that occurred between Dole's sweep of the early March primaries and the end of the contested part of the Republican campaign. The emphasis is on how television news media redefined the context of the campaign and expedited the withdrawal of Dole's remaining rivals.

I evaluate the Republican campaign and its televised news coverage in the eighth section and link them to the theory of mediated incumbency that I advanced in chapter 1. It is my intention to demonstrate that this campaign, despite the existence of several unique features, actually exhibited many of the recurring patterns that characterize opposition party campaigns in elections with strong incumbents. These patterns include the television news media practice of focusing attention on the most divisive events and personalities within the opposition party's campaign while depicting the incumbent in a far more favorable light. The eventual result is that the incumbent develops a lead over his challenger, or maintains an existing one that proves insurmountable in the general election.

THE INVISIBLE PRIMARY

The period of time referred to here as the invisible primary encompasses the year 1995 and includes the initial announcements by the candidates of their intentions to seek the Presidency and their subsequent efforts to raise the monies and generate the requisite levels of activist support necessary for contesting primary elections. It also includes the televised news coverage of those activities.

Most potential candidates now announce their intentions to seek the Presidency or to remain on the sidelines during the year preceding the actual election. This is a relatively new phenomenon and is a consequence of the party reforms of the late 1960s and early 1970s. In contrast, John Kennedy announced his 1960 presidential ambitions in January of that same year and was the first candidate in that election to make such an announcement. Today, a candidate who waits that long will almost certainly lose the nomination. Aspirants for the Presidency now need several months, perhaps even as much as one year, to prepare for the early primary elections.

Expansions in the number of primaries and the enactment of new fundraising laws have encouraged longer campaigns. In 1968, the Democrats required state parties to develop more open and timely procedures for choosing their national convention delegates. The procedures now require that all Democratic voters must have an opportunity to participate in the choice of delegates. They can accomplish this by voting for President or by voting for delegates. Previously, party officials or committees usually chose the delegates. Under the earlier rules, candidates often secured nominations by convincing party leaders such as governors, state chairmen, or congressmen to deliver the support of their state's delegation directly to them. Many state parties soon discovered that a primary election was one of the best means of compliance with the new rules. Consequently, the number of states with presidential primaries expanded from perhaps a dozen in 1960 to approximately forty in 1996. States are not required to have primaries, however. About ten states now select their delegates through caucuses, a procedure that enables party members to vote directly for delegates. Party members in Iowa, for example, attend precinct caucuses in February and elect delegates for county conventions. Those delegates, in turn, select other delegates for state conventions who then choose the delegates who attend the national conventions. With these changes, presidential candidates can no longer win the support of a state's delegation merely by securing the personal backing of a few key party leaders. They must now run well in that state's primary or caucuses. In order to succeed, candidates and their supporters must motivate and organize thousands of political activists, a task that often takes a considerable amount of time.

With respect to fundraising, Congress enacted the Federal Election Campaign Act in 1972. The law was designed to limit the contributions and expenditures of presidential candidates and to provide some public funding for campaigns. The law limited a candidate to spending only $12 million on a nomination and $20 million in the general election. These totals were to be revised annually for inflation, however. The revised totals for 1996 were $36 million and $60 million, respectively. Political Action Committees (PACs) could contribute only $5000 to a candidate while contributions by individuals could not exceed $1000. These numbers are not readjusted for inflation and are therefore the same today as they were in 1972. Moreover, a candidate could spend only $50,000 of his own money on a presidential bid. The law also provided for federal matching funds in nomination campaigns. If a candidate raised $100,000 in small individual contributions, with small meaning $250 or less, that candidate qualified for matching funds. The federal government would match, dollar for dollar, all small individual contributions raised by the candidate. Finally, the federal government would provide the monies for the general election campaigns of the nominees of the major parties with no additional fund-raising permitted. As occurred with the expansion in the number of primaries, these changes also lengthened the campaigns as candidates now needed to contact far more people than before in order to raise the necessary funds.

As a note to readers who may be unfamiliar with federal requirements, this law applies to candidates, not political parties. The parties can solicit large contributions, that is, more than $5000, from individuals and organizations and can spend that money without regard to the restrictions the law places on candidates. These unlimited contributions to parties led to the troubles faced by the Democratic National Committee during and after the election.

These changes have helped make the invisible primary an integral part of modern nomination campaigns because they force candidates to devote the greater part of the year preceding the election to fund-raising and organization building. It is within this context that the campaign for the Republican nomination began during the early months of 1995.

There were eventually eleven candidates in the field, with Dole being foremost among them. He had a distinguished public career, one that included involvements in previous national campaigns but one that was also concentrated in Congress. He was elected to the House of Representatives in 1960 and remained there until 1968 when he won the first of his five Senate terms. Dole did not limit his activities exclusively to Congress, however. He was also a prominent member of his party during these years, serving as national chairman from 1971 to 1973 and as Gerald Ford's running mate in 1976. He made the first of three presidential bids in 1980 but lost to Ronald Reagan in the New Hampshire primary, and withdrew. He found another opportunity for leadership later in 1980 when the Republicans gained control of the Senate. He became chairman of the Finance Committee and used his new office as a strategic position for advancing Reagan's tax cutting plans. Dole became the Senate Majority Leader in 1985, then Minority Leader in 1987 after the Democrats won control of the chamber. He remained in that position until January 1995 when he regained the Majority Leader's office after the Republican congressional takeover. Dole held this position throughout the invisible primary and the contested part of the nomination campaign. He resigned from the Senate in June 1996 in order to devote full time to his presidential bid.

Dole also sought the Republican nomination in 1988. He fared better this time although he was still unsuccessful. He defeated George Bush in the Iowa caucuses but finished second to the Vice President in the New Hampshire primary. By this time the struggle for the nomination and the right to be the Republican successor of Ronald Reagan had narrowed to Dole and Bush. Bush took a commanding lead after winning an array of primaries in March. These outcomes encouraged Dole to withdraw and to concentrate his political efforts in the Senate instead. The defeat of Bush in 1992 opened the door for Dole to make another try for the Presidency.

It is rare for a major congressional leader to win a presidential nomination because he often lacks many of the political skills needed for creating followings from diverse groups of party activists. Nonetheless, Dole's previous experiences as a party chairman and national candidate had given him far greater personal contact with party activists than is typical of congressional leaders. As a consequence, he avoided the problems that congressional leaders often face when running for President and was actually able to use his congressional experiences as an electoral asset.

Dole's rivals were generally unknown to much of the American public at the beginning of the campaign and none ever came close to matching his standings in public opinion surveys. They included three Senators— Phil Gramm (Texas), Arlen Specter (Pennsylvania), and Richard Lugar (Indiana)—Congressman Bob Dornan (California), Governor Pete Wilson (California), former Governor Lamar Alexander (Tennessee), television commentator Pat Buchanan, radio talk show host Alan Keyes, publisher Steve Forbes, and businessman Morley Taylor. An interesting feature of this list is the names it does not contain. Several prominent officials of the Bush administration who might have been strong candidates decided against running. These included Vice President Dan Quayle, Secretary of Defense Dick Cheney, Secretary of Housing and Urban Development Jack Kemp, and Chairman of the Joint Chiefs of Staff Colin Powell. The first three announced their decisions early in 1995 while Powell waited until November. Quayle, Cheney, and Kemp attributed their choices to a lack of money while Powell said he did not wish to pursue a more partisan public career at this time. The absence of these four helped make Dole's victory easier since he had no immediate challenger for the role of front-runner or for the leadership of the party establishment. He responded by uniting a substantial part of the established leadership of state and local parties behind his candidacy long before the primaries even began.

Two indicators often demonstrate the progress of the invisible primary, the amount of money raised and the strength of poll standings attained by the candidates. Dole came out ahead in both, particularly the latter. Candidates must file periodic reports of their financial resources with the Federal Election Commission. The reports of January 1996 indicated the extent of Dole's success. He had already raised $24.8 million and had qualified for an additional $9.3 million in matching funds, thus giving him a grand total of $34.2 million. The only candidate in either party with comparable funding was Clinton whose combined total of contributions and matching funds was $35 million.

Phil Gramm had raised more money than any of Dole's rivals as his combined total of contributions and matching funds was $27.4 million; in contrast, Alexander's was $13.2 million, Buchanan's $10.7, and Lugar's $6.9. Two other candidates, Wilson and Specter, had already withdrawn from the campaign while Dornan, Keyes, and Taylor would soon do the same as each had failed to raise the requisite $100,000 in small contributions needed for qualifying for matching funds. One candidate was in better financial shape than all the others, however. Steve Forbes had decided to bypass the matching funds and to spend $25 million of his own money on his presidential effort.

This was possible because of a decision by the U.S. Supreme Court in 1976. In *Buckley v. Valeo*, a case relating to the constitutionality of the Federal Election Campaign Act, the court ruled that Congress could limit the size of the contributions that a candidate could accept but it could not limit the amount of money that an individual may spend. Such limits would violate free speech. In a rewriting of the law to conform to the court's standards, Congress created an incentive for candidates to adhere to the financial requirements of the law. A candidate had to agree to the expenditure limits in order to receive matching funds. By renouncing matching funds, Forbes could spend as much of his own money as he wanted in seeking the nomination rather than only $50,000 as provided in the law.

The polls provided yet another indication of Dole's strength. Gallup–CNN–USA *Today* conducted ten polls during 1995 which measured support for the Republican candidates. The first, completed April 6, included the names of the nine candidates who had already announced their intentions to run while excluding Forbes and Taylor who had not yet done so. Dole held first place with 46 percent of the vote while Gramm was second with 13 percent and Buchanan third with 8 percent. The others ranged between 1 and 6 percent. The results of six additional polls taken between May and September were similar. Forbes was included for the first time in September. This survey had Dole at 46 percent, Gramm at 9 percent, Buchanan at 8 percent, Forbes and Wilson at 4 percent apiece, and all others between 1 and 3 percent. The final poll of 1995, concluded on December 18, had Dole in first place once again, this time with 49 percent. Gramm was second with 13 percent while Buchanan held third with 9 percent. The support for these three candidates was similar to what it had been in April, but the support for Forbes had doubled to 8 percent since September. The support for the others ranged from 1 and 3 percent and was also unchanged from earlier polls.

One reason for the stability of the polls was that Dole was virtually the only candidate who attained any televised news coverage throughout most of the year. Television news media reported extensively on his fights with Clinton over Medicare and the budget. Contrastively, they rarely looked at the other candidates except to report about their initial announcements or failing campaigns. Moreover, they did not focus attention on the campaign until the last few weeks of 1995. In fact, they spent more time on Powell's November announcement of noncandidacy than they did on most of the announced candidates' entire year's activities. One of the few instances when television news media actually showed some interest in the other candidates was on October 12 when they reported that a New Hampshire debate had been lackluster and poorly attended. One network, CBS, had short excerpts of Dole, Buchanan, Forbes, and Alexander speaking while NBC showed Buchanan attacking Powell who had not yet announced his plans. On that same evening, ABC reported from Iowa on how the candidates were not connecting with voters. The overriding theme in all three reports was of how poorly the candidates were faring.

The Republican candidates were not completely shut out from all televised news coverage during the budget fight, however, as they actually received some attention on the final days of the first government shutdown. The event that led to this was a straw poll at a Republican state meeting in Florida. Phil Jones (CBS) introduced the November 19 story by remarking that "Florida Republicans ballyhood this as the most important GOP event of 1995. There were nine candidates but Senators Dole, Gramm, and former Tennessee governor Alexander were the ones who fought the hardest for the 3400 votes." Jones followed the usual pattern that television news media use when reporting about contested nomination campaigns. He identified Dole as the front-runner and then quoted Gramm who proclaimed that it was "a two-person race" after finishing second behind Dole. Dole won with 33 percent of the vote, Gramm had 26 percent and Alexander came in third with 23 percent.

Television news media also expressed some interest in the other candidates on December 30 when Gwen Ifill (NBC) previewed the nomination battle. The network placed her report shortly after they had updated viewers about the budget talks. This update contained a scene of the three principal players—Clinton, Dole, and Gingrich—seated at a White House conference table. The network prefaced Ifill's report with a picture of their election year logo "Decision 96." The use of the logo informed viewers that an election-related story was about to follow. Ifill's report contained visual images of each of the six major candidates speaking at one of his recent campaign appearances. She identified each candidate with his most important theme. She identified Dole as an advocate of a balanced budget, Gramm as a strong opponent of Clinton's economic policies, Lugar as running on the character issue, Alexander as an outsider, Forbes as an advocate of the flat tax, and Buchanan as a spokesman for conservative values. After identifying Dole as the front-runner, Ifill added that the other five were striving to become his main rival. She concluded in a manner similar to that of earlier news reports by telling the audience that most voters say they want change but did not seem to be finding it with these candidates.

The year of the invisible primary ended much as it had begun, with Dole the overwhelming front-runner and preferred candidate of much of the party establishment. He had been endorsed by nineteen governors by the end of the year while the remaining governors had declined to endorse anyone. His greatest asset had been his visibility as Senate Majority Leader.

His party had advanced a major legislative agenda and he had been one of its leading advocates. *Washington Post* reporter Dan Balz said Dole's visibility "gave him the opportunity to prove his commitment to the legislative agenda of the Republican revolution and kept him at the center of the political debate in the country as his rivals struggled for attention" (1995, 14).

There is an irony here, however. Dole may very well have secured the Republican nomination partly because of the extensive televised news coverage he attained by virtue of his Senate leadership during a time of significant partisan controversies. He attained far more news coverage from his position than all of his rivals acquired from their combined campaign efforts. Dole led his rivals in the polls at the outset of 1995, held his lead throughout the year, raised more money and acquired more endorsements from important party officials than any of them. The irony is that the news coverage that helped make Dole the Republican nominee is precisely the same coverage that helped defeat him in the general election. It also helped turn Bill Clinton, the embattled President of early 1995, into a strong incumbent by the end of that same year. Clinton's new strength of November 1996 came partly at the expense of Senate Majority Leader Robert Dole.

THE EARLY WEEKS OF 1996

The NBC news report of December 30 also implicitly summarized the campaign as it stood at the beginning of 1996. Of the eleven original candidates, two had already withdrawn, three more had failed but had yet to officially quit, while six others remained viable. Of these six, Dole still retained his earlier position of front-runner while the other five were striving to become his major adversary. Gramm had seemed the most likely candidate to become that adversary during much of the invisible primary of 1995, and television news media had responded accordingly by often depicting him in that role. He had finished second in the Florida straw poll and had raised more money and shown more support in national surveys than all other candidates except Dole. But Gramm no longer appeared as the best prospect to emerge as Dole's leading adversary by the time the campaign finally reached January 1996, however. By now, most of his money was gone and his poll standings were declining. He had spent lavishly on such activities as fundraising itself and by conducting several expensive campaigns in states that had non-binding straw polls such as Florida while failing to generate much enthusiasm among the majority of

Republican voters. Dole initially had considered Gramm as his leading adversary but he would soon shift his attention to Forbes.

The campaign took place on two different fronts during the late months of 1995 and the first weeks of January 1996. One was in Washington, D.C., and was reported extensively to the nation by television news media while the second was in the early test states and was just beginning to attain national attention. The early test states are those with the initial caucuses or primaries, Iowa and New Hampshire, that frequently serve as important steps in the winnowing process. The campaign as shown through the cameras of the national television networks focused on Clinton and Dole as they fought their budgetary battles and attempted to define the national agenda and the stakes of the general election. Dole was the only Republican candidate who attained much attention from network television during this time. Voters who resided in places other than the early states, and whose knowledge of the campaign was thereby limited primarily to what they learned from the national news media, watched Dole as he appeared as the one and only Republican alternative to Clinton. The remaining candidates did not seem to exist.

The campaign was different in the early test states, however, as the other candidates had many more opportunities for reaching voters. While Dole dominated the national news with his congressional activities, his rivals devoted much of their time and money to Iowa, New Hampshire, and a few other states with early votes. The campaign was underway in these states by November with the candidates making personal appearances and advertising extensively in local media. The distinguishing characteristic of this second front was the relative equality that existed between Dole and his rivals. Several of the other candidates spent far more money or time, or both, in these states than Dole, and they attained votes that greatly exceeded their standings in nationwide polls. Their strong showings helped make the campaign appear more competitive than it actually was. There was another aspect to this part of the campaign that was to prove important, however. Dole had a virtual monopoly on the information about the candidates that was available to the rest of the nation because of his battles with Clinton and because of the fact that his rivals were concentrating their resources almost exclusively in these early states. This would be a strong contributing factor in his ultimate triumph because his rivals could not compete equally or effectively in all states. Eventually, all of them failed to make the national breakthroughs in the early states that they had wanted, and were out of money as a result. The campaign did not extend much beyond the early states.

There are two general strategies that candidates can use in seeking a party nomination. One is the establishment strategy where the candidate uses the invisible primary as an opportunity for developing support within state and local party organizations. He seeks the support of party leaders and elected officials, which often translates into greater contacts with experienced political workers, improved access to local money, and significant personal endorsements. An important prerequisite for successfully employing such a strategy is for the candidate to have a strong initial base of support within the party establishment before he seeks the Presidency. He must be an incumbent, or the surrogate of an incumbent, or someone with many years of involvement with state and local party organizations. If successful, the candidate can then rely upon this support and compete effectively in virtually every state's primary or caucuses. Some of his supporters may also seek election as national convention delegates and will thereby link their efforts at attaining votes with his, thus allowing the two efforts to complement one another. Republicans who have successfully used this strategy in contested nominations of the recent past have been Nixon (1968), Ford (1976), Reagan (1980), and Bush (1988). Ironically, Dole had been a victim of this strategy in 1988 when Bush, as the candidate of the Reagan administration, won the backing of numerous Republican officials, including the governors of three early primary states: John Sununu (New Hampshire), Carroll Campbell (South Carolina), and James Thompson (Illinois). By 1996, Dole could rely upon his many years of personal involvement in party affairs to win the support of most party leaders.

The second is the outsider strategy. Here, an aspirant begins the campaign as a candidate without a constituency. His goal is to find a constituency either by motivating one that already exists but which does not presently look to him as its leader, or by creating a new one from a variety of interests or causes. Television news coverage often becomes one of his most vital resources. The outsider is relatively unknown at the outset of the campaign but he compensates for this problem by concentrating his limited monies and most of his time in a few early test states where he can compete on more even terms with any establishment candidates. His goal is to run well in these states in the hopes that television news media will respond to his good showing by focusing more attention on him afterwards. This expanded coverage should then provide the outsider with the personal exposure that he wants throughout the nation to motivate or create his needed constituency. In 1976, Jimmy Carter became one of the most successful candidates ever at using this strategy. His campaign now serves as the model that many outsiders wish to emulate. Others who have attained limited success with this strategy are George Bush (1980) and Gary Hart (1984). Each ran well in Iowa and then used the resulting news coverage to become the leading adversary of the front-runner: Bush against Ronald Reagan and Hart against Walter Mondale. Neither was able to translate his Iowa showing into a nomination, however. Each of Dole's rivals of 1996 used this outsider strategy.

Dole's dominance of the national news continued through the first half of January as the networks continued focusing attention on the budget battle. The few news reports that actually looked at the campaign were also mostly about Dole. For example, correspondent Phil Jones referred to Dole as the front-runner in a CBS report of January 4. His report contained scenes of Dole speaking about the budget while two other candidates, Gramm and Buchanan, appeared in secondary roles where they attacked him. Three days later NBC had a similar report with Gwen Ifill, speaking from New Hampshire, stating that Dole was the front-runner. Gramm, Buchanan, and Alexander attacked Dole for his alleged willingness to compromise with Clinton. On that same day ABC analyst Jeff Greenfield identified Dole as the front-runner and predicted that he would win the nomination quite early during the year. These correspondents worked from the same theme, Dole was the front-runner and central political actor in the campaign while his rivals derived their importance mainly by opposing him. These rivals were merely obstacles that stood between Dole and the nomination.

There was an abrupt change in the network coverage on January 12, perhaps one that Dole himself influenced. The networks began directing far more attention to Forbes and started depicting him as if he were Dole's major adversary. They apparently were not going to wait for another month until the vote in Iowa to designate the second candidate in the race, they were doing it now. They began what was to eventually become a significant expansion in the coverage of Forbes that would extend through the Iowa vote. A report by Jackie Judd (ABC) was typical of this pattern. Her major theme was that Dole had started running a series of televised attack advertisements about Forbes in Iowa and New Hampshire. He was doing so because Forbes apparently was gaining on him. Forbes had campaigned extensively in these states for several weeks, mostly through television attack ads directed at Dole. The response by the Dole campaign, with televised attacks about Forbes, seemed to alert the national media to the fact that Dole was now taking Forbes seriously. In response, the networks began doing the same.

Network reporters used this new interpretation in their news reports of the next day, January 13. Each saw Dole as the front-runner and Forbes as his new leading adversary. Gwen Ifill (NBC) described Forbes as the major challenger to Dole while she reviewed a candidate debate from the previous evening. She also included scenes of Dole attacking Clinton and of Alexander, Gramm, and Buchanan attacking Forbes over his proposed flat tax. Tom Foreman (ABC) identified Dole as the front-runner and then referred to him as a longtime Washington insider. He followed by saying that Forbes was gaining on Dole and concluded his report with scenes of Buchanan and Alexander denouncing Forbes. Bob Schieffer's (CBS) approach was similar as he included scenes of Dole, Gramm, Alexander, and Buchanan attacking Forbes. One day later, on January 14, CBS analyst Joe Klein added to this interpretation by saying that Dole was the front-runner but that someone would finish second to him in Iowa and that Dole would then have to start defending himself. Klein concluded by remarking that Forbes was spending millions on advertising. The media message now seemed clear, front-runner Dole would win Iowa while the other candidates were fighting for second place. The second-place finisher would then become Dole's leading adversary and the campaign would be redefined as a race between two candidates only. Forbes was now well on his way to becoming that second candidate.

Forbes remained a major topic of news reporting for several more days with two networks focusing their attention on him on January 15. The CBS report was mostly biographical while the one by ABC focused on Forbes' main issue, the flat tax, with some analysis of its strengths and weaknesses. The report included scenes of Alexander, Dole, and Buchanan speaking about the weaknesses of the tax. These networks looked at Forbes again on January 21 and used the reporting formula that had become commonplace by now. They identified Dole as the front-runner, discussed Forbes and his advocacy of a flat tax, and followed with scenes of other candidates, Gramm and Alexander this time, attacking Forbes. There was another and somewhat more implicit theme in these reports than mere commentary about the merits of a flat tax. While Dole and Forbes seemed to be occupying the more significant roles of front-runner and leading adversary, respectively, the remaining candidates were quickly moving into the realm of becoming the "others." They seemed to be newsworthy only in relation to the critical remarks they made about the two principal candidates. Television news media rarely telecast scenes of Gramm, Alexander, or Buchanan speaking of anything other than their reservations about Dole or Forbes. The three had already been relegated to the sidelines of the campaign. Moreover, Lugar had disappeared from network news almost entirely.

The fact that television news media were casting Forbes as Dole's major adversary was not merely a matter of their creation, however, for there was objective evidence that he was actually gaining support. First, there was the reaction of the other candidates to his efforts. The increased news attention started when Dole began his negative attack ads, as mentioned above. The polls also provided some support for Forbes' gains. A January 15 poll by Gallup–CNN–USA *Today* indicated that Dole had the support of 55 percent of Republicans, the highest number he had recorded since the polling had started in April 1995, while Forbes held second place with 12 percent. Gramm, Buchanan, and Alexander ranged between 3 and 6 percent each. Forbes continued to gain in the polls that followed. The poll of January 29 showed Dole leading him by 47 percent to 16 percent with the other candidates each recording 8 percent or less.

One of the major themes in news reports about the other candidates was how poorly they were doing. On January 17 ABC carried a special report about the financial condition of the candidates entitled "The Greenback Primary." It told about the methods the candidates were using in fundraising, how much money each had actually raised, how much was on hand, and the amount of federal matching funds each was entitled to receive. Jim Wooten (ABC) also identified Dole as the front-runner while adding that Forbes planned to spend about $25 million. Wooten then depicted Alexander as struggling and Buchanan as unlikely to win but who would probably influence the final outcome.

Television news media changed their reporting themes for several days after this when Clinton gave his State of the Union Address on Tuesday, January 23, while Dole provided the Republican response. The contrast between the two was vivid, with Clinton performing much the better. A major news theme that developed from these speeches was that Dole had been ineffective in responding to Clinton. Several of his rivals used this as an opportunity for attacking him. The networks included scenes of Buchanan, Alexander, and Gramm speaking against Dole on January 24 and of Dole who felt obligated to defend himself. Meanwhile, Clinton received fairly positive coverage from the networks while campaigning in Louisville. Lisa Myers (NBC) and Rita Braver (CBS) both referred to Clinton's strong speech while John Cochran (ABC) and Phil Jones (CBS) remarked about the negative tone of Dole's speech. Clinton appeared as an upbeat and successful national leader while Dole was spending his time defending himself from the attacks of his intra-party rivals.

The televised depiction of the campaign as essentially a battle between Dole and Forbes continued after the State of the Union Address and related news coverage. Gwen Ifill (NBC) reported on January 25 that Dole was slipping because of his poor performance in responding to Clinton although she still identified him as the front-runner. She continued by depicting Forbes as Dole's major rival. Buchanan was the only other candidate who received any coverage in this report, and he was only seen attacking Forbes. Forbes was also the focus of the political reporting on CBS this day with Phil Jones reviewing him. Two days later, Bill Greenwood (ABC) reported about Dole's campaign in New Hampshire and included scenes of both Dole and Forbes attacking one another. This pattern continued once again in two ABC reports on January 29. Dean Reynolds reported that Forbes was gaining in the polls and now had a chance to win in New Hampshire, while John Cochran focused on Dole and said that he was facing strong competition from Forbes and was even trailing him in one poll. On the same day, David Bloom (NBC) said that Forbes was gaining ground on Dole. One day later, ABC and CBS reported about Dole attacking Forbes for his performances as a Reagan administration official while NBC reviewed some of the attack ads that Forbes had been using against Dole in Iowa and New Hampshire.

The emphasis on Dole, Forbes, and the others acting in their stereotypical roles continued to dominate televised news reporting during the first week of February although CBS supplemented its coverage by running a series of daily profiles of each of the six major candidates. Nonetheless, even CBS directed most of its campaign coverage toward the horserace. On February 1 all three networks reported that Forbes had taken the lead from Dole in New Hampshire, at least according to a new poll from the *Boston Globe*. Forbes had 31 percent, Dole 22 percent, with Buchanan, Alexander, Gramm, and Lugar recording 11, 9, 7, and 3 percent, respectively. Each network then used this result as an opportunity for reminding viewers that Forbes was gaining on Dole. These same themes continued on the next day as Eric Engberg (CBS) reported about the extensive television advertising that Forbes had already purchased in Iowa while David Bloom (NBC) reviewed the content of Forbes' advertising and showed how it was both pervasive and misleading. He also reported that many Iowa businesses had been unable to find time available for their own advertising since Forbes had purchased about 42 percent of all that had been available. This same day, Lisa Myers (NBC) reviewed Forbes' stands on abortion, taxes, gay rights, and the proposed balanced budget amendment. One day later, on February 3, Bloom reported that Dole was struggling to remain as the front-runner and that Forbes was gaining ground. His report included scenes of Gramm, Buchanan, and Alexander acting in their roles as the "other" candidates by attacking Forbes.

There was one unusual test of candidate strength that preceded Iowa this year, however. Louisiana Republicans had decided, partly in response to pressures from Gramm, to elect some of their national convention delegates in seven congressional district caucuses on February 6. They would choose the remainder of their delegates in a March primary. While most candidates ignored these caucuses, Gramm and Buchanan decided to contest them. They were a disaster for Gramm. He had helped bring them about because he thought he could win, but he now appeared headed for an almost certain defeat. Television news media reported this and implicitly began the practice of removing Gramm from the category of "other" candidate and placing him instead into the new role of "failed candidate" who should withdraw. Jack Smith (ABC) was the first correspondent to report about this, doing so on February 3. Smith also looked at the Louisiana efforts of both Gramm and Buchanan in another report on February 6 and spoke again of how poorly Gramm was likely to fare. The other networks soon emphasized this same theme. Dan Rather remarked that a poor showing by Gramm could finish him.

Buchanan captured thirteen delegates in Louisiana while Gramm gar-nered only eight. This outcome served as the major political news story of the next day. In a report in which the themes were similar to those of the other networks, Russ Mitchell (CBS) said that Gramm had been the driving force in bringing these caucuses about and that he had anticipated a win. His failure now meant that he must finish among the first three in Iowa or would have trouble remaining a viable candidate. Kevin Phillips, working as an analyst for CBS, identified Gramm as a loser. Contrastively, Buchanan received more favorable coverage from the networks but they were not yet ready to proclaim him as a major player in the campaign. Mitchell identified him as an ultra-conservative. The news reports from the other networks were similar as Tim Russert (NBC) predicted that Gramm would drop out of the campaign while Lisa Myers (NBC) referred to Buchanan as an ultra-conservative.

THE IOWA CAUCUSES

With the conclusion of the Louisiana vote, network reporters began directing their attention almost exclusively to the Iowa caucuses, which were only five days away. They continued with their efforts at stereotyping the candidates into categories, but they also employed one new theme in the final days before the vote. They stopped looking at Forbes as if he was the rising new challenger and Dole's leading adversary. His campaign was beginning to stall as voters were increasingly becoming skeptical about him and seemed particularly concerned about his lack of experience and his massive spending from a personal fortune. They also doubted the wisdom of the flat tax and had been influenced by the strong personal criticisms that other candidates had raised about Forbes. Some of those doubts were related to issues important to religious conservatives, such as abortion. Network reporting soon reflected Forbes' changing status. As Forbes began to look more like a loser, the reporting became more adversarial and critical. For example, Eric Engberg (CBS), reported on February 8 about the problems related to the flat tax in a special topics segment entitled "Reality Check." His report also included comments by Brookings Institution economist William Gale who said the tax would not cause the economic renaissance its proponents promised and it might even increase the deficit. There was another indication of Forbes' changing status on an NBC report of February 8 when the network cast him in the secondary role of attacking Buchanan. The major NBC story for this day was about Buchanan's efforts to appeal to Iowa's religious conservatives. Jim Wooten (ABC) also reported about religious conservatives one day later and featured both Buchanan and Gramm while disregarding Forbes.

Despite these changes, the Dole as front-runner and Forbes as leading adversary theme continued receiving the largest amount of news coverage in the final days before the Iowa vote. Phil Jones (CBS) focused his report of February 9 on Dole with Forbes once again cast in the adversary role, while John Cochran (ABC) reported that Forbes had accused Dole of running a telephone smear campaign against him by engaging in push polling. Push polling occurs when voters are asked hypothetical questions in a manner that may plant suggestions about the character and integrity of one or more candidates. For example, one might ask a question such as "would you think more, less, or the same of candidate A if you learned that he has a criminal record?"

The quantity of news coverage expanded considerably during the final days before the caucuses and resulted in even more emphasis on the horserace theme. This expansion also provided the other candidates with more opportunities for attaining news coverage than had been available to them previously. Despite this additional attention, network reporters did not alter any of their usual themes. Two networks, ABC and CBS, looked more closely at Alexander on February 9. Neither saw him as a likely winner nor did they even treat him as if he was a leading contender. Instead, each viewed him as simply one of the others. Michele Norris (ABC) said that Alexander was the candidate of voters thinking "none of the above," while Russ Mitchell (CBS) remarked that the negative campaigning by the leading candidates was encouraging undecided voters to look more closely at Alexander. In addition to viewing him as a secondary candidate, the networks also placed their reports about Alexander after the ones that focused on Dole, Forbes, and Buchanan.

Television news media reiterated these familiar themes on February 10 when ABC began its telecast by identifying Dole as the front-runner, Forbes as the second strongest, and the rest as the others. This network then juxtaposed four field reports about the candidates according to the status that it had just pronounced for each of them. The first, by John Cochran, focused on Dole. Cochran described Dole as leading in the polls and included scenes of him both campaigning and attacking Forbes. Dean Reynolds then reviewed Forbes. He depicted Dole as the front-runner while adding that Forbes was slipping because of his inability to win support from Christian conservatives. This report also contained scenes of Gramm, Buchanan, and Alexander campaigning. Two reports followed, including one by analyst Hal Bruno who said that Dole would win, that Forbes would finish second, and that the other candidates were fighting for third place. The others were in a three-way fight for survival, Bruno added. Finally, John Donvan discussed Lugar's limited prospects. By now, Lugar had fallen far behind the other candidates and seemed to have virtually no chance of finishing among the top five. Perhaps to indicate his low status, ABC separated this report from the other three by several minutes and used that time for news unrelated to the campaign. The reports about the stronger candidates had appeared during the first few minutes of the telecast while the one about Lugar came in the final minutes. This placement indicated that Lugar was no longer a part of the actual race and that one should count him out as a serious player. The juxtaposing of news reports on the other networks was similar to that of ABC this day. One of them, CBS, began by reviewing Dole and depicting Gramm, Buchanan, and Alexander as his rivals. The network then looked at Forbes and showed him attacking Dole for alleged telephone smear tactics. Similarly, NBC began by illustrating Dole's actions, then considered Forbes, and concluded its coverage by looking at Gramm, Buchanan, and Alexander together in the same report.

Television news media reemphasized these familiar themes and used this same positioning of the candidates in their programming of the following day. Phil Jones started the CBS coverage by identifying Dole as the front-runner and by saying that the battle in Iowa was now for second and third place. He added that Gramm was struggling and concluded that anyone finishing lower than third would likely be out of the campaign. Russ Mitchell followed and proclaimed Dole the front-runner while casting Forbes in a more limited capacity than before in which he only commented about Dole. Finally, NBC also identified Dole as the front-runner while reminding viewers that the other candidates were fighting for second place. This network concluded its reporting by adding that Forbes was losing ground while Alexander and Buchanan were gaining. The ABC approach was similar as this network reviewed Dole first, Forbes second, and Buchanan and Alexander third and fourth, respectively.

This pattern of juxtaposing news reports by the status of the candidates continued on February 12, caucus day. Gwen Ifill started for NBC by saying that Iowa was the first real test of the campaign, that the real race was to run second to Dole, and that the caucuses would help weed the field to only three or perhaps four candidates. She then included several scenes of Dole, whom she identified as the front-runner, and short remarks by Forbes, Alexander, Gramm, and Buchanan. The likely Dole victory was also the theme of Jim Wooten's ABC report. This network was the first to identify Buchanan as Dole's latest leading adversary, at least with respect to the upcoming primary in New Hampshire. John Cochran remarked that Buchanan was Dole's main rival in that state. Dean Reynolds then focused on what he described as Forbes' stalled effort in Iowa and concluded his coverage by saying that Forbes might not do better than fourth. This network followed with reports about Alexander and Buchanan. Catherine Crier told viewers that Alexander had run a low-key campaign in Iowa and had spent eighty days campaigning in the state. Michele Norris said that Buchanan had been helped in Iowa by his recent victory in Louisiana. The CBS themes were similar with Phil Jones predicting a victory by Dole while Russ Mitchell directed attention to the remaining four candidates.

Dole won, but his margin was far from overwhelming. He attained 26 percent of the vote compared to 23 percent for Buchanan and 18 percent for Alexander. Forbes suffered a significant setback as he acquired only 10 percent while Gramm finished fifth with 9 percent and was eliminated as a candidate. Network reporters continued emphasizing the horserace theme in their coverage and soon reminded their viewers that the campaign was far from over. Lisa Myers (NBC) called Dole's victory anemic. She said that he was weaker now than he had planned to be. She also referred to Dole's problems of 1988 when he had taken these caucuses, and with more support than he had shown this year, only to lose the New

Hampshire primary to Bush. Myers said that Dole was now worried about Buchanan whom she then identified as his new leading adversary. She also described Buchanan as an ultra-conservative.

One can see a good indication of how quickly television news media change their stereotypes without abandoning their paradigms in the NBC report that followed the one by Myers. The report, by Gwen Ifill, looked at the campaign of the second place finisher and new leading adversary, Buchanan. The report's content is not as important as its positioning. Buchanan had suddenly moved from his previous status where he had merely been one of the others to a new status where he now received second billing in the daily coverage. By virtue of finishing second, Buchanan had won the "right" for more daily news coverage from the networks and for a higher position in their status hierarchy of candidates. No longer would he be a mere critic of the two principal contenders: he was now Dole's main rival for the New Hampshire primary. In addition, television news media demoted Forbes from his once lofty role. The only information that NBC provided viewers about the man who had previously held this second spot was quite unflattering as Tom Brokaw mentioned that Forbes had spent $458.44 for each vote that he had received in Iowa. With the results of Iowa now available, television news media attempted to redefine the campaign by altering their characterizations of several candidates, particularly Buchanan and Forbes. They did not alter their reporting patterns, however. The first news report on the networks' telecasts during the days preceding the Iowa vote had often focused on Dole while the second ones had considered Forbes and the third ones, if there had been any third ones, the others. The revised hierarchy now had Dole first, Buchanan second, and the others third.

The news reports for ABC on February 13 were similar to those of NBC as this network also redefined the campaign by identifying Dole as the shaky front-runner and Buchanan as the new leading adversary. This network also referred to Alexander and Forbes but characterized them only as the others. John Cochran described Alexander as upbeat while adding that Forbes was heading to New Jersey in order to create some new television commercials. Finally, CBS varied slightly from this new juxtaposing of candidates as it began by first reporting that Gramm was withdrawing. It then conformed to the patterns of the other networks, it focused attention on the weaknesses of Dole's victory and then depicted Buchanan as his new leading adversary.

The outcome in Iowa raises some concern as to whether television news media were accurate in their perceptions of the candidates' strengths and in their interpretations of the meaning of the campaign. They began their coverage by initially defining the race as a battle between Dole and five others with the real contest being for second place. They seemed to be viewing the Iowa battle as if it were an athletic tournament where five candidates were fighting for the right to advance to the semifinal round where one could then face Dole for the "title." The eventual second-place finisher was not obvious at first, so television news media treated all five of Dole's rivals as equals, as one can see in the NBC overview of December 30. Forbes' extensive advertising efforts, his subsequent rise in the polls, and Dole's immediate response through negative ads soon altered reporters' perceptions and convinced them that Forbes would finish second. They responded by depicting the campaign as if it actually was a battle between front-runner Dole, his leading adversary Forbes, and the others. This assumption eventually proved questionable when the Forbes effort stalled, or perhaps reflected the true nature of its limited support, in the days preceding the vote. Television news media started redefining the campaign during those last days primarily as a battle for second place with the identity of that one candidate still not apparent. They did not find that candidate until after the votes had actually been cast. In fact, there never really had been a number two candidate in the race. Television news media believed they had needed one in order to describe the campaign as an exciting battle between high profile actors. They assumed that an adversary really existed and structured their reporting accordingly, despite the fact that the identity of the adversary seemed elusive. They would continue this practice in New Hampshire.

THE NEW HAMPSHIRE PRIMARY

The next early test was the New Hampshire primary on February 20. The campaign was quite volatile at this time as voters often shifted their support from one candidate to another on an almost daily basis. One can see evidence of this volatility in the daily tracking polls taken in New Hampshire by Gallup–CNN–USA *Today* during the last days of the primary campaign. This group conducted nine such polls between February 11 and 19.

The first poll indicated that the levels of candidate strength that had existed just prior to the last days of the Iowa caucuses corresponded to the patterns of television news coverage at that time. This poll had Dole and Forbes tied for first place at 25 percent each with Buchanan at 19 percent and Alexander at 11 percent. The two other major candidates, Gramm and

Lugar, appear to have been finished as each recorded only 4 percent. Dole initially gained some support in the polls taken shortly after his Iowa victory as he recorded 28, then 31, and finally 32 percent over the first three days. His support declined afterwards to 28 percent, then to 27, to 26, to 24, and finally to 23 percent. He finished second in the actual primary with 26 percent of the vote. Forbes had a very different pattern as his support declined daily. His initial showing of 25 percent diminished to 21 the next day, then to 17, 14, 13, and finally to 12 percent. It remained at this level for the rest of the primary campaign, totaling 13 percent in the final poll and 12 percent of the actual vote. He finished in fourth place. Buchanan quickly advanced to fulfill his new role as the leading adversary of Dole. His initial showing of 19 percent grew steadily and soon reached 25 percent. He attained 26 percent in the final poll and won the primary with 27 percent of the vote. Alexander also gained steadily from his initial 11 percent and eventually reached his peak of 20 percent in the final poll. He ran somewhat ahead of that in the primary as he took third place with 23 percent of the vote.

Television news media started focusing directly on New Hampshire on Wednesday, February 14. After reporting Gramm's decision to withdraw, they continued the same patterns of coverage that they had used in Iowa. They stereotyped the candidates into roles and then structured their reporting to conform to those roles. This pattern was evident in a CBS report that day by Phil Jones. Jones began by showing scenes of Dole attacking Buchanan, whom he now claimed was his main rival, and then followed with Buchanan attacking Dole. The other candidates, Forbes and Alexander, occupied only supporting roles in this report.

Forbes had emerged as the leading adversary, at least from the perspective of television news media, in January. With this, he became the target of greater media scrutiny and of attacks by his rivals. Buchanan now encountered this same fate as several controversies erupted over the final days preceding the New Hampshire vote. The first, reported on February 15, involved a charge that a Buchanan manager had spoken at an anti-gun control rally in Colorado where he had met with some white supremacists. Network reporters showed scenes of Dole accusing Buchanan of running a campaign of hate and bigotry. There was a related story one day later as the Buchanan campaign staff in Florida dismissed a woman because she was presently active in the National Association for the Advancement of White People, an organization that reporters identified as white supremacist (NBC and ABC).

The increased scrutiny was not limited to Buchanan as television news media directed some attention to Alexander. Two networks, CBS and NBC, had critical reports about his income on February 15 and 16, respectively. The two reports focused on how Alexander had used inside opportunities while in office to increase his personal wealth. This contradicted Alexander's efforts aimed at creating a public image where he appeared as a political outsider. He had even used a red plaid shirt as his campaign symbol.

The closeness of the Iowa vote and the New Hampshire poll standings encouraged the candidates to become even more critical of one another. Since television news media prefer to direct their attention to the most divisive features of campaigns, the competitiveness of the primary led them to direct even more of their reporting to the personal attacks of the candidates. This practice may have encouraged the candidates to become even more critical of each other. On February 15, network correspondents reviewed an acrimonious debate of the previous evening. John Cochran (ABC) said that today was "the morning after the bloodletting." He added that Dole had taken the most arrows because he was the front-runner. This report had scenes of Buchanan and Alexander attacking Dole and recent footage of some of the negative advertising that was dominating New Hampshire television. Cochran concluded by adding, "Keep it up, say Democrats, and Bill Clinton can campaign on the character issue." Perhaps as a way of underscoring this point, this network followed with a report about negative campaigning that included interviews with several disaffected voters who seemed angry at both the Republican campaign and its candidates. The other two networks had similar news reports about the debate and included attack comments by Dole, Buchanan, Alexander, and Forbes (CBS and NBC).

Two days later, on February 17, Gwen Ifill (NBC) described New Hampshire as "a make or break state." She said polls showed that Dole had slipped, that Forbes was fading, and that Alexander and Buchanan were on the move. In a scene that was quite obviously made for television, Alexander talked about negative campaigning while holding a pair of high boots that he said he needed for the campaign. Ifill then added that Dole had the support of former Governor John Sununu and current Governor Steve Merrill. She followed with scenes of recent television commercials where Merrill attacked both Alexander and Buchanan. The other networks also had scenes of the candidates attacking one another. Gramm, who by now had endorsed Dole, condemned Buchanan for using what he said were racist appeals in the Louisiana campaign (ABC). The correspondent, Michele Norris, referred to polls that said one-third of voters thought Buchanan was too extreme. Russ Mitchell (CBS) reported about charges that Dole was using push polls against Buchanan. His report also contained scenes from negative ads from the different candidates.

The media perception of the prospects of the candidates as the primary approached and of the status hierarchy among them was quite evident on the NBC telecast of Sunday, February 18. This network had four field reports with one for each of the major candidates. The placement of the reports corresponded to the exact order of finish of the candidates in Iowa and of the standings by those candidates in current polls. Dole was first, Buchanan second, Alexander next, and Forbes last. The reports also reiterated the themes about each candidate that television news media had been using in recent days. Lisa Myers focused on Dole who spoke of his economic plans while being endorsed by Gramm. Myers identified Dole as the front-runner and said he was expecting a protracted fight for the nomination, but also believed that he would win it if he could capture New Hampshire. Gwen Ifill described Buchanan as shadowing Dole in the polls and targeting angry voters and working-class Republicans. She then added that Buchanan's rivals were saying he was too conservative to beat Clinton and that he would have trouble winning the support of moderate voters. David Bloom informed viewers that Alexander was surging in the polls and was riding a backlash about negative advertising. Bloom also referred to some of the recent controversies about Alexander's personal finances. He concluded by adding that Alexander's campaign was short of money and was not raising it fast enough to compete much longer. Tom Brokaw followed by summarizing Forbes' stands while including scenes of him campaigning. Brokaw then referred to Forbes' rapid reversal of fortune in recent polls.

The coverage by the other networks was similar to that of NBC, including the emphasis on divisive themes. The first report on ABC was about the present poll standing of the candidates. Peter Jennings said the campaign was mean and that people were talking about negative advertising. He added that Dole would likely be a scant winner. The media emphasis on negative features was also apparent on CBS as Dan Rather called the campaign "an increasingly down and dirty fight." Phil Jones described Buchanan as Dole's rival on the right and included scenes in his report of the two attacking one another. Finally, Dan Rather interviewed Gramm who attacked Buchanan for his support from racists, particularly from former Ku Klux Klan leader David Duke.

Television news media continued with these same themes on February 19, the final day before the primary. The race was too close to call, ABC reported, with Dole and Buchanan tied for first and with Alexander and Forbes fighting for third. Despite this closeness, John Cochran identified Dole as the front-runner and the establishment candidate who had overwhelming support from most New Hampshire politicians. Cochran added that Dole's campaign seemed to lack excitement and that his rallies appeared as flat as his native Kansas. The report about Buchanan followed, in second place, in conformity with network patterns of recent days. Michele Norris said Buchanan wanted a new party and was offering "raw American First populism" and was "making hay with people who fear the future." She added that his oratory was anti-establishment, in contrast to that of Dole. In a third news report on ABC, Jim Wooten said all four of the major candidates had been attempting to appear as outsiders but Buchanan had been the most successful at doing so. He identified Dole as an insider. In a report with themes similar to those of the other networks, Phil Jones (CBS) described the campaign as "tight, volatile, and nasty," with Buchanan surging and "keeping up with what other Republicans saw as radical rhetoric." Jones said Buchanan was looking for an upset but Dole was still expected to win the primary. Jones focused much of his report on reviewing some of Buchanan's past speeches, including his call for a security fence along the Mexican border, his 1992 references to a cultural war, and his opposition to the Persian Gulf War.

Each network reported directly from New Hampshire on primary day, February 20, with NBC describing Buchanan as the new front-runner after projecting him as the winner. Dole was still the nominal front-runner in the opinion of ABC, however. The NBC report also said that Buchanan had a hard-core base and was helped in the primary by economic troubles in the state. This network added that Dole had the best organization for the rest of the campaign but this defeat would cause some psychological damage to his effort. Kevin Phillips (CBS) stated that Buchanan would not be the nominee and that the party could split. He added that the Buchanan movement was much broader than the Republican Party, as demonstrated by the recent candidacies of Jesse Jackson, Ross Perot, Ralph Nader, and even that of Buchanan himself, as all were alternatives to the two-party system. Buchanan had scored a big win and had now hit the Republican Party like a lightning bolt, Phillips continued. He would find trouble outside New Hampshire because people did not believe he could win and thought that he was too extreme. The theme of the CBS reporting was that the nomination had now narrowed to Dole and Buchanan. Alexander had too little money to seriously contest the remaining primaries while Forbes was effectively out of the race.

The early tests were now over and the winnowing process was well underway. What had once seemed a complicated battle among eleven announced candidates had narrowed into a two-way struggle between an embattled front-runner from the party establishment, and his leading adversary who was the spokesman for a variety of anti-establishment forces that existed within the party. Dole and Buchanan had recorded a first and a second place finish in the two early tests and had, with the assistance of television news media, redefined the campaign as limited only to their candidacies.

While voters in Iowa and New Hampshire had seen the candidates firsthand, voters in the rest of the nation had little contact with any of them except through mass media, and particularly television. The Gallup–CNN–USA *Today* polls suggest that the reporting patterns discussed here may well have affected the perceptions of voters in places other than these early test states. These polls showed Dole leading all candidates on January 7 by a substantial margin but with no one candidate clearly identifiable as his leading adversary. Dole had 47 percent of the vote at that time with Forbes holding 11, Gramm 10, Buchanan 7, and Alexander 2 percent. The poll of February 25, taken shortly after the New Hampshire primary, had Dole in first place but his support had declined to 41 percent. Buchanan had moved into second with 27 percent while Alexander had 14 and Forbes 8 percent.

THE BATTLE FOR SOUTH CAROLINA

The closeness of the votes in Iowa and New Hampshire suggested that the nomination might remain unresolved for months. In a twist of events, however, the struggle lasted for only a few weeks more and effectively ended with the South Carolina primary on March 2. The reason for this abrupt change of fortune was that two campaigns, conducted under very different circumstances, had been taking place simultaneously with the candidates now required to shift their attention from the first of them to the second. The first campaign had been the struggle in the two early test states that had attracted the personal attention and financial resources of the candidates and the attention of television news media. The second, virtually unnoticed, was occurring in the remainder of the nation. Dole was the undisputed front-runner in this second campaign and was generally unchallenged by anyone. While several candidates had contested Iowa and

New Hampshire on relatively even terms, Dole was the only candidate who was prepared to compete in this second campaign. He had survived the battles in the early test states and was ready to eliminate his remaining rivals within a matter of weeks.

Buchanan appeared to have successfully employed the outsider strategy, discussed previously, with his showings in Iowa and New Hampshire. Despite such appearances, he had actually failed in this endeavor and his candidacy would soon collapse. He would be unable to transform the expanded televised news coverage that resulted from his showings into a strong national constituency or even into a clear role as the leading adversary of front-runner Dole. He had emerged as the second strongest candidate within a very short period of time, perhaps less than one week, and had accomplished this through intense competition with other candidates whose support had been only slightly weaker than his own. As a result, his hold on second place was tenuous. Television news media had already looked at both Gramm and Forbes at various times as the number two candidate in the race. They had stopped making such characterizations during the final days before the Iowa vote and the caucuses had not provided them with a clearly identified candidate to fill that role. Television news media had considered Buchanan as one of the "others" in the race for much of the year. They had viewed both Buchanan and Alexander as candidates whose major roles had simply been to attack the principal contenders, Dole and Forbes. The only constant theme in news coverage thus far was that Dole was the front-runner. The identity of his leading adversary seemed to change weekly with Buchanan now getting his turn in the limelight.

While television news media may have started viewing Buchanan as Dole's leading adversary, voters in the rest of the nation still saw the campaign as one involving front-runner Dole opposed by several relatively unknown aspirants. None of these aspirants, including Buchanan, had developed the constituencies that would have enabled them to win the nomination. Moreover, Alexander and Forbes were not yet ready to withdraw and thereby limit the battle to only Dole and Buchanan. They would continue their efforts for several more weeks and would attain just enough television news time to keep the race from becoming exclusively a two-candidate affair. Dole had won the invisible primary and had survived the early tests. By now, he had more money, organizational support, and personal exposure in the remaining states than any of his rivals. Despite their extensive activities in the early test states, Dole's rivals had not penetrated the political consciousnesses of many of the nation's Republican voters. Dole could now rely on his superior resources and personal recognition and eventually wear down his rivals in a war of attrition.

The post-New Hampshire phase of the campaign began on February 21, the day after the primary. Television news media tried to depict the battle as a two-candidate affair but soon found that the presence of Alexander and Forbes posed obstacles. They focused more attention on Buchanan than before and also placed the reports about him in more prominent positions in their daily telecasts. Russ Mitchell opened the CBS political reporting on February 21 by depicting the campaign as "shifting into higher gear" with Buchanan at the head of the pack. Mitchell added that money was starting to roll into what had previously been a poorly financed effort. He continued by saying that all was not good news for Buchanan as many party insiders were against him and were starting a stop Buchanan movement. Phil Jones (CBS) followed by saying that Dole was now in a fight for survival but added that he would fight on. Linda Douglass provided the third report for CBS this day as she stated that Alexander was trying to depict himself as the only candidate who could unite social and economic conservatives and win the election. The other networks followed scripts similar to that of CBS with the first political report on each network focusing on Buchanan and with the second on Dole. Both networks had scenes of the two leading candidates commenting about one another and illustrated Alexander only in a secondary role (ABC and NBC). None of the networks focused any attention on Forbes this day.

Network correspondents continued to make Buchanan the subject of their news reports over the next two days with Mike Jensen (NBC) reporting on February 22 of controversies surrounding his economic proposals for international trade. Jensen interviewed several business owners who said they would be hurt by them. Jensen included some past quotes of Buchanan speaking about import quotas, NAFTA, and the recent financial bailout of the Mexican government by the United States. Brit Hume (ABC) directed attention to divisions that appeared to be developing within the Republican Party over the Buchanan candidacy. He also included remarks by Gingrich and Lugar about how they believed the party would be damaged by a Buchanan nomination and that it could suffer major losses in Congress. All three networks reported about the daily comments of Buchanan and Dole on February 23 while generally ignoring the other two candidates.

Three states—Arizona, North Dakota, and South Dakota—were holding primaries on the following Tuesday, February 27, so television news media responded on February 24 by directing attention to these upcoming battles while including scenes of both Alexander and Forbes campaigning in other states. The most important televised imagery this day was of Dole and Buchanan attacking one another with Buchanan even referring to Dole as "Beltway Bob" (NBC). Alexander had declined to contest these three states so he campaigned in South Carolina instead. Forbes was in Delaware and expected to win an uncontested primary in that state before heading for Arizona (NBC).

Dole was clearly in trouble in Arizona, said Mike von Fremd (ABC) on February 25, and a highly publicized endorsement he received that day from Barry Goldwater would not likely help. Von Fremd added that Dole had led his rivals by about twenty percentage points in polls taken two months earlier but the lead was gone, a result he attributed to Forbes' negative advertising and Buchanan's personal barbs. While Dole appeared with Goldwater, Buchanan generated some interesting imagery of his own by attending services at a conservative church and by speaking against gun control while wearing a pistol and western clothing (ABC, CBS, NBC). Forbes attained some favorable coverage this day by virtue of his victory in Delaware. He captured 33 percent of the vote compared to 27 percent for Dole and 19 for Buchanan (NBC).

Correspondents' emphasis on the more divisive aspects of the campaign continued on February 26 when they reported about controversial staff changes in the Dole organization and with CBS describing a new poll in which 46 percent of Republicans said that Buchanan was too extreme. With February 27 being election day, each network directed much of its attention to Arizona, the site of the only primary with several candidates actually competing against one another. Dole, Buchanan, and Forbes contested Arizona while Dole was the only candidate who had devoted any significant effort to the Dakotas. Jim Wooten (ABC) said that Arizona was a ripe opportunity for Buchanan to wreak havoc while adding that Dole was worried because he believed he had not worked hard enough in the state. Wooten concluded by saying that Dole's candidacy was struggling. He also described Forbes as optimistic about his chances and included a scene of Alexander speaking in Massachusetts. In other ABC political reports, Tom Foreman said Dole was running well in the Dakotas while Dean Reynolds added that Arizona could be a breakthrough state for Forbes and that a good showing might help his chances in the New York primary scheduled for nine days later. Forbes was quite optimistic about his chances and even predicted victory.

Forbes apparently had good reasons for his optimism as he won with 33 percent of the vote compared to 30 percent for Dole and 28 percent for

Buchanan. While he made a significant comeback from his disappointing fourth place finishes in Iowa and New Hampshire, Forbes would not find Arizona to be his breakthrough state. It was his last hurrah. One day later, NBC reported that the Arizona triumph had cost Forbes approximately $40 per vote. Even someone with his extensive wealth could not afford many more victories at this cost. Dole, meanwhile, had some good news this day as he scored two sweeping victories in the Dakotas. He acquired nearly 45 percent of the vote in South Dakota and about 42 percent in North Dakota while finishing far ahead of everyone else.

The campaigning and media emphasis shifted to the next primary, South Carolina. The race was a demolition derby, remarked Lisa Myers (NBC) on February 28. She said Forbes can now claim he is the front-runner, Dole is confident about winning South Carolina, Buchanan is planning an ambush, and Alexander is seeking to get back in the stream. Aaron Brown (ABC) looked at differences in the economic appeals of Dole and Buchanan. Dole was supported by much of the growing high tech and foreign trade industries, he said, while Buchanan was appealing to people hurt by the declining textile industry. The other networks had similar economic reviews over the following two days and emphasized these same themes. All networks reported on February 29 about what Phil Jones (CBS) called an "ugly" debate between the four candidates where they spent much of their time attacking one another. The news reports also included one scene where Buchanan defended the flying of the confederate flag from the state capitol.

South Carolina was a Dole breakthrough, said Mike von Fremd (ABC) on March 2. It could be the defining moment of the campaign, Phil Jones (CBS) stated. The voting had not concluded by the time the networks began their evening broadcasts, so none actually attempted to project a winner. Instead, the correspondents reported about the day's exit poll. According to von Fremd, the poll indicated that Dole was running well and the issues he had campaigned on—taxes, economics, and the deficit— were the most important to the state's voters. Contrastively, Buchanan had campaigned on the trade issue but the poll demonstrated few voters found it important. Buchanan had not been helped by what von Fremd described as his strident anti-abortion stand. A majority of Republican voters said they did not want a plank in the party platform calling for a human life amendment to be added to the constitution. The amendment and plank were major goals of religious conservatives. In addition, the poll also showed that about half of the Republican voters thought Buchanan was too extreme. Network reporters also employed imagery to emphasize this point as they included scenes from an anti-Buchanan demonstration in Massachusetts where Buchanan had spoken at a rally that day (CBS and NBC). Buchanan had also been hurt because he seemed to be losing the Christian vote to Dole in South Carolina. Dole said he had supported the agenda of the Christian Coalition at a 100 percent level for the past three years, Jerry King reported (ABC). The exit polls and related media analysis appeared correct as Dole won the primary with 45 percent of the vote. Buchanan finished in second place with 29 percent while Forbes had 13 and Alexander 10 percent. This victory allowed Dole to leave South Carolina with momentum, said Phil Jones (CBS).

The themes of televised news reporting changed after this and became very similar to what they had been in early January. Once again, television news media depicted Dole as a strong front-runner while virtually reducing his remaining rivals to the status of "losers." The major theme that surfaced over the next few days was that Dole would win the nomination while the remaining candidates would soon fail. Themes of this nature are not unusual for they reflect one of the major functions that television and other news media now play during the latter stages of contested nomination battles. Correspondents redirected their reporting in ways that helped generate a consensus of support behind the candidacy of the front-runner and obvious winner. Dole had demonstrated that he was the most viable candidate while each of his rivals had apparently failed. Network reporting conformed to this pattern and helped bring the race to a speedy conclusion. From this point on, network reporters treated Dole as the winner.

For example, on Sunday March 3, the first political news report on ABC focused on Dole with John Cochran using the term front-runner twice while Linda Douglass (CBS) described Dole as the resurgent front-runner. Lisa Myers (NBC) called his victory "commanding," and added that his rallies were now upbeat. Dole was also helped by the fact that he had won an uncontested primary in Puerto Rico this same day, a fact mentioned on the various network telecasts. In contrast, the media emphasis on the failures of Dole's rivals was particularly noticeable with respect to Alexander. Catherine Crier (ABC) raised the question of "What's Next?" One scene showed Alexander in church, but Crier commented he would need more than prayers in Georgia. Georgia was one of eight states holding primaries on March 5 and was the one state of the group where Alexander had campaigned extensively. While the reports about Buchanan and Forbes were not as focused on failure as those about Alexander, they were unfavorable nonetheless. Dean Reynolds (CBS) reported about the latest efforts of Forbes and said he was attempting to stay in the race at all costs and was now picking targets in several states, including New York.

The changing status of the candidates was apparent once again in the news reporting of Monday, March 4. Each network made Dole the subject of its first election-related report and told viewers that he would do well in the primaries of the next day and perhaps even win them all. They even had scenes of him receiving an endorsement from Gingrich. In contrast, Buchanan and Forbes appeared only in scenes where they attacked Dole. The emphasis on Alexander's failures continued as John Cochran (ABC) said he might leave the race if he did not do well the next day.

The reporting on election day, March 5, once again focused on the likelihood that Dole would run well, although this analysis was also based on exit polling. Gwen Ifill (NBC) spoke of a raucous race for the nomination while adding that Dole would likely win all of the day's eight primaries. She said Dole had fractured Buchanan's base by winning over many of the religious and economic rally motivated voters. Jim Wooten (ABC) described this as an enormous day for Dole whom he depicted as cheerfully optimistic. Even Buchanan was quoted saying as much. Wooten remarked that Alexander was short of money and might soon quit the campaign while adding that Forbes would continue his campaign in the New York primary two days later. The struggle for the nomination was not yet over, however, as two additional reports this day suggested what was likely to come. Richard Threlkeld (CBS) reported from Rochester about Forbes in New York while Lisa Myers (NBC) looked at a problem that would resurface in news reporting many times before the year ended, women and the Republican Party.

There has been much discussion since 1980 about the alleged existence of a gender gap in voting, where women vote more Democratic than men. Myers reported about the difficulties the Republican Party was having in winning the support of women voters in this year's election. Senator Olympia Snowe (Maine) placed part of the blame on Buchanan and the Christian Coalition by saying their anti-abortion views were driving women from the party. Myers concluded by saying men were about evenly divided between Clinton and Dole while women preferred Clinton by a margin of eighteen percent. This is a pattern of support that would remain consistent for the rest of the year (see chapter 4).

Indeed, the day was Dole's as he swept to victory in all eight primaries. His support ranged from a low of 40 percent in Vermont to a high of 64 percent in Rhode Island. His triumphs included Colorado, Connecticut, Georgia, Maine, Maryland, and Massachusetts. Buchanan's best showing was in Georgia where he attained 29 percent. Forbes ran best in Connecticut with 21 percent while Alexander's high was in Rhode Island with 19 percent. He had finished second behind Dole only because Forbes and Buchanan had not been on the ballot. There could no longer be any doubt, Alexander's campaign was over.

THE FINAL WEEKS

Dole's victories in ten primaries during the first days of March virtually ended the nomination campaign. He was the only candidate who had a national following sufficiently large enough to provide him with any realistic chances of contesting every primary. His rivals could run well only by devoting massive amounts of time and resources to selected states. Forbes had run fairly well in Iowa, New Hampshire, Delaware, and Arizona only after saturating those states with television advertising. Alexander and Buchanan had run well only in those places where they had spent many weeks in personal campaigning. Buchanan had campaigned in his best states four years earlier when he had opposed George Bush. No candidate could possibly hope to sustain intense efforts like these in every state, particularly in light of the fact that each week would bring on another group of primaries. Fifteen more primaries would be taking place over the next three weeks. Dole, however, could compete. His years of national involvement in the Republican Party in a variety of capacities had helped him become a well-known and popular candidate among his own partisans in virtually every part of the nation. He did not have to devote weeks to personal campaigning or spend millions on television advertising in order to run well in a primary. The major task for Dole in every state was to expand into victory what probably would have been a decent second place finish that he could attain with limited efforts. He had done that in Iowa and South Carolina while narrowly falling short in New Hampshire and Arizona. His defeats had been close, not devastating, and had been balanced by good performances elsewhere.

In a sense, the early tests of 1996 were artificial. Several candidates devoted virtually all of their time and money to competing in a small number of states in the hopes that a good finish in one or more might translate into the massive media coverage that had propelled the unknown Jimmy Carter to the Democratic nomination in 1976. There were two major differences between 1976 and 1996, however. The scheduling of caucuses and primaries in 1976 had been less compact than it was in 1996. The Iowa caucuses of 1976 had occurred in late January, one month before the New Hampshire primary. The two were separated by only eight days in 1996, however. Second, there had been no front-runner for the Democratic nomination at the outset of 1976. Consequently, Carter merely needed to finish ahead of his rivals in Iowa in order to claim the vacant front-runner role. There was already a front-runner for the 1996 Republican nomination before Iowa, however, and it was Dole. Even a victory by Buchanan in New Hampshire did not alter the fact that Dole was the national front-runner who was more well-known, who had raised more money, who had attained more endorsements, and who had a stronger campaign organization than all other candidates. Carter finished first in Iowa in late January, claimed the vacant front-runner position immediately, then received a month of sustained news coverage as the leading Democratic candidate, and finally verified his new role by winning the New Hampshire primary. There was little doubt that Carter was indeed the front-runner and the probable nominee after his victory in New Hampshire. One cannot say this of Buchanan. He was still struggling after his New Hampshire victory to even claim the leading adversary role and could not hope to compete with Dole in every one of the 25 primaries scheduled for March. This incredible schedule overwhelmed Dole's rivals and effectively drove them from the field.

Television news media changed their news themes after this latest group of victories by Dole and started treating him as the virtually certain nominee. They also directed more attention to the theme that the other candidates were losers who should now abandon their failed efforts. Two of those rivals, Lugar and Alexander, actually withdrew from the race on March 6 and immediately endorsed Dole. Phil Jones (CBS) began his network's coverage of the day's political news by reporting that Dole looked unstoppable for the nomination. Jones included some upbeat scenes of Dole campaigning and then described Buchanan as a defiant loser, a term which also served as a subtitle for the report about him. Dole attained another important endorsement this day, that of Governor George W. Bush of Texas whose state would be one of seven holding primaries on March 12. Each network also had scenes of Dole meeting with both Governor Bush and his father, the former President. Despite Dole's primary sweep, Buchanan was not yet ready to leave the race. He told Dan Rather that Dole could not win the support of Perot voters and that Dole was clueless about what was happening in the nation. Buchanan then attacked Dole over NAFTA and trade while saying that corporate layoffs were occurring in order to increase the stockholders' profits. He also attempted to personify his campaign with a cause when he said that it was not about a man, but was instead about values.

There was a curious irony this day, and it received some fairly extensive news coverage. Former congressman and Bush housing secretary Jack Kemp endorsed Forbes while claiming that Forbes had the best tax plan of all candidates. Kemp's endorsement was designed to help Forbes in the March 7 New York primary and actually encouraged reporters to focus more of their attention on that battle. Jeff Greenfield (ABC) soon reported about Dole's campaign in New York, including his support from the state's Republican organization and its leaders Senator Alfonse D'Amato and Governor George Pataki. Greenfield's report included visual images of party workers campaigning door-to-door for Dole. Greenfield added that Forbes had little organizational support in the state and was therefore relying almost exclusively on television. Organizational support is particularly important in New York because voters cannot cast ballots directly for candidates. They are limited to selecting individual delegates instead. Dole eventually swept the primary and won all 93 delegates.

Television news media continued to cast Dole as the imminent winner of the nomination in their coverage during the following week and even began devoting more airtime to his upcoming confrontation with Clinton. Russ Mitchell (CBS) reported from Texas on March 9 about how Dole might fare with Perot voters in the general election while ABC considered the problems that Dole might face in his choice of a Vice President. On March 12, Jim Wooten (ABC) reported from Florida about the differing views that Cuban voters had of Dole and Clinton. Older voters seemed to like Dole for his opposition to Fidel Castro while younger ones were more attracted to Clinton because of his stands on education and the environment. The fact that this network was considering voter preferences for the general election was an indication of how it viewed the Republican campaign. Despite their new emphasis on Dole's upcoming confrontation with Clinton, however, television news media continued reporting about the efforts of his remaining rivals. Dean Reynolds (ABC), Russ Mitchell (CBS), and Gwen Ifill (NBC) reviewed Forbes and Buchanan but their reports followed those about Dole and were shorter in duration.

To the surprise of no one, Dole won all seven primaries on March 12, thereby bringing his number of victories for March to eighteen. His support ranged from 48 percent in Louisiana to 60 percent in Mississippi. He also captured the primaries in Florida, Oklahoma, Oregon, Tennessee, and Texas. The day was a disaster for both Buchanan and Forbes. Buchanan's strongest showing was in Louisiana, a state whose caucuses he had won earlier. He attained only 33 percent of the vote. His worst was in Florida where he tallied only 18 percent. Forbes did even worse as his support ranged from a high of 20 percent in Florida to a low of 8 percent in both Mississippi and Tennessee.

The Republican candidates virtually disappeared from network news for the next two days as Clinton dominated the airwaves when he traveled to Egypt for an anti-terrorism conference. He also went to Israel and appeared in a number of made-for-television scenes. These included a visit with schoolchildren, a meeting with Prime Minister Shimon Peres, and a trip to the grave of Yitzhak Rabin. There were only two news items of any significance concerning the Republican candidates during Clinton's trip. One was about Forbes withdrawing and endorsing Dole while the other was about Dole returning to Washington. One news report about the latter contained some visual imagery that may well be one of the best illustrations of why a challenger encounters such enormous difficulties in defeating a strong incumbent. John Cochran (ABC) said Dole planned to campaign against Clinton from his leadership position in the Senate. Governor John Engler (Michigan) had been in Washington this day, March 14, to promote the creation of block grants to the states for Medicaid and welfare spending. Dole wanted congressional approval for the measures. If Congress responded by doing so, Dole could take credit, Cochran said. If Clinton vetoed the proposals, however, Dole could then blame him and use the vetoes as campaign issues. The two final scenes in Cochran's report included an image of Clinton sitting at his desk in the Oval Office followed by a scene of Cochran pointing toward the Capitol Building while referring to it as Dole's home. Clinton appeared as an individual President while Dole was associated with the faceless building that represents what many people believe to be an impersonal government.

The withdrawal of Forbes now reduced the campaign to only two candidates and removed all doubt that Buchanan was indeed Dole's leading adversary. In fact, he was the only adversary. Seven primaries remained in March, however, with those in the Midwestern states of Illinois, Michigan, Ohio, and Wisconsin scheduled for the nineteenth. Three Western primaries from California, Nevada, and Washington would take place the following week on the twenty-sixth. Thirteen additional primaries remained afterwards, but they were scheduled for much later dates, mostly in May and June. Buchanan appeared in some of these states but continued to fall further and further behind Dole. Television news media treated him more and more as a defeated candidate who should leave the battle than as a viable contender. Buchanan also attained very limited news coverage because network correspondents were already focused on the general election campaign.

Dole's final efforts as a candidate at this stage of the election year occurred in California during the final days preceding that state's vote. He left Washington to campaign in California for a few more days and directed his remarks toward Clinton rather than Buchanan. He advocated the B-2 bomber and the death penalty and visited a state prison where he called for an end of lengthy appeals by convicted felons. He ended his efforts on Monday, March 25, with a rally in Russell, Kansas, where he once again attacked Clinton. As expected, Dole won all of the late-March primaries. His votes ranged from a low of 51 percent in Michigan to a high of 66.4 percent in Ohio. He won in California with 66.1 percent while Buchanan attained only 18 percent. Buchanan concluded his failed campaign shortly afterwards while Dole returned to Washington where he would begin the next phase of his doomed battle with Clinton.

CLINTON AND THE REPUBLICAN PRIMARIES

One of the more important influences on the outcomes of elections with strong incumbents is the successful effort by the incumbent to project a televised image of statesmanlike leadership on his part during the most divisive phases of the opposition party's nomination campaign. This certainly applied in 1996. The major themes of televised news during the first two weeks of January that involved Clinton and the Republicans were related to the budget battles, as discussed previously. Coverage of the Republican campaign changed in mid-January when network correspondents started focusing on Forbes as the probable leading adversary of Dole. This was also when Clinton began appearing more frequently in the unifying statesman role and less as a combative partisan involved in budget struggles.

Clinton went to Bosnia on January 13 and met with American troops in a number of highly photographed scenes. The Republicans were engaged in a bitter debate in Iowa at the time and received much more critical coverage. Clinton preempted the news about the Republican candidates two days later when he spoke in Atlanta in honor of Martin Luther King, Jr.'s, birthday and again five days later when he spoke at the funeral of Barbara Jordan. He continued preempting the Republicans during the following week when he gave his State of the Union Address. The address itself and its aftermath were the leading political news stories for three days; the day before the address when correspondents speculated about what

Clinton might say, the day of the address when they reviewed what he would say, and the day after the address when they analyzed what he had said while evaluating how poorly Dole had performed in the Republican response.

Clinton launched his campaign in New Hampshire on the second of February and visited the state for two days. He was the topic of the lead political stories on both CBS and ABC on the second and of NBC and ABC on the third. These networks had scenes of him shaking hands with voters, touring a school classroom, speaking at a rally, and commenting to reporters about the death of the first American soldier in Bosnia. Ann Compton (ABC) added that Clinton was leading all of his Republican rivals in the state. The newscasts moved on only after they were finished with Clinton and showed the Republicans in Iowa engaging in some of the strongest personal attacks yet against one another.

Clinton did not leave the campaigning in Iowa and New Hampshire entirely to the Republicans during the final days before the votes in those states either. He received very good televised news coverage while speaking at an upbeat rally in Iowa the weekend before the caucuses and at another rally during the following weekend in New Hampshire (CBS). John Palmer (NBC) said that Clinton was using the rally in New Hampshire as an opportunity to test themes that he might use in the general election. Clinton had also spent some of the time between the Iowa and New Hampshire votes in highly photographed appearances where he inspected recent flood damage and spoke with victims. He spent two days, February 14 and 15, in Washington and Oregon (ABC) and the sixteenth in Pennsylvania (NBC). He had several opportunities to respond to international problems during the last week of February as well. He went to California for a trade meeting with Japanese Prime Minister Ryutaro Hashimoto on the twenty-sixth. Clinton used this trip as an opportunity to speak before large and enthusiastic rallies and to attack Buchanan's trade proposals. Moreover, the controversy surrounding the Cuban attack on several planes of an anti-Castro exile group based in Miami also occurred during this time. Clinton's comments continued to preempt Republicans and even helped to turn their campaign actions into matters of secondary news interest for three consecutive days.

The campaign for the nomination of the opposition party was relatively short in 1996 compared to the more exacting ones of 1964, 1972, and 1984 when the incumbents were also unopposed for renomination. Despite this, Dole suffered the political consequences that usually befall the nominees of opposition parties in elections with strong incumbents. It is virtually impossible to win a nomination in elections of this type without falling so far behind the incumbent that victory in the general election becomes unattainable. Such was the fate of Dole. Three polls taken by the Gallup–CNN–USA *Today* group indicate how the events of the nomination campaign, including Clinton's numerous attempts to present a statesman-like image of leadership while the Republicans were fighting one another, actually weakened Dole's prospects. Clinton led Dole by 54 percent to 43 percent in the poll of December 18. This poll had been taken shortly after the start of the second government shutdown. While many voters may have initially blamed the Republicans for the shutdowns, as shown in the previous chapter, they were beginning to distribute that blame somewhat more evenly in January. The poll of January 15, taken about the time that the budget issue had finally disappeared from network television, indicated that the race was once again too close to call. Dole had 49 percent while Clinton had 48 percent. The battles over Medicare and the budget had provided Clinton with a temporary advance but he could not sustain it without some additional help. The Republican campaign provided that help. Clinton took the lead for good during this time as he led Dole by 54 percent to 42 percent in the poll of March 17. This poll was completed about one week before Dole finished his primary election efforts with his victory in California, and three days after John Cochran had talked of how Dole was planning to use his position of Senate Majority Leader as a means of opposing Clinton. Dole's new strategy eventually proved useless, however, since the campaign was actually over by this time. Clinton had already secured his second term by winning the rhetorical battle over the budget and by then successfully projecting imagery during the divisive Republican campaign where he appeared as a qualified statesman more deserving of the Presidency than his embattled rival from the opposition party.

CHAPTER 4

THE SEVEN MONTH GENERAL ELECTION CAMPAIGN

Dole's extensive string of primary election victories during March brought about a relatively early end to the Republican campaign. With the conclusion of the California primary on March 26, Dole had more than enough delegates to claim victory. Moreover, each of his rivals had accepted this verdict and had concluded his candidacy. With this, the general election campaign was underway by the beginning of April, and as a consequence, would develop into one of the longest political and media battles of recent history.

My purpose in this chapter is to describe and evaluate the seven month general election campaign while directing particular attention to the manner in which television news media interpreted political events and candidate statements and then explained them to their viewers. I also look at the final distribution of votes as recorded in the Electoral College and among specific population groups as determined by network exit polls. There are five sections in this chapter; this introductory one, three that direct attention to the different chronological parts of the campaign, and a final one that describes and evaluates the vote of November 5 and links it to the nation's recent electoral patterns. The first chronological section is about the campaign during the four-month period between the conclusion of the primary election season and the beginning of the two national party conventions in August. This is an unusual period of time in presidential elections because in most years at least one of the nominations remains undecided. Moreover, the campaign for that undecided nomination is often at the very peak of its intensity and divisiveness between April and mid-summer. In most elections with strong incumbents, this is also when the eventual nominees of the divided opposition party suffer most from the recurring patterns of televised news coverage and become virtually unelectable. The unusual feature that marked this time during 1996 was that the general election campaign was already underway but was quite incomplete. The eventual nominees were limited in what they could do because the $60 million in federal funds that each was counting on to finance his effort would not be available until he had been nominated by his party in August. Moreover, Dole did not even have a running mate. The candidates responded to these circumstances by developing the themes and strategies they would later use while television news media focused much of their attention on short-term events that proved interesting for only a limited number of days.

The second chronological section is about the campaign during August, the month of the national conventions. The Republicans began on Monday, August 12, while the Democrats convened two weeks later on the twenty-sixth. Both conventions were four-day affairs. The conventions were unusual in that both were far more scripted for television and emptied of any real or imagined controversies than those of other years. Despite this lack of content, the quantity of televised news coverage of the candidates was far more extensive during this one month than at any other time during the year.

The third chronological section directs attention to the post-convention phase of the campaign, the time after Labor Day. Labor Day traditionally marks the beginning of the general election campaign in most years, but it occurred on September 2 in 1996, which was only four days after the final day of the Democratic convention. It also marked the time when many news organizations, such as the Gallup–CNN–USA *Today* group, began their daily tracking polls to measure the progress of the candidates. This period encompassed the final two months of the campaign year and included the three nationally televised debates.

The general patterns of televised news reporting that occurred during these seven months were similar to those of the nomination period. Television news media once again spent far more time responding to the initiatives and statements of the candidates and to breaking stories about criminal trials and corruption rather than to efforts aimed at generating information about topics other than polling. When they did generate their own information, they either looked at the finances of the candidates and parties or to the electoral prospects of the two candidates and their support from particular states or groups of voters.

Television news media employed five primary themes in their reporting. The amount of time they devoted to each theme varied through the different chronological periods and sometimes even within the same week. Nonetheless, there were few instances where the networks focused much attention on any themes other than these five. One theme was that of statesman. Reporting of this nature occurs when candidates seek to project imagery where they appear as non-partisan unifying leaders rather than as aspirants for office. Most reporting associated with this theme focused on Clinton. Television news media frequently showed him responding to foreign events or to tragedies such as airplane crashes, bombings, floods, or church burnings. In addition, Clinton often appeared statesmanlike in several media-oriented events that he generated specifically for the campaign, such as White House bill signing ceremonies. Contrastively, television news media directed very little attention to Dole where he appeared statesmanlike. His most important opportunity occurred on his final day in the Senate when the networks included imagery of his past activities while reflecting on his 35 years in Congress.

The most widely employed theme was the daily behavior of the two candidates. This included scenes of the leading actions and statements of each candidate on any particular day. Examples are Clinton's announcement of yet another new presidential initiative or an attack by Dole on Clinton's policies, character, or administration. Television news media often showed the candidates speaking before large crowds of enthusiastic supporters and telecast some of the imagery that the candidates had employed in their efforts at enhancing their personal appearances. The imagery was not limited to that advanced by the candidates in their daily appearances, however. It sometimes extended to the content of paid television advertising. The networks often reviewed Clinton's and Dole's advertising.

A third theme was the contrast between the candidates. Clinton and Dole, and various other people and institutions associated with them, often appeared in contrast to one another. This occurred in such circumstances as the budget battle, the State of the Union Address and Republican response, the acceptance speeches by each candidate on the final night of his party's convention, and the nationally televised debates in October. Television news media used these opportunities to compare the candidates and evaluate their performances. Moreover, the contrasts extended to the candidates' wives who spoke at their respective conventions and to their running mates who debated in October.

Corruption and ethics served as a fourth theme. On several occasions, television news media looked at a number of alleged scandals of the Clinton administration, including Whitewater, the secret FBI files, and foreign fundraising. They looked at Dole's fundraising as well. Much of the network reporting about this theme was related to external, that is, non-campaign, developments rather than to actions taken by the candidates. Clinton's troubles attracted media interest only when they were the result of major courtroom actions or congressional hearings. Television news media actually took the initiative on one related topic, however—the parties and their special interest money. Each network broadcasted a series of reports during both national conventions where they focused attention on the extensive contributions the parties were receiving from corporations and lobbyists.

The final theme discussed here is the one that often attracts the greatest criticism of television news media, the horserace. The networks reported extensively about how well Clinton was doing; how he had united the fractious Democrats; how well he was running in traditional Republican states; and how poorly Dole was faring. They depicted Dole as conducting a disorganized campaign and of trailing in many nationwide and statewide polls and in those among specific groups such as women. The horserace reports informed television viewers that Clinton was ahead and would win while Dole was trailing far behind and would lose. The networks often accompanied their reports with comments that Dole was not "gaining any ground" on Clinton and that his time was "running out."

My first step in explaining the final results of the election is to describe the state-level outcomes as seen in the vote of the Electoral College. In particular, I direct attention to the votes of individual states and to the voting patterns of groups of states. I follow by looking at the long-term significance of these patterns in relation to elections of the recent past for both President and Congress and of the prospects for both political parties in the next presidential election, 2000. I conclude by looking at the votes of various social groups as measured by the exit polls of the Voter News Service and link them to the personal and partisan appeals of Clinton and Dole and to the strength of Clinton's incumbency.

THE PRE-CONVENTION CAMPAIGN

The pre-convention campaign, the events that were part of the general election season but which occurred before the party conventions, is the topic of this section. This four month period was an unusual feature of the 1996 election, since comparable periods rarely occur in most election years. In a number of ways it was unique to 1996. It was unusual for both parties to conclude their nominations by April 1, at least in the sense that the eventual winners were obvious and with all other candidates withdrawing from the contests. It was also rare for both parties to hold their conventions in August; this is a relatively late time. The usual pattern is for one party to convene in mid-July with the other meeting in early or mid-August. One can attribute the unusual times for the 1996 conventions to the scheduling of the Atlanta Olympic Games during the last half of July, which is a relatively early date for the Olympics. The Summer Games of 2000 will be held in mid-September at Sydney, Australia, which is a more typical time for them.

While the existence of this pre-convention campaign was indeed unusual, it was consistent with what was to occur in the months ahead. Each candidate employed the same themes in his speeches and actions that he would use during the latter stages of the campaign. Moreover, television news media developed and employed the same themes in their daily coverage that they would use later. The networks focused more attention on the daily appearances and statements of the candidates than they did on any other topic. They also focused on several themes that helped define the nature of the campaign itself. The most important were of Clinton acting in the statesman role and speaking in an upbeat manner before crowds of enthusiastic supporters; of both Clinton and Dole facing significant ethical difficulties; of Dole attacking Clinton while promising an alternative vision of leadership; and perhaps most important, of Dole always trailing Clinton in the polls and heading for an almost certain defeat in November.

One of the most important advantages that an incumbent possesses when seeking reelection is his ability to project imagery where he appears as a statesman leading the nation rather than as a politician seeking office. Clinton used this rhetorical aspect of the Presidency quite effectively during these four months. One of his first successes came on April 4 when he spoke in Oklahoma City to commemorate the first anniversary of the bombing of a federal building that had killed 168 people. He appeared as the nation's leader rather than as its chief Democrat, and used this opportunity to speak to the depth of the emotional feeling that millions held for the families and friends of the victims.

Clinton also appeared statesmanlike through his foreign policies and related travels. He visited Japan and Russia in April and enjoyed the opportunities for televised imagery that often accompanies presidents in these circumstances. He spoke with leaders and ordinary citizens while abroad, toured sights, and signed a new agreement with Russia on April 20 to limit nuclear testing (ABC). He met with Shimon Peres (CBS) and Yasir Arafat (NBC) at the White House on April 30 and May 1, respectively. The bombing by terrorists of a barracks at an Air Force base in Dhahran, Saudi Arabia, on June 25 with a loss of 19 American lives also provided Clinton with additional statesmanlike imagery. The bombing was the leading news story on all networks that day with Clinton speaking to reporters from the White House where he denounced terrorism (CBS and ABC). He headed for Europe on June 26 to attend the annual conference of the world's major free economies, the G-7 group. Television news media focused particular attention on his comments as they related to the problems of terrorism (NBC). After returning, Clinton traveled to Florida where he spoke at two memorial services in honor of the Saudi Arabian bombing victims. He spoke of the sacrifices of the servicemen and said that the nation would find and punish those responsible (ABC). He expressed, once again, the grief that much of the nation held for victims of political violence.

The statesmanlike imagery was not limited to foreign affairs, it extended to Clinton's initiatives concerning arson attacks at Southern black churches. He used his weekly radio talk show of Saturday, June 8, to announce an expanded federal law enforcement effort aimed at finding the arsonists responsible for fires at over thirty churches. He complemented his address by appearing with the ministers of some of the affected churches at a White House press conference and photo opportunity later that day (ABC). Television news media soon supplemented Clinton's initiative and began focusing more attention on the problem. On Monday, June 10, CBS reported about the arsons and the federal efforts to find the perpetrators. The network also included scenes of Clinton speaking about the problem. Clinton encouraged the networks to focus on race-related arson again two days later when he toured a South Carolina church that had been rebuilt after an arson attack. He prayed with religious leaders, denounced the arsonists, and called on the nation to support its churches (CBS).

Clinton continued generating statesmanlike imagery through the summer months. He met with the new Israeli Prime Minister Benjamin Netanyahu at the White House on July 9 and traveled to Atlanta on the nineteenth for the opening of the Olympic Games (ABC and CBS). Two networks, ABC and CBS, showed him speaking to the American team while NBC, the network that televised the games, broadcasted scenes of the Clinton family during the initial ceremonies. Clinton also appeared statesmanlike during the events related to the explosion of TWA Flight 800 on July 18. Television news media first reported of the tragedy with Clinton saying we should not jump to conclusions about terrorism until all the facts were known (ABC). Clinton went to New York on July 25 where he spent more than three hours with the families of the victims. Several of these people praised his actions while speaking before television cameras. Clinton used this opportunity to announce the immediate implementation of new safety requirements for airlines (CBS). He commented about terrorism once again on July 27 when the leading news story was the bombing at the Olympics. He told reporters that the federal government would catch those responsible (ABC).

There was a second aspect to the statesmanlike coverage of Clinton during this time, however, this being the media treatment of Dole. After taking a short break following his California victory, Dole began his general election effort against Clinton in mid-April. Despite the fact that the news coverage he had attained thus far had been somewhat less damaging than that usually attained by challengers in elections with strong incumbents, Dole still encountered a problem similar to those faced by all such challenges. When a President appears in a statesmanlike manner, the challenger comes across as little more than an aspirant for office. He cannot create imagery where he appears as the statesmanlike equal of the President. This assumes that the challenger can even attain any televised news coverage during these times, a feat not always possible. Dole attained little news coverage during the events related to the Saudi Arabian bombing. Moreover, ABC and CBS telecast a series of reports about Dole's contributions from the tobacco industry while Clinton was in Europe commenting about terrorism. Dole also attained limited news coverage on those days when television news media initially focused on new tragedies such as the Olympic Park bombing or the crash of Flight 800.

It is, of course, difficult for a challenger to appear statesmanlike since this role often belongs exclusively to the President. One can see the difficulties a challenger faces in the manner in which television news media covered Dole when he was statesmanlike, on the day he resigned from the Senate. After returning from the primaries with the nomination secured, Dole planned to use the Majority Leader position to outline an alternative approach to governing. This strategy soon failed, however. Senate Democrats were unwilling to cooperate and instead delayed the passage of much of the legislation Dole wanted. Virtually nothing Dole sought had any chance of passing without extensive fighting between the two parties. Such fighting would remind voters of the gridlock that had dominated Congress for so many years. It would also work in Clinton's favor whenever he campaigned against Congress as he had been doing for much of the year. In response, Dole announced on May 15 that he intended to resign from the Senate in early June (ABC).

Dole's final day in the Senate was Tuesday, June 11. Television news media made his resignation their lead story as each network commented about his 35 year congressional career while including remarks by his colleagues of his accomplishments and leadership. While this certainly was a day when Dole looked very good, reporters' comments often detracted from the statesmanlike imagery. Jeff Greenfield (ABC) talked about what Dole would need to do in order to win the election. His theme was that leadership in Congress rarely translates into support in a presidential campaign. Dole would need to appeal to voters in ways that differed from his actions as a legislative leader, Greenfield added. In addition, reporters also commented about the abortion controversy within the Republican Party and of Dole's likely response to it.

Despite the obvious fact that he had already secured the nomination, Dole could not avoid news coverage that focused on divisive problems within the Republican Party, particularly abortion. The most important unresolved controversy was the platform language relating to abortion. Christian conservatives wanted the platform to openly oppose abortion and call for a constitutional amendment granting states the power to outlaw it. Moderate Republicans, realizing their minority status within the party, instead wanted language more tolerant of opposing views. They certainly had no hopes of defeating the abortion plank. The inclusion of the tolerance language was their major goal and one which the Christians opposed with equal fervor. Dole was soon trapped in this controversy. As a consequence, television news media had a divisive theme they could use when reporting about the Republican convention.

The first televised reference to the controversy was on June 11, the very day Dole resigned from the Senate (ABC). John Cochran said Dole wanted the more inclusive language. Additional news reports followed over the next few weeks. The news of June 20 came from Texas where pro-life forces were attempting to deny Senator Kay Bailey Hutchinson a seat in that state's national convention delegation because of her pro-choice views (ABC). News relating to her candidacy and abortion stand continued on June 21 when Dean Reynolds (ABC) reported from the Texas Republican convention and included interviews with several of the principal actors in the battle. John Cochran (ABC) reported about the platform language this day and about Dole's efforts to change it. Dole had met with Henry Hyde, chairman of the platform committee and a major congressional leader of pro-life forces. The two apparently agreed to alternative language.

The controversy continued into the next day as both Ralph Reed, Executive Director of the Christian Coalition, and Pat Buchanan spoke before the Texas convention about the need for an unequivocal pro-life position in the platform. The pro-life activists eventually won control of the Texas delegation, although Hutchinson did win a delegate position. In a related story about the party divisiveness theme, ABC replayed some of the controversial remarks Buchanan had made at the 1992 national convention where he said the nation was in a cultural war and the Republican Party needed to take sides.

The abortion issue returned to network television on July 1 after Dole hinted he might select a pro-choice running mate. After summarizing Dole's remarks, Phil Jones (CBS) profiled two pro-life Christian groups, the Christian Coalition and Focus on the Family. Opposition to abortion was the driving force among Christian conservatives and they would become angry if the Republicans adopted the tolerance language, Jones added. He included some critical comments by Buchanan in his report. On July 12, Cochran (ABC) once again reported about the continuing attempts by Dole and Hyde to alter the platform language, a task Dole could no longer accomplish. Cochran also interviewed Ann Stone, a leader of the pro-choice Republicans, and Gary Bauer of Focus on the Family. Neither was particularly satisfied with Dole's recent statements.

While Clinton attained relatively favorable coverage for his statesman-like appearing actions, he fared less well with the ethical and legal problems of his administration. Television news media occasionally reported about a number of Clinton's problems relating to the Whitewater scandal and of a new controversy, the requests to the FBI by White House staff members for confidential personnel files about several hundred prominent Republicans. Dole was unable to take advantage of these developments, however, since network reporters discussed his fundraising problems and looked at his contributions from the tobacco industry. Television news media did not look at Clinton's fundraising troubles until later in the year.

The first ethical issue that attracted the attention of television news media was the Whitewater related trial in Arkansas of James and Susan McDougal and the new governor of the state, Jim Guy Tucker. Clinton had testified about his associations with them in April, although television news media had not reported about the content of his videotaped remarks at that time. This story became newsworthy once again on May 9 after

Clinton's testimony was shown in court and again on May 28 when the trio was convicted. Clinton conducted an impromptu press conference on the White House lawn after the verdicts were announced. The theme of the various news reports was that Clinton had not been charged in connection with the scandal but, as Jackie Judd (ABC) added, these convictions were likely to bring new life to the Whitewater story just when public interest in it was declining. It seems she was right. On June 6, CBS focused on Whitewater by televising Alfonse D'Amato's remarks about the needs of his investigative committee for more information. Media interest in Whitewater increased once again on June 17 when the final report of D'Amato's committee was due. The story this day was about Hillary Clinton's possible involvement with the missing billing records that had been found recently in the White House. Bill Clinton denied that Mrs. Clinton had been involved in any wrongdoing (ABC). One day later Jackie Judd reported that the committee's Republicans were "very harsh" about her role while Democrats defended her actions by saying the investigation was politically motivated. More Whitewater news followed on June 19 when Bruce Lindsay, a Clinton campaign aide, was named as an unindicted co-conspirator in the upcoming trial of two bankers who allegedly had made illegal contributions to the 1990 Clinton campaign for governor (ABC).

The news emphasis finally shifted from Whitewater, but Clinton soon found himself in new political trouble when a controversy developed about the White House personnel files. Television news media reported about some matter related to this problem virtually every day between June 23 and July 2 and continued occasionally afterwards. They began each day by reviewing the latest events associated with White House security aides Craig Livingstone and Anthony Marcesa, and, if relevant, the investigation by the Senate Judiciary Committee into the matter (ABC, CBS, NBC). The story began to conclude on July 8 when Clinton stated the collection of the files had been a mistake and the problem had been corrected (ABC). It finally concluded on July 12 when CBS reported that Clinton had apologized to approximately 300 Republicans whose files had been observed by Livingstone.

There was also some air time devoted to Dole and his problems. John Cochran (ABC) reported on April 21 about a scandal involving a Republican fundraiser and business owner from Massachusetts who had given several of his employees cash reimbursements for their contributions to Dole. Television news media continued with the financial theme on June 27 when they reported that both Dole and the Republican Party had been receiving extensive contributions from the tobacco industry. The party had already attained about $3.4 million during 1996 with Dole himself getting about $400,000. The Republican Party and its candidates were now getting about 84 percent of all contributions made by the tobacco industry (CBS). The tobacco-related news coverage was not limited to reports about contributions. Dole had to defend himself from criticism over remarks he had made about tobacco not being addictive. The news reports included imagery of a Democratic Party worker dressed as a cigarette and carrying a sign that read, "Butts for Bob" (CBS). The CBS report was on a single evening news program while ABC had a one-hour prime time special program on June 27, which included an interview with Dole. While these reports failed to prove the existence of any significant ethical problems that might have denied Dole the Presidency, they mitigated Clinton's problems by suggesting they were not unique and that Dole's ethics probably were not much better.

While television news media may have focused some of their summertime attention on a few controversies associated with the candidates, particularly with Clinton, they appear to have done so primarily in response to short-term events. They exhibited little sustained interest in these matters over the course of the campaign. They directed attention to Whitewater only (1) when Clinton testified on videotape, (2) when the tape was shown in court, (3) when the jury returned guilty verdicts, (4) when the Senate committee investigating Whitewater issued its final report, and (5) finally, when Bruce Lindsay was named as an unindicted participant. They considered the files controversial only when (1) the problem initially surfaced, (2) when the central roles of Livingstone and Marcesa were established, and (3) finally, when the Senate investigated the problem. The news reports about Dole's tobacco related contributions were also driven by events. They occurred only after various political action committees had to file mandatory listings of their political contributions. Some of these committees were associated with the tobacco industry. Interest in Clinton's and Dole's ethical troubles was always short-lived, often taking place for only a few days at a time, and ended quickly without new developments. Television news media quickly redirected their attention elsewhere. Moreover, Clinton acting in the role of President and Dole acting in the role of challenger had many opportunities to encourage television news media to focus their attention on other matters. The abilities of presidential candidates, and an incumbent in particular, to create imagery or to respond to breaking events in very public ways virtually guaranteed that ethical issues would occupy only a limited part of the news agenda. Television news media quite simply found many more topics worthy of their attention.

The third theme of televised news was of Dole attacking Clinton over a variety of issues of his choosing and of Clinton responding rapidly to those attacks. Dole began the series of daily battles on April 20 when he attacked Clinton for appointing federal judges whom he claimed were too liberal and too soft on crime. Clinton responded almost immediately by saying that Dole had voted to confirm 98 percent of them (ABC). After this exchange, television news media spent the next few days focusing on Clinton's visit to Russia, the candidates' ethical problems, and the standings of the candidates in the polls. The campaign returned to charges and countercharges on April 29 when Dole focused his attacks on the 4.3 percent increase in the gasoline tax that Clinton had successfully sought in 1993. The recent and sharp increases in gasoline prices should lead to the repeal of this tax, Dole argued. The media battle over the tax continued for several days. On May 3, Dole said he was planning Senate hearings favoring repeal (NBC). The battle took on a new dimension as Democratic Leader Daschle spoke on the seventh of preventing any vote on the tax until the Senate considered an increase in the minimum wage. Dole was visibly angry at these developments (CBS). Clinton gained the advantage on the eighth when he said he would accept the tax changes if he also received the wage increase bill. He said he would sign both if there were no "poison pills" in them (NBC). The gas tax and wage battles disappeared from network news shortly after these exchanges and neither issue resurfaced again.

The next battle was over welfare reform. Phil Jones (CBS) reported on May 20 that Dole had attacked Clinton for stealing Republican ideas on welfare. Jones remarked that Clinton planned to speak in Wisconsin the following day and had recently spoken favorably about that state's welfare changes. Dole was trying to prevent Clinton from preempting his own efforts, Jones added. Dole was scheduled to be in Wisconsin one day after Clinton. Clinton countered Dole's remarks by saying he had advocated welfare reform for the past fifteen years and the issue was not one where "no Democrats need apply." Television news media reported about Dole's efforts to raise the welfare issue for two more days while including imagery from his Wisconsin remarks. They then dropped the issue about as quickly as they had focused on it. The issue returned to network news on July 30, although this time it was Clinton who attained most of the coverage. The House of Representatives had approved the welfare reform bill and was sending it to Clinton for his signature. The general theme of various media analyses was that Clinton would likely be helped because Dole could no longer use the issue against him (ABC and CBS).

A new round of topics developed in early June as Dole raised the issue of a 15 percent tax cut for everyone, a theme that was to become a major part of his campaign appeal (CBS). Clinton soon seized the initiative, however, as he used his commencement address at Princeton University to call for a tuition tax credit for college students (NBC). Clinton then announced plans on June 7 for reductions in closing costs for new home purchases. This proposal would reduce the cost for first time buyers by about $200 (ABC). Clinton followed by directing attention to the church arsons and dominated the political news for several more days.

There was a sharp reduction in news coverage of the candidates after these developments as television news media directed their attention to the Republican debate over abortion and to Clinton's difficulties over the personnel files. The most important candidate-related news over the next few days was about the appearance of Clinton and the lack of one by Dole at the national convention of the NAACP. Clinton spoke before the organization on July 10 where he said he would veto any attempt by Congress to repeal the Brady Law concerning handgun control. Television news media complemented these visual images by telling their viewers that Clinton had strong support among black voters. They also commented, as did several black leaders, about Dole's refusal to speak before the convention (CBS and NBC).

Another round of battles for media attention occurred during the final days of July when the candidates exchanged comments over the conduct of the television and movie industry. Clinton spoke on the twenty-ninth at a conference he had called, and announced an agreement between the Federal Communications Commission and the television industry in which the industry agreed to provide three hours of children's programming weekly (CBS). Dole had his turn the next day as he spoke in Hollywood before the Motion Picture Association. He praised them for producing films over the past year that contained less sex and violence than before. Following his report of this event, Phil Jones (CBS) included remarks by several prominent critics of the movie industry, including Jack Valenti and Gene Siskel, about the probable effects of political jawboning. They said the most effective pressures would be market-related, not political.

The standings of the candidates in the polls and their prospects for victory was the fourth major theme of news reporting during these summer months. Television news media started directing attention to this theme shortly after Dole began campaigning in April. They often told their viewers about how poorly Dole was faring and how well Clinton was doing. One can see an example of this in the ABC telecast of April 27 when Jerry

King remarked that Clinton was running well and had united his party. This unity had paid off because it enabled Clinton to take a number of moderate stands on controversial issues that Republicans often used to attack Democrats, such as welfare and crime. King also reviewed the Democrats' advertising efforts as they sought to link Dole to the unpopularity of Newt Gingrich and the Republican Congress. The advertising referred to a Dole-Gingrich Congress. In addition, King said Dole was trailing far behind Clinton, perhaps as much as twenty percentage points. In another report, John Cochran remarked that Dole was low on money and that some Republican leaders wanted him to resign from his position of Senate Majority Leader so he could then escape the negative image of Congress, which they believed was harming his efforts. A resignation would also provide Dole with far more time for campaigning directly against Clinton, Cochran concluded.

This theme was reiterated by ABC on May 15 when Dole actually announced his resignation plans. Cochran said Dole had become the victim of Democratic stalling tactics and was falling even more behind in the polls. On July 14, ABC reporters John Cochran, Sam Donaldson, Cokie Roberts, and George Will, commenting on *This Week with David Brinkley*, spoke of how inept the Dole campaign was and of how Dole could well lose the election. Finally, CBS reported on July 24 about a joint appearance in Pennsylvania of Dole and Susan Molinari who had recently been named as the Republican convention keynote speaker. Sandra Hughes (CBS) focused on the gender gap among voters and on how poorly Dole was faring among women. She referred to a CBS poll showing Dole trailing Clinton by a margin of 58 percent to 36 percent among women.

This unusual summertime campaign concluded at the end of July. It was a strange period, dominated by scenes of Clinton in staged appearances where he looked statesmanlike, by media reports of personal scandals, and by Dole engaging in several unsuccessful attempts to criticize Clinton on a variety of issues that failed to generate long-term interest by either news reporters or voters. Despite all of this activity, the standings of the candidates in the polls hardly changed at all. They were virtually the same at the end of July as they had been at the start of April; Clinton was ahead and on his way to another term.

THE NATIONAL CONVENTION PERIOD

The campaign changed dramatically after the beginning of August. The candidates and their parties engaged in far more election-related activities during this month than they had at any time before. Television news media responded accordingly by devoting more airtime to political activities in August than they did in any other month of 1996. One can divide this month into two halves based on the content of political news and the scheduling of the conventions. Dole and the Republicans dominated the news during the first half, while Clinton and the Democrats did so during the second. The patterns of news reporting for both halves were similar; each candidate attained extensive coverage in the week prior to his party's convention and in the week of the convention itself. Each candidate's best coverage came on the final night of the convention when he gave his acceptance speech before both partisan and national audiences. This was the greatest single opportunity each candidate would have during the year to appeal directly to the nation's voters.

The first news reports of August concerning Dole were driven by an event he created, the announcement of his economic plan with a 15 percent tax cut as the centerpiece. The reports were rarely favorable and often raised questions about the feasibility of the proposal. One network, CBS, reported on August 2 that Dole would be announcing his plan three days later on the fifth. Ray Brady (CBS) then reviewed Clinton's economic record and concluding that the tax cuts he had fought for and attained in 1993 had contributed to greater economic growth by reducing both the deficit and subsequent borrowing. This eventually helped lower interest rates and fuel economic growth. This network then showed imagery of Clinton speaking about his successes in creating more jobs, and included a scene of him signing a bill at the White House. A second network, ABC, also reviewed Dole's plan on August 2. John Cochran referred to unnamed critics who said the plan would increase the deficit and help only the rich. These two networks continued their analysis on the fourth with sharp comments about the plan from economists and government officials. The major theme of their criticisms was that the tax cut would expand the deficit and increase interest rates without stimulating the economy.

The lead story on all three networks on Monday, August 5, was Dole's actual announcement of the plan. Once again, television news media focused on the controversies associated with it. They quoted various critics as saying the plan would increase the deficit and slow economic growth. In addition, Clinton attained some fairly extensive coverage of his own when he stated that his program had reduced the deficit while Dole's would undermine his accomplishments. One network, ABC, also reported about the new Democratic television commercials attacking Dole's plan while another, NBC, reported that Dole was trailing in the polls and hoped this plan would improve his chances.

Television news media redirected their attention to the abortion controversy during the final days preceding the Republican convention. Their major theme was the part Dole was playing in resolving the language issue and how this might affect his chances. The controversy was the lead televised political story on August 6, the Tuesday before the convention. The platform committee had voted to reject the tolerance language that Dole had negotiated previously with Henry Hyde. Tom Brokaw began the NBC newscast by remarking that abortion was blowing up in Dole's face. This network used the wording "Backing Down" as the title for its report about Dole's troubles over the tolerance language. Dan Rather started the CBS telecast by describing the day's actions as a "cave-in, a roll-back, and a defeat" for Dole. Peter Jennings began the ABC program by saying that the day's activities had been a power struggle about abortion with zero tolerance being the view of the party. Television news media also carried the public comments of such abortion adversaries as Ann Stone and Ralph Reed. Stone said the platform committee was telling pro-choice Republicans they were not welcome. Reed, obviously delighted with the results, told his supporters "this is a pro-life party." Governor William Weld (Massachusetts) talked about leading a floor fight to change the abortion language. Meanwhile, Dole addressed the committee by video and directed his remarks primarily to his economic plan. Television news media were focused on abortion, however, and showed little interest in Dole's other concerns.

Television news media also focused their attention on abortion during the opening day of the convention, August 12, as all three networks broadcasted scenes of three prominent pro-choice Republicans—William Weld, Olympia Snowe, and Pete Wilson—being booed by pro-life delegates as they spoke with reporters. Peter Jennings (ABC) called attention to the booing while NBC profiled and interviewed two women Republican activists from Texas. One was a pro-life delegate who was opposed to any employment outside the home, while the other was a business executive who recently had been defeated for a delegate position because of her pro-choice position. The network (NBC) followed this report with one about the communications plans of the Christian Coalition for keeping track of the convention actions of about 500 pro-life delegates who were affiliated with the coalition. On August 13, CBS carried a report from Wichita, Kansas, about the abortion controversy in this city, which had undergone extensive picketing and even a shooting within recent years.

Neither side appeared satisfied with Dole on the issue. The next day, Wednesday August 14, all three networks reported about the abortion controversy and showed scenes of Ralph Reed saying from the podium, "Let me say it so there can be no doubt. The Republican Party is a pro-life party and as long as we're here it always will be." In addition, John Cochran (ABC) said the party was trying to avoid a debate on abortion because a debate might lead to remarks similar to the cultural war references Buchanan made while speaking at the 1992 convention that some Republicans believe contributed to the party's defeat in that year's election.

The focus of reporting soon shifted to Dole's choice of a running mate. Network reporters profiled several potential candidates during the week preceding the convention with Jack Kemp, John Engler, and Senators Connie Mack (Florida) and John McCain (Arizona) receiving the most attention. They concentrated on Kemp on and after the ninth when Dole finally made his choice known. The Kemp selection was the dominant news story for two days as the networks continued profiling him. The networks also interviewed optimistic Republicans and telecast scenes of Dole speaking in Russell, Kansas on the tenth when he actually announced his decision. There were extensive scenes of the two candidates appearing together and of Kemp campaigning with supporters, including instances where he passed a football. The imagery was very favorable to Dole and television news media responded by telecasting it as such. This was some of the best coverage that Dole had attained in months.

The coverage of the Republican convention began in earnest on August 11 when Dole arrived in San Diego. The most prominent scene this day was of Dole and Kemp arriving by boat in the harbor area. Later, Dole talked about his tax plan while Kemp employed a football metaphor by saying Dole was the quarterback while he was the blocker. This pattern of coverage was typical of what was to follow over the next few days. Network reporters would review scenes of the two candidates speaking before state delegations and other Republican groups each day, with the supporting imagery generally optimistic and favorable. The leading speakers during the convention were Nancy Reagan, Susan Molinari, McCain (who nominated Dole), Elizabeth Dole, Kemp, and Dole himself. Television news media broadcasted their speeches live during prime time, and then reviewed the major aspects of them on the evening news telecasts of the following day. Mrs. Dole attained an unusual amount of media attention and public praise for her unusual but effective approach when she spoke from within the audience rather than from the podium as is typical for convention speakers. The high point of the convention was Robert Dole's acceptance speech on August 16.

The Republican candidates dominated political news for several days following the convention as they conducted a cross-country campaign trip where they emphasized the themes of lower taxes and personal trust. Dole and Kemp traveled to Denver, Springfield, Pittsburgh, and Buffalo and spoke before large and enthusiastic crowds of supporters. They were joined by Colin Powell on August 20 in Louisville at the convention of the Veterans of Foreign Wars, and in Nashville for a meeting of black journalists two days later. Dole also attained some favorable coverage on the twenty-fifth when he spoke at a well-attended rally in Chicago on the eve of the Democratic convention. With this, except for several news reports of him gaining support after the convention only to lose it following the Democratic conclave, Dole virtually disappeared from network television for the rest of August while Clinton and the Democrats dominated the news.

Clinton began his convention efforts in New York City on Sunday, August 18, with a public celebration of his fiftieth birthday. He followed with a new media-oriented event each day until the convention convened eight days later. He was interviewed by Dan Rather on the nineteenth and emphasized his many years of activity on welfare reform. He spoke at a White House ceremony the next day and signed the minimum wage bill into law. He said the law would increase opportunity, responsibility, and community. Brit Hume (ABC) described these words as the theme for both the Democratic convention and the Clinton campaign. Jim Miklaszewski (NBC) said Clinton had used the South Lawn at the White House for the signing ceremony because the Rose Garden was not large enough to accommodate all the guests. Clinton was also photographed with a number of families and children.

Clinton continued his campaign of media-related events the next day, Wednesday the twenty-first, when he announced plans to "lower the boom" on the tobacco industry and, as described by Pete Williams (NBC), to challenge Dole on the issues of regulation and addiction. The actual announcement of rules from the Food and Drug Administration (FDA) would occur two days later and would be aimed at the selling of tobacco to children. The FDA would label cigarettes as drug delivery devices and nicotine as an addictive drug. This would allow new regulations on tobacco sales and advertising. Clinton also conducted another South Lawn made-for-television bill signing ceremony on the twenty-third, with recent changes in health insurance law being the formal cause of the gathering. This law prohibited companies from denying insurance to people who changed jobs or had preexisting conditions (CBS). Clinton continued his bill signings with welfare reform on the twenty-fourth. He said this law would give people a second chance but would not become a way of life (NBC). He formally announced his new tobacco regulations one day later which, not surprisingly, was the lead news story on all networks. Gore actually dominated the news this day. He arrived in Chicago and spoke at an outdoor rally about the economic record of the Clinton administration.

Clinton began a highly publicized and extensively photographed four-day train trip from Huntington, West Virginia, to Chicago on August 25. He visited six states, including Kentucky, Ohio, Michigan, and Indiana, in addition to West Virginia and Illinois, and spoke at a number of stops along the way. The train was named the 21st Century Express in recognition of his campaign theme of "A Bridge to the 21st Century." He attacked Dole's economic plan on the first day by saying it would lead to higher deficits, higher interest rates on homes and credit cards, and that more cuts similar to those he had vetoed recently would likely follow. He also used the theme of opportunity, responsibility, and community in this Ashland, Kentucky, address. Brit Hume (ABC) described Clinton as a cheerful chief executive.

Clinton also dominated the airwaves the next day when he spoke in Columbus, Ohio, about his plans for expanding the Brady Law to prevent gun sales to people convicted of stalking, harassment, and domestic violence. One network, ABC, followed its report about Clinton by examining the effectiveness of the Brady Law. Rebecca Chase said about 85 felons were prevented daily from purchasing guns.

Two other news themes this day also helped bring about some favorable television coverage for Clinton, with one being a report about a possible deal between the federal government and the tobacco companies over regulation. The coverage most favorable for Clinton occurred when Rita Braver (CBS) said he had done more to regulate tobacco than any previous president. The CBS coverage was also favorable as Linda Douglass (CBS) reported about what she described as an enthusiastic and well-received speech on woman's rights that Hillary Clinton had delivered before a group of women delegates in Chicago.

Clinton continued his media blitz on August 27 when he spoke in Pontiac, Michigan, about education. He advocated more money for Headstart and Americorps, expanded school technology, and college tuition tax credits. His plan would cost about $3.4 billion (NBC). He concluded his train trip one day later by talking about the environment. With a stream as a backdrop, he announced a $1.9 billion program for cleaning up toxic waste dumps (ABC).

The convention was underway by now, so Clinton's media efforts gave way to the actions of others. Two of the more important convention speeches were those of Hillary Clinton on August 27 and Gore on the twenty-eighth. In their reviews of Mrs. Clinton's speech about families and children, television reporters gave particular attention to her comments where she challenged the family values agenda of conservative Republicans, "We are all responsible that children are raised in a nation that doesn't just talk about family values but acts in ways that value families." These same reporters seemed more interested in Gore's political future than in his immediate remarks, however. They depicted his speech as an opportunity for building support for his own presidential bid in 2000. Cokie Roberts (ABC) described Gore's day as a "laying on of the hands" while Rita Braver (CBS) proclaimed Gore as the Clinton administration's leading Republican basher and included some past scenes of him attacking Dole and Gingrich. Television news media showed particular interest in the part of Gore's convention speech when he referred to the suffering and death of his sister from lung cancer.

While Clinton had succeeded in dominating the airwaves for several days with highly favorable news and imagery, he could not control everything. The news of Thursday August 29, the very day of his acceptance speech, was dominated by a scandal involving political advisor Dick Morris. Morris was the architect of many of Clinton's strategies, including his earlier battles with Congress over Medicare and the budget. He resigned from his position shortly after a supermarket tabloid claimed that he was associating with a prostitute and had discussed several of his conversations between himself and Clinton with her. The news about Morris was pervasive this day and remained important for about two days afterwards. It proved to be of only temporary interest, however, and completely faded from network news by the end of August.

Despite this setback, Clinton's favorable news coverage continued. One day after the Morris resignation and the conclusion of the convention, television news media focused their evening news reports on Clinton's acceptance speech and new imagery of both Clinton and Gore campaigning on a post-convention bus trip in Missouri. This trip, although far less elaborate than the highly photographed one the Democratic candidates had taken with their wives in 1992, lasted for two more days and included stops in Kentucky and Tennessee.

Televised news coverage of any campaign would hardly be complete without the usual attention that reporters give to the horserace. The first such coverage in August was on the eleventh when ABC reported that

Dole had gained no ground on Clinton with his choice of Kemp and was currently trailing by a margin of 56 to 37 percent. On the fifteenth, in a report originating from Denver, David Bloom (NBC) discussed how Dole was running poorly in Colorado. He interviewed three moderate Republicans who expressed reservations about Dole and concluded by telling viewers that Clinton was leading in that state.

The first network polls that reflected the phenomenon known as the convention bounce, which is when a candidate gains support because of the extensive news coverage of his party's convention, occurred on August 14 when two networks reported Clinton leading Dole by only ten points. One network, ABC, had Clinton ahead by 52 to 42 percent while NBC had the differences at 46 to 36 percent. Five days later CBS had similar numbers, showing Clinton ahead of Dole by 54 to 42 percent compared to 59 to 36 percent shortly before the convention. On August 22 NBC added one additional poll to the collection that showed Dole trailing Clinton by only ten points, 48 to 38 percent. The bounce did not last long, however. The Gallup–CNN–USA *Today* polls showed a volatile but relatively stable period during August. Their final July poll, taken on the twenty-eighth, had Clinton in front of Dole by 50 to 35 percent. Dole reduced that margin to 48 to 41 percent on August 18 but the numbers reverted to totals of 51 to 38 percent favoring Clinton during the final days of August. Once again, a major part of the campaign had passed with very little change occurring in the measured support for either candidate.

The horse-race coverage was also present during the Democratic convention. One network, NBC, reported from the Chicago suburb of Lagrange on the twenty-fourth. Mike Boettcher said the city was a bellwether in that it had voted for every winning presidential candidate over the past sixty years. Boettcher, supporting his remarks by interviewing some area residents, suggested that Clinton was presently ahead and would probably carry the city. The horserace reports continued on the twenty-seventh as ABC summarized its latest poll and said Clinton was regaining some of the support Dole appeared to have acquired during the Republican convention. The next day, the latest poll from CBS also showed Clinton regaining his earlier standing. These various polls had Clinton leading Dole by approximately 15 points. Clinton also attained a convention bounce as a poll by NBC, reported on August 31, had him ahead by 21 points. In a reverse of emphasis, ABC directed its attention on the thirtieth to Dole's weak support in Orange County, California. This county is the heart of suburban Los Angeles and is the home of a conservative Republican voter base, John Cochran informed the audience. Reagan had spoken at a rally here in 1984 attended by 50,000 people while Dole had just spoken at a rally that attracted only 3,000, Cochran added. Cochran remarked that Dole would need a big vote in this Republican county if he had any hope of winning California. He concluded by referring to Clinton's leads in both the state and nation.

While television news media devoted most of their reporting during the convention period to the candidates, they did not limit themselves to merely illustrating the staged events described above. They investigated one issue that promises to be of significant interest for some time to come, campaign finance. They included a number of special topics reports in their daily newscasts about the influence of big money in the affairs of each party. The titles were "Follow the Dollar" (CBS), "In Depth" (NBC), and "The Money Trail" (ABC). On August 12, ABC showed lobbyists attending a Republican gathering with an admission fee of $100,000. Brian Ross included pictures of security guards attempting to block television cameras from revealing the identities of those in attendance. Ross also showed tobacco company executives holding lavish parties for Republican office-holders with Newt Gingrich among them. One day later, CBS reported that the Republican Party was using $13 million it had received from corporations and individuals to help pay for its convention. This report contained scenes of delegates attending yacht parties and sitting in reserved seats at the Del Mar thoroughbred racetrack. On August 14, NBC had similar images and commentary and even had pictures of free mugs that Budweiser had given the delegates with the slogan "lower beer taxes" printed on them.

Television news media gave the Democrats equal time and used the same special topics and titles when reporting about big money interests within that party. They included scenes of private parties and corporate jets in their newcasts. Brian Ross (ABC) focused his report of August 27 on Arthur Coit, President of the Laborers' International Union, a man Ross claimed had a history of connections with underworld figures but who was now making large contributions to the Democrats. One day later, Ross looked at the lobbying and contributions by Native American gambling interests seeking more favorable federal legislation. He gave particular attention to the efforts on their behalf by former party treasurer Patrick O'Connor and concluded by saying, "Few people want to talk about the simple fundamental fact that access to the Clinton White House as well as the Republican Congress is now quite available for the right price."

Despite these harsh themes, the news coverage of the two candidates and parties during August was generally quite favorable. Each party had the opportunity to present itself to the nation in ways that some reporters, Ted Koppel (ABC) for example, called political infomercials. The candidates created vast amounts of upbeat and optimistic imagery where they appeared before groups of enthusiastic partisans while speaking favorably about themselves and their prospects for victory. While August may have contained some of the most widely reported political events of the year, it was not a time of significant changes in support for the candidates, however. Clinton and Dole left the convention period much the same as they entered it, with Clinton holding the large and apparently insurmountable lead he had developed during the latter part of 1995 and the primary election season of 1996.

THE POST-CONVENTION CAMPAIGN

The post-convention campaign encompasses the events of September, October, and the first few days of November. In light of what occurred between April and August, this was only the final chapter in a seven month struggle between Clinton and Dole and is treated accordingly here.

Television news media emphasized the same themes during these final months as they had earlier. They continued displaying the imagery and broadcasting the statements that the candidates created in their daily efforts, particularly those which originated from Dole's singular actions as the Republican nominee and from Clinton's dual actions as both the Democratic nominee and the individual leader of the nation. As occurred previously, Clinton's most important statesmanlike appearing actions occurred when he responded to international troubles or met with foreign leaders.

Clinton's actions did not always appear statesmanlike, however, as television news media focused attention on some of the questionable fundraising activities of his campaign. While most reports with this theme were negative in tone, they appear to have done little damage to Clinton's chances or to have helped Dole much. Since television news media had looked at his fundraising problems earlier, Dole was unable to gain any significant electoral advantages from the troubles of the Clinton campaign.

A new theme that had not been present earlier emerged during these two months, the performances of the candidates in face-to-face confrontations. There were three televised debates in October: two involving Clinton and Dole and one between the Vice Presidential candidates. The only other instance when Clinton and Dole seemed to appear together, although they actually had not, was in January when Clinton delivered his

State of the Union Address and Dole provided the Republican response. Reporters seem incapable of resisting the urge to compare the candidates' performances and to assess how their campaigns might be affected when they appear in contrasting circumstances such as debates. They responded accordingly and provided plenty of commentary and analysis after each debate about the performances and prospects of all four candidates.

The horserace story, and particularly of Clinton winning and Dole losing, continued as a major news theme. Its most prominent usage occurred in news reports about the outcomes of media-generated polls which indicated that Dole was trailing Clinton throughout the nation, within individual states, and among important groups of voters such as women. This theme was even present during the debates as television news media conducted polls immediately after each of them and reported the results to their viewers within minutes of the debates' conclusions. Every post-debate poll suggested that the Democratic candidate had "won" the evening's confrontation.

A final theme, and one that was somewhat new, was that Perot was essentially finished as a significant political actor. Television news media focused attention on Perot only infrequently and treated him as a sideshow to the real action. They depicted him as a struggling candidate who had no realistic chance of duplicating his performance of 1992 or even of attaining enough support to establish the Reform Party he had hoped to start as an electoral vehicle of consequence for the future.

The statesmanlike theme proved to be the most helpful for Clinton. It surfaced immediately after the conclusion of the Democratic convention when he needed to respond to events in Iraq. Television news media reported on August 31 that the Iraqi government was sending troops into the northern part of that nation in order to intervene in a dispute among rival Kurdish factions. The Iraqi action violated the terms of the cease-fire agreement from the Persian Gulf War. Clinton placed American troops in the region on high alert and then informed news reporters and the nation of his actions during a campaign appearance with Gore in Tennessee (CBS). One day later, Clinton stated that he would not tolerate the recent attack that the Iraqi government had just made against a Kurdish city. He ordered a missile attack against selected military targets in Iraq on September 2 (CBS). Network correspondents described the attack itself and then evaluated Clinton's actions and statements of the previous days in their news reports of the third (ABC and CBS), while Tom Brokaw (NBC) informed his audience on the fourth that Generals Colin Powell and Norman Schwarzkopf supported Clinton's actions. With this, the Iraqi story temporarily receded from network news but returned briefly as a secondary item on September 8, 11, and 14. These events helped Clinton in two ways: they made him look statesmanlike, and they removed Dole from the news. While Clinton was responding in a statesmanlike appearing manner to a foreign crisis, Dole was unable to find any realistic opportunities for seriously questioning Clinton's actions. He could do little more than offer supportive statements while arguing that Clinton had waited far too long to act.

The problems that a challenger faces in attaining equal news coverage with the incumbent during a foreign policy crisis were quite evident in the media treatment of the two candidates on Labor Day. Clinton was the topic of the first two news reports on each network. The first reports focused on his actions concerning Iraq while the second ones dealt with his appearance in Milwaukee that day at a labor rally (CBS and NBC). He was also photographed with members of the Green Bay Packers football team (ABC). Television news media then focused their attention on Dole and showed him speaking about taxes before a large crowd in St. Louis. While the coverage of Dole was actually quite favorable, the juxtaposition of scenes of him speaking as a politician immediately after Clinton had already appeared in the statesman's role made Dole the media loser of the day.

Foreign affairs soon disappeared from the news and did not return until late September and early October when events in Israel brought that area of the world into focus once again. This also provided Clinton with opportunities for creating statesmanlike appearing imagery. The lead news story on September 26 was of new violence between the Israeli army and the Palestinians over the opening of a new tunnel on the Temple Mount in Jerusalem built by the Netanyahu government. The various news reports also contained Clinton's remarks about the need for the two sides to bring about a cease-fire (ABC and CBS). The news emphasis on foreign affairs resumed three days later as the lead story was of Clinton's plans to host a White House conference between Arafat and Netanyahu during the following week. Correspondents described how Clinton had been involved in quiet diplomacy over the preceding days in order to bring this about (NBC and CBS). The most important political stories during the next two days, the first and second of October, were about the White House summit. Each day, television news media began their evening telecasts with scenes of the Middle Eastern leaders meeting with Clinton and then followed with Clinton remarking about the possible good outcomes of the talks. Dole, in contrast, could only say Clinton was engaging in diplomacy by photo op

(CBS). As in early September during the Iraqi crisis, television news media generally ignored Dole during the summit. After the conclusion of the talks on October 3, Dole finally attained some news coverage when he attacked Clinton's foreign policies relating to Haiti, Bosnia, Iraq, and Israel and mentioned Clinton's alleged inability to maintain adequate levels of military spending.

Clinton's news coverage throughout September remained quite favorable. Television news media quickly directed their attention to economic matters after the Iraqi crisis concluded, and once again, Clinton responded in ways that made him appear as a highly successful incumbent. On the sixth, the Department of Labor released statistics showing that the annual unemployment rate had declined 5.1 percent, the lowest in seven years. Clinton took credit for this, an improvement he attributed to his taxing and spending changes of 1993, and added that the economy was on the right track. Jim Miklaszewski (NBC) remarked that the unemployment rate had been 7.8 percent only four years earlier when Clinton first ran for President. Corporate profits were at a 28-year high and wage levels were rising, he added. With a reference to a line from Ronald Reagan, Miklaszewski concluded his report by saying that most people believe they are better off today than they were four years ago. The good economic news continued for Clinton on September 24 when the Federal Reserve Board announced plans for holding interest rates constant. Miklaszewski called this "good news for Clinton," and added that new economic information showed incomes had increased while poverty had declined. Clinton commented about these developments on the twenty-seventh while campaigning in Texas.

The campaign returned to the law and order theme for several days in mid-September with Clinton raising the issue this time. He was endorsed by the Fraternal Order of Police on September 16. This endorsement came about because of Clinton's anti-crime record, for his support of the Brady Law, for his successful efforts at banning assault weapons, and for his program of financial aid for hiring additional law enforcement personnel at the local level. Clinton spoke before a group of uniformed officers while receiving the endorsement (ABC).

Dole attempted to seize the law and order theme from Clinton but failed. He actually had planned to devote this week, according to ABC, to emphasizing law and order but Clinton's actions had seriously hindered his efforts. Dole responded by attacking Clinton on the sixteenth for appointing liberal judges to the federal courts, and followed on the seventeenth by touring an Arizona prison that worked convicts in chain gangs. Dole spoke about the needs for cutting drug use, for prosecuting violent juveniles as adults, and for requiring prisoners to work (CBS). One day later, he used a video from a 1992 Clinton interview as an opportunity for attacking the President on drugs.

The crime issue remained in the news for three days with each candidate making a number of promises, but it disappeared on the eighteenth when Clinton changed the topic. He used the institutional powers of the Presidency and signed a bill creating a new national monument of 1.7 million acres (CBS and NBC). The environment replaced law and order as the leading news theme as several congressmen of differing views offered their opinions on Clinton's actions. Clinton then returned to creating imagery through more bill signing ceremonies as he approved a military pay increase at the White House on September 23 and signed a new test ban treaty at the United Nations one day later.

There was an interesting political irony on the twenty-eighth, and it provided Clinton with more good news. Congress had just completed its work on the budget for fiscal 1997 with the passage of reconciliation legislation. With two hard-fought budget victories from previous years already behind him, Clinton attained yet another in 1996. The final legislation provided an additional $6.5 billion in spending that he had wanted for education and social programs. While campaigning in Rhode Island and Massachusetts on the twenty-ninth, Clinton took credit both for the increased spending and for the bipartisan efforts that led to the passage of the new budget (NBC).

The television coverage of Dole during September was nearly as extensive as that of Clinton, but the themes were quite different. While Clinton often appeared statesmanlike when dealing with foreign policy problems or announcing new federal programs, Dole continued acting like an adversarial politician. Network reporters usually directed attention to Dole's daily actions as a candidate, to his frequent attacks on Clinton, and to how poorly he was faring in the polls. Dole spoke in Ohio on September 5 and emphasized education (ABC) and in Pennsylvania on the eighth when he talked about abortion (NBC). He returned to Ohio on the thirteenth and spoke about economics, attended a stock car race in North Carolina on the seventeenth (CBS), and attacked Clinton's drug policies in Los Angeles on the eighteenth (NBC). He was in St. Louis on September 25 and talked about school scholarships for low income people (CBS) He raised the economic issue once again while campaigning in Florida on the twenty-eighth (NBC). Despite these appearances, however, Dole's best day for news coverage, although certainly not planned, may very well have been the nineteenth when every network had scenes of him slipping and falling from an unsecured podium.

Television news media devoted a considerable amount of their time in September to discussing Dole's weaknesses as a candidate. For example, after Dole had spoken in St. Louis on Labor Day, John Cochran (ABC) added that the odds were against him winning the election. Three days later, Phil Jones (CBS) reported that Dole's economic plan did not appear to be catching on with voters. Jones also referred to a new CBS poll that indicated only 23 percent of voters believed Dole would actually cut taxes if elected while 64 percent did not believe he would. On the same day, ABC showed Dole campaigning in Ohio, with Cochran adding that his chances of carrying the state were not good because of a robust economy. Clinton appeared to be ahead here, Cochran concluded. This theme of Dole's troubles continued on September 7 when he spoke in Pennsylvania about his economic plan, with Kelly O'Donnell (NBC) saying that his chances in that state were not good and that he was struggling to gain attention.

Dole spent September 11 in Washington, D.C., where he met with Republican congressional leaders in order to reassure them that he did have a chance to win. Lisa Myers (NBC) said the meeting was poorly attended but many Republicans were concerned about the prospect of losing Congress. The juxtaposing of news reports in the evening network telecasts during this time also did not help Dole. On the twelfth NBC reported about possible American military action in Iraq with Clinton saying the United States would enforce the no-fly zone. This network then exhibited its election year political logo, "Decision 96," with Tom Brokaw adding, "now to campaign 96." David Bloom then followed by reporting Dole was struggling and was seeking a new way to boost his efforts. He was reportedly ready to "take off the gloves" and engage in negative campaigning against Clinton, Bloom continued. This news report also showed scenes of Dole speaking about Clinton's negative advertising and included several excerpts from recent Clinton television commercials attacking Dole and Gingrich. Bloom added that Dole was trailing Clinton by fifteen percentage points in the latest NBC poll. In a related story on September 15, Jeff Greenfield (ABC) commented that this year's campaign was dull because it was not close. A campaign has to be close in order to be exciting but Dole was constantly trailing Clinton, Greenfield concluded.

The unfavorable news coverage and interpretation of events that usually accompanies a losing candidate continued for Dole when a controversy developed over the decision of a bipartisan commission to exclude Perot from the debates. Perot attained some of his limited news coverage when he attacked the commission. He also announced that he would file a lawsuit demanding that he be included or the debates be cancelled. The lawsuit was of little consequence and eventually failed. Perot blamed Dole for his exclusion and television news media appeared to agree. Dole now had to defend his actions. He had wanted the debate limited only to Clinton and himself because Perot's presence would limit his own opportunities for directing viewers' attention to the differences between himself and Clinton (ABC). Network reporters also suggested that Clinton had gained from the scheduling. They derived this conclusion from the fact that the commission decided to hold only two presidential debates, to be concluded by mid-October and to have one of them take place in a town hall format. This is exactly what Clinton had demanded. He had wanted only two debates, with the second ending about three weeks before the election, and with one to occur in the town hall setting where he is at his best.

The horserace coverage resumed on September 23 when ABC began its telecast with an introductory picture of Dole and the caption of "Struggling." Brit Hume said Dole was attempting to find a new theme that would move him ahead in the polls. The most recent ABC tracking poll had Clinton with a fourteen point lead, 54 percent to 40 percent. Hume added that Dole had made no gains since Labor Day and was doing well in only thirteen states. This report included scenes of Dole campaigning in Virginia with Hume adding that Republicans rarely worry about winning this state but Dole now needed to. In an additional ABC report this day from Michigan, where Dole planned to campaign the next day, Dean Reynolds said Dole appeared to be in trouble here. The more unionized areas were strongly for Clinton while Dole was not running well in the Republican suburbs. Voters appeared satisfied with the economy, did not believe Dole's anti-Clinton attacks, and were not buying his tax plan. They also blamed him for the government shutdown, for the mean-spirited behavior in Congress, and for the proposed cuts in Medicare. Dole was also having trouble with women over the abortion issue, Reynolds added. He concluded by saying that Dole was struggling and trailing. One day later NBC carried a similar report with Tom Brokaw telling viewers that Dole was trailing Clinton nationally and was ahead in only eight states, with Texas presently too close to call. Several days later on the twenty-eighth Dan Rather (CBS) introduced a campaign report by saying that Dole was running poorly in California. This report included comments by Senator Diane Feinstein who said the California economy was working quite well for Clinton. Feinstein also referred to a recent *Los Angeles Times* poll showing Clinton with a seventeen percent statewide lead.

One network, ABC, demonstrated once again on September 28 how the juxtaposing of reports about the actions of a strong incumbent and of his hapless challenger can help to generate a consensus of support in favor of the incumbent. This network began its political reporting by focusing attention on Clinton's latest attempts to arrange a White House meeting between Netanyahu and Arafat. Upon completion of that storyline, ABC changed its emphasis to the election and reviewed the poor condition of the Dole campaign. Peter Jennings reported that Clinton would probably win and then showed a map highlighting the seven states where Dole was running ahead. Jennings added that Clinton was running well in states that often vote Republican.

Television news media devoted more of their airtime in September to the horserace theme, and particularly to Dole's weak prospects of victory, than they did to any other topic. They reiterated it time after time, often employing it only days after having done so previously. Moreover, they often juxtaposed this theme with reports and imagery of Clinton appearing statesmanlike. After showing Clinton responding to a foreign policy problem, they would remind viewers that Dole was losing. When they showed Clinton at the White House signing a new law, they would tell voters that Dole was losing. They would show Clinton campaigning in a state that usually votes Republican and then inform viewers that Dole would probably lose the election. They would show Dole campaigning in more competitive states and then inform their audience of how poorly he was running in that same state. This pattern of juxtaposing imagery of a highly successful president leading the nation and winning the election against reports of how poorly Dole was running and statements that he was losing would continue with even greater intensity during October.

While much of the September news coverage about Dole focused on his losing campaign, at least a substantial part of it concerned his daily activities. One cannot say the same about the coverage of Perot. Other than with events related to the debate controversy, television news media virtually ignored Perot and used the horserace theme on the few days that it actually considered him. For example, ABC reported on the eighth that Perot was starting his media advertising campaign but then added that he was garnering only 8 percent support in their latest poll.

As had been true in August, support for the candidates remained remarkably stable during September. The Gallup–CNN–USA *Today* group began its daily tracking polls on Labor Day and continued them throughout the campaign. Clinton's support during the month ranged from a low of 48 percent on the twenty-sixth and twenty-seventh to a high of 57 percent on the thirtieth. His daily average was 53.7 percent. Dole's support ranged from 32 to 39 percent with a daily average of 35.3 percent while Perot's fluctuated between 4 and 8 percent with a daily average of 5.5 percent. These monthly averages were not far from the final election outcomes, although they were somewhat higher for Clinton and lower for both Dole and Perot. The September poll standings were not much different from those of earlier months of the campaign, however.

The actions of the candidates and television news media changed little in October as "Dole losing the election" remained the leading theme of television news. This theme was even more pervasive than it had been in September. On October 4, for example, network correspondents focused their attention on the preparations by the candidates for the first debate of Sunday, the sixth. Jim Wooten (ABC) said that some unnamed Republican critics were calling Dole's campaign efforts unfocused and unorganized and were complaining that he was shifting from topic to topic instead of making one central theme. Wooten added that Dole was speaking to relatively small audiences with very few important Republican politicians in attendance. He then included a scene of Clinton speaking in the rain to a crowd in Seattle estimated at 10,000 people. Finally, the anchor of the day's telecast, Forrest Sawyer, told the audience that Dole was trailing Clinton by fifteen points in the most recent ABC tracking poll.

Television news media directed much of their reporting during the second week of October to the debates, including the one between the Vice Presidential candidates on the ninth. They reported about preparations, analyzed the performances of the candidates, and conducted post-debate polls. With this, they returned to the theme of Dole's troubles. Each network looked at Dole's alleged dissatisfaction with Kemp's debate performance on the tenth and particularly with his failure to attack Clinton. On the eleventh, CBS reported that Dole was planning character attacks against Clinton and included some imagery of him making such an attack. Former education secretary William Bennett spoke to reporters about a possible Whitewater related indictment of Clinton after the election (CBS). In addition, ABC reported about the guidelines that the Dole campaign had given to its surrogate campaigners regarding how they should attack Clinton. Four days later, NBC reported about the so-called soccer moms, people who might provide the decisive votes in the election. Correspondent Lisa Myers defined soccer moms as white suburban women with children who are worried about problems of child raising and work.

Most of these women had voted Republican in the past but now supported Clinton over Dole by a margin of 59 to 31 percent, Myers said. She then interviewed several women and concluded her report by saying that many women were alienated from Dole because of the actions of Newt Gingrich and the content of the Republican platform. These women did not believe Dole understood their problems. Gwen Ifill (NBC) followed by looking at the efforts of Clinton organizers in Arizona to recruit Republican women to work in their campaign.

Television news media returned to the debate theme on October 16 when they raised the question of whether Dole would attack Clinton in that night's confrontation. One network, ABC, reported about the history of character attacks in past elections while referring to the possibility that Dole might use them. Jim Wooten concluded that such attacks seldom work and that candidates who engage in them usually suffer. John Cochran met with a panel of twelve undecided voters from Pennsylvania who disapproved of character attacks and appeared likely to react quite negatively toward Dole if he decided to use them.

Network reporters focused their attention on Dole's continuing troubles on the seventeenth, the day after the debate. Several of them spoke of how well Clinton had done, with Rita Braver (CBS) remarking that his California campaign speech of today was a victory statement. Her report contained some imagery of Clinton speaking before large crowds of jubilant supporters. Brit Hume (ABC) noted that Clinton did not seem bothered by Dole's personal attacks during the debate. He added that Dole was not running well and was using these attacks because other issues that he had raised were having little effect. Television news media continued with this horserace theme on the nineteenth when John Palmer (NBC) reported that the Clinton staff believed the campaign was over and that Clinton needed to focus more of his attention on helping Democrats take control of Congress. One day later, John Donvan (ABC) suggested that Dole realized he could not win and now seemed more interested in helping Republicans retain control of Congress. Donvan's report included scenes of Dole campaigning in New Hampshire, a place he described as a small state the Republican Party rarely loses. In addition, Peter Jennings said the latest ABC tracking poll had Clinton ahead by 52 percent to 40 percent.

The reports about Dole's troubles continued throughout October, with television news media placing more emphasis on his growing anger over his apparently failing efforts. Dan Rather (CBS) said on the twenty-third that Republican congressional candidates had been told by the national party to distance themselves from the Dole campaign. Each network reported one day later about Dole's unsuccessful attempts at encouraging Perot to withdraw and endorse him. Perot refused and responded by attacking both candidates instead. Several network reporters described Dole as angry over these developments, partly because of his problems with Perot and partly because he could gain no ground on Clinton (CBS and NBC). Dole campaigned in Alabama this day where he attacked Clinton, the media, which he called liberal, and even voters because they apparently were unwilling to wake up and understand what Clinton was doing. Jim Wooten (ABC) commented that Dole was desperate. On the twenty-fifth, Dan Rather said that Dole was "pumping up the attacks, especially on the press." Phil Jones (CBS) stated that Dole was fighting for his political life in Texas, where he had spoken that day, and in a number of other Republican states. He continued by saying that Dole was frustrated with both the press and voters and that many Republicans were frustrated with him because of his poorly run campaign. This network also included some imagery of an incident that vividly demonstrated the powers of incumbency and the obstacles that Dole faced as a challenger. Dole was speaking at a rally in Louisiana when the television station covering him suddenly cut away in order to show Clinton's plane arriving. The horserace theme continued on the twenty-sixth when David Bloom (NBC) reported from California. He said that new statewide polls showed Dole trailing Clinton by twenty points. Bloom then raised the question of whether Dole had any chance at all of carrying the state. One day later, John Donvan began an ABC report by saying Dole was gaining no ground against Clinton and was now trailing by 15 percent in this network's latest tracking poll.

Other than horserace stories, television news media focused most of their remaining coverage of Dole during October on his daily actions and particularly on his use of the character issue. Dole attacked Clinton on the thirteenth over the FBI files (CBS), on the fourteenth for his contributions from Indonesian bankers, and on the fifteenth for Whitewater and other legal troubles of members of his administration (NBC). The frequency of news reports about Dole's electoral prospects actually declined during the final days of the campaign, although several network correspondents continued mentioning the results of their tracking polls. Instead, they focused attention on two other themes; Dole's 96-hour marathon trip on the eve of the election, and the growing troubles within the Democratic Party and Clinton campaign over questionable contributions from Indonesian banking sources. Nonetheless, the damage to Dole had already been done.

In an October 27 commentary that demonstrated how television news media had already determined the outcome, Jeff Greenfield (ABC) provided five reasons why Clinton would win. The reasons shared the assumption that Dole had failed to offer any serious threat to Clinton's prospects. Greenfield started by saying that the Republican takeover of Congress had prevented other Democrats from opposing Clinton for the nomination, thus giving Clinton an opportunity to unite his party. Decisions by Colin Powell and other prominent Republicans to bypass the campaign had the effect of making Dole the strong front-runner, Greenfield said. He continued his remarks by saying that many voters blamed the government shutdown on Republicans and Dole in particular. Greenfield's fourth reason was the emergence of Pat Buchanan as Dole's leading opponent in the primaries. This had helped consolidate the Republican establishment behind Dole early in the year. Finally, Dole's decision to resign from the Senate had deprived him of a position from which he could stake a claim of alternative leadership to Clinton. Dole had reduced his stature to that of a mere candidate by resigning from the Senate, Greenfield stated. While Greenfield's reasons were probably accurate, they also provided another indication of the dominant theme in network news during the final weeks of the campaign. Television news media would show Clinton in upbeat and staged imagery where he appeared statesmanlike and then tell their viewers that Dole was a loser. There seemed to be no way that Dole could escape from this dilemma.

The series of events in late October relating to the financial troubles of the Clinton campaign complemented Dole's attacks, and may have helped tighten the race. Dole attacked Clinton on the twenty-first for receiving contributions from the Lippo Corporation (ABC and NBC). Two days later, all three networks reported of plans by the Federal Election Commission to investigate the problem. They began reporting about a new but related problem on the twenty-ninth, the efforts of former Democratic National Committee operative John Huang to raise money for the Clinton campaign from Chinese sources (ABC). They reported extensively about Huang's actions for several days and even referred to Secret Service logs indicating he had visited the White House 65 times (CBS). Clinton remained silent while this controversy developed but finally commented about it on November 1. He said his campaign had followed the rules and had done nothing illegal. He added that the rules should be changed but blamed Dole for six years of filibusters that had defeated any campaign reform bill (NBC).

Despite the fundraising controversies, the televised news coverage of Clinton during the final five weeks of the campaign was quite favorable, as one might very well expect of a strong incumbent leading his challenger in the polls. Clinton continued acting in an upbeat and confident manner and created numerous events from which television news media could broadcast statesmanlike imagery of him. The first televised news reports of October featuring Clinton involved the White House conference between Arafat and Netanyahu. After this, Clinton campaigned in New Hampshire on the seventh before a group of 2,500 corporate chief executive officers while receiving their endorsement (ABC). He spoke in New Mexico on the thirteenth and took credit for the fact that crime was at a ten-year low, according to a new FBI report. He told his audience that the crime bill he had advanced in 1993 was partially responsible. In addition, he signed a bill providing for greater penalties for using rohypnol, the so-called rape drug (CBS).

Clinton continued these efforts after the final debate, always speaking before large and enthusiastic crowds. He was in Orange County, California on October 17, in Ohio on the twenty-first, in Michigan on the twenty-second, and in Alabama on the twenty-fourth. This last appearance included an emotionally moving scene where a young woman questioned Clinton about his pro-choice abortion position while telling him of her pro-life views. After he had spoken to her, his comments were inaudible for news coverage, she smiled and hugged him (CBS). Clinton was in Atlanta on the twenty-fifth and focused on the youth vote (CBS). He spoke in St. Louis on the twenty-eighth where he took credit for reducing the annual deficit from the $290 billion figure of the last year of the Bush Presidency to a current level of $107 billion (NBC). He emphasized his economic record one day later in Columbus, Ohio (ABC) and at the Alamo on the second (NBC). He concluded his campaign in New Hampshire on the fourth, the state he said had saved his chances for the Presidency in 1992 (ABC).

The standings of the candidates in the Gallup–CNN–USA Today tracking polls did not change much during October or the first week of November. Clinton's support ranged from 48 to 57 percent during the last five weeks of the campaign, with a daily average of 52.3 percent. This differed only slightly from his September average of 53.7 percent. Dole also remained fairly consistent as his support ran between 32 and 41 percent, with a daily average of 35.9 percent. This was nearly identical to his 35.3 percent average during September. Perot appears to have gained slightly, however. His daily totals ranged between 4 and 11 percent with an average of 6.5, which was one percent above his September average. The fact that he had begun a more active campaign may have contributed to this increase. The final survey had Clinton winning the election with 52 percent of the vote, Dole in second place with 41 percent, and Perot third with 7 percent. Dole made some fairly sharp gains during the final week as he moved from 35 percent on October 30 to 41 percent four days later. He appears to have gained much of the undecided vote.

THE GENERAL ELECTION RESULTS

This section directs attention to the final outcome of the election while focusing on three distinct but related topics. The first is the aggregate pattern of national and state voting. The focus is on the outcomes by states and geographic regions as recorded in the vote of the Electoral College. The second topic is a discussion of the meaning of these results in relationship to the aggregate voting patterns that have operated in this nation over the past few decades. The discussion includes a review of the prospects of these patterns resurfacing in the near future. Finally, the third topic includes a review of the outcome of the vote by the behavior of various social groups. The data used here are from the Voter News Service election day exit poll taken by news media organizations.

The outcome of the election came as no surprise to most observers as Clinton won a second term by a substantial but not overwhelming margin. He attained 49.2 percent of the popular vote and 379 electoral votes from 31 states and the District of Columbia while Dole had 40.8 percent of the popular vote and 159 electoral votes from 19 states. Perot finished third with 7.8 percent of the popular vote and no electoral votes. Clinton and Dole increased their party's share of the popular vote from 1992 with Clinton's expansion in support for the Democrats being nearly twice that of the Republican gains. Clinton had won 43.0 percent of the vote in 1992 while George Bush had taken 37.4 percent. Clinton increased the Democratic support by 6.2 percent while Dole ran 3.4 percent better than Bush. These gains came at the expense of Perot whose support declined significantly from the 18.9 percent that he had attained in 1992.

One way of observing the patterns of state outcomes is to observe the nation by geographic region. In doing so, I use four regions—the Northeast, Southeast, Midwest, and West. The Northeast consists of the New England states of Maine, New Hampshire, Vermont, Massachusetts, Connecticut, and Rhode Island, and the Middle Atlantic states of New York, New Jersey, Pennsylvania, Delaware, Maryland, the District of Columbia, and West

Virginia. The Midwest is comprised of the Great Lakes states of Ohio, Indiana, Illinois, Michigan, and Wisconsin, and the Great Plains states of Minnesota, Iowa, Missouri, North and South Dakota, Nebraska, and Kansas. The thirteen-state West consists of the Rocky Mountain states of Montana, Idaho, Wyoming, Colorado, Utah, Nevada, Arizona, and New Mexico, and the Pacific states of California, Oregon, Washington, Alaska, and Hawaii. The Southeast includes the South Atlantic states of Virginia, North Carolina, South Carolina, Georgia, and Florida, and the South Central states of Kentucky, Tennessee, Alabama, Mississippi, Arkansas, Louisiana, Oklahoma, and Texas.

By far, Clinton's strongest region was the Northeast. As previously, Clinton once again carried every state in this region. Moreover, his margins were extensive and suggested that the growing Southeastern orientation of the Republican Party may be reaping electoral benefits for the Democrats. Clinton defeated Dole nationally by a margin of 8.4 percent of the popular vote, but he beat his Kansas rival in every Northeastern state by a much greater margin. He more than doubled the size of his nationwide margin over Dole in New York, New Jersey, the District of Columbia, and every New England state except New Hampshire. These results were not unique, for the Democrats also fared better in Northeastern congressional elections than they did in any other region. They won 60 House seats in the Northeast in 1996 compared to 39 for the Republicans. These outcomes suggest that the Clinton victory in this region did not derive from a temporary deviation supportive of a strong incumbent but instead was reflective of a voting pattern where the Democratic Party is the regional majority. The Democratic nominee in 2000 should run quite well in the Northeast.

Clinton's second strongest region was the Midwest where he carried seven states. He won Michigan, Ohio, Illinois, Wisconsin, Minnesota, Iowa, and Missouri, exactly the same seven states he carried in 1992. His margin over Dole was greater than 8.4 percent in five of them. His margin in Ohio and Missouri was lower. The congressional voting in the Midwest was more competitive than it was in the Northeast as the Republicans carried the region with 55 seats in the House compared to 50 for the Democrats. The results in the West were comparable to those of the Midwest as seven states in this region supported Clinton. They included California, Oregon, Washington, Hawaii, Nevada, New Mexico, and Arizona. Clinton had won six of those states, Arizona excepted, in 1992. Two Western states that Clinton had won in 1992, Colorado and Montana, voted Republican this time, however. Perot had run particularly well in the

West in 1992, and his loss of support became the Republicans' gain, according to exit poll data compiled by the Voter News Service. Four states that Clinton won—California, Oregon, Washington, and Hawaii—supported him by a margin greater than his national total of 8.4 percent. Western voters divided their House seats by a margin of 51 to 42 in favor of the Republicans. Clinton ran well in the Midwest and West primarily because he was a strong incumbent rather than because he was the Democratic nominee. The fact that a majority of the votes in the Electoral College from these two regions went to the Democratic candidate while a majority of the seats in the House remained with the Republicans demonstrates that some of Clinton's victory margin resulted from the strength of his own incumbency rather than from partisanship. Clinton used the rhetorical and institutional powers of his office and constructed a personal constituency that exceeded the political appeal of his own party.

The Southeast was the one region that Clinton lost to Dole, just as he had lost to Bush in 1992. Clinton won only five of the region's states—Florida, Kentucky, Tennessee, Arkansas, and Louisiana—and defeated Dole by more than 8.4 percent only in Arkansas and Louisiana. Two states changed their partisanship from 1992. Clinton carried Georgia in 1992 while Bush won Florida. The Republicans dominated the House in 1996 as they captured 82 Southeastern seats while limiting the Democrats to only 55. These results correspond to the support the Republicans showed in the Southeast in the congressional elections of 1994, and provide yet more proof of the contention that the Southeast is the nation's most Republican region.

One of the more remarkable features of the elections of 1992 and 1996 is the stability of voting patterns across the states and regions. Clinton won the Electoral College votes of a majority of the states in the Northeast, Midwest, and West in both elections. Except for the five states listed above, each state voted for Clinton in both elections or voted against him in both elections. The major difference between the outcomes of these two elections in most states was the size of Clinton's margins. He increased the size of his victory margin in the states he carried while decreasing the magnitude of his defeats in the states he lost. The last time the partisan distribution of states was this similar between two consecutive elections was in the second Eisenhower victory of 1956, when four states changed their votes from 1952. Eisenhower gained three new states while losing one.

Is there a parallel between the elections of the 1950s and 1990s? This is a difficult question to address at this time, but recent outcomes suggest an answer. The election of 1996 marked the fifth time in the post-war period that a political party has won a second consecutive term. Each of the four previous elections, Eisenhower (1956), Johnson (1964), Nixon (1972), and Reagan (1984), was characterized by the fact that the incumbent won another term by a margin that was greater than what his party had attained four years earlier or would attain four years hence. These elections were personal triumphs by strong incumbents that could not be replicated by either the incumbent himself, Johnson (1968), or by the surrogates of retiring incumbents Nixon (1960), Humphrey (1968), or Bush (1988). Only Bush won, and his margin of victory was far less than Reagan's. The stability of the vote between 1952 and 1956 proved to be temporary as the Republican majority of those elections soon disappeared after Eisenhower's retirement. The same result may very well happen again as the Democratic strength shown in the two Clinton victories might not be repeated in 2000. If the Democrats extend their control of the Presidency beyond the Clinton years, recent history suggests they will do so by a popular vote margin smaller than the one attained by Clinton in 1996, that is, 8.4 percent over the Republican nominee.

The two Clinton victories destroyed the so-called Electoral College lock that Republicans believed they had created and maintained since the election of 1968. The Republicans based their claim on the argument that enough Southeastern, Great Plains, and Western states would vote for their candidate that the party might win the Presidency through the Electoral College even if it lost the popular vote in a close election. Let us assume the Republicans could reduce the Democratic margins of 1996 in each state by exactly 8.4 percent in the election of 2000. This would create a virtual tie in the popular vote. If an Electoral College lock actually existed, the Republicans would win the election. This would not happen, however, as the Democratic candidate would acquire 286 votes compared to only 252 for the Republicans (Tables 4.1 and 4.2).

While state and regional voting patterns may yield some valuable insights about the divisions of American politics, they often merely disguise underlying patterns of voting behavior that may prove far more revealing. The states and regions often differ from one another in the composition of their electorates. As a consequence, it is important to supplement the above discussion with an observation of the voting patterns of various social groups that are fairly prominent throughout the nation. Exit polls of the Voter News Service focused on such groups. The gender gap that received so much attention during the campaign did exist and it played a significant role in the outcome. Women provided Clinton with his margin of victory as they supported him by 54 to 38 percent. This support was most pronounced among working and unmarried women. Working women voted for Clinton by a 56 to 35 percent margin while women who did not work divided their preferences more evenly. They voted for Clinton by a margin of 46 to 43 percent. Unmarried women supported Clinton by a 62 to 28 percent margin while married women voted for Clinton by a narrow margin of 48 to 43 percent. In contrast, men backed Dole by an even narrower margin of 44 to 43 percent (Table 4.3).

Clinton and Dole divided the usual partisan-oriented categories of voters as one might expect, with Clinton running better among racial minorities, lower income people, labor union members, Democrats, and liberals, and with Dole doing particularly well in less populated areas and among white Protestants. These results are consistent with those of most elections. Partisanship is only one factor in an election, however, as many voters make their choices partly on the basis of their personal assessments of the particular candidates. This is when the features of candidate-centered campaigns, particularly those associated with the rhetorical skills and institutional powers of a strong incumbent, are most important. With respect to their personal assessment of the candidates, voters wanted a president who was in touch with the 1990s (mentioned by 89 %), or who had a vision for the future (77 %), or who cared for people like themselves (72 %), preferred Clinton over Dole. Voters who felt that the President should be honest and trustworthy (84 %) were strongly for Dole. Clinton's strongest issues were education (78 %), Medicare and Social Security (67 %), and the economy (61 %), while taxes (73 %), foreign policy (56 %), and the budget deficit (52 %) worked best for Dole. Clinton ran best among voters who had decided on their choice at least one month before the election (53 %), a group that included 69 % of all voters, while people who made their decisions within the final week of the campaign were more favorable toward Dole (41 %, compared to 35 % for Clinton). This latter group included only 17 % of voters, however. The exit poll confirmed many of the assumptions that the candidates had used in the campaign; Clinton became a strong incumbent by opposing Republican attempts to weaken Social Security, Medicare, and educational programs. He was helped by the estrangement of many women from the conservative ideology of the Republican Party. Dole found his strongest support from conservative voters who favored reducing the activities and funding of the federal government and who were among the most pessimistic of people about the nation's future (Table 4.4).

Table 4.1
Clinton's Strongest States

States Clinton Won by More than 8.4 percent of the Vote.

	Clinton's Margin		Clinton's Margin
Northeast			
Maine	21.7	New York	29.5
New Hampshire	10.1	New Jersey	18.2
Vermont	23.0	Pennsylvania	9.3
Massachusetts	33.9	Delaware	15.3
Rhode Island	33.7	Maryland	16.2
Connecticut	18.6	West Virginia	14.9
District of Columbia	78.6		
Midwest			
Illinois	17.7	Michigan	13.4
Iowa	10.5	Wisconsin	10.6
Minnesota	16.5		
West			
California	13.4	Oregon	8.5
Hawaii	26.3	Washington	13.1
Southeast			
Arkansas	17.2	Louisiana	12.2

Table 4.2
Clinton's Weakest States

States Clinton Won by Less than 8.4 percent of the Vote.

	Clinton's Margin		Clinton's Margin
West		**Southeast**	
Arizona	2.3	Florida	5.8
Nevada	1.1	Kentucky	0.9
New Mexico	7.6	Tennessee	2.4
Midwest			
Missouri	6.4	Ohio	6.2

States Clinton Lost to Dole.

Southeast		**Midwest**	
Virginia	-1.9	Indiana	-5.6
North Carolina	-4.7	North Dakota	-6.9
South Carolina	-5.8	South Dakota	-3.5
Georgia	-1.2	Nebraska	-8.8
Alabama	-7.0	Kansas	-18.3
Mississippi	-5.1		
Oklahoma	-7.9		
Texas	-5.0		
West			
Alaska	-18.5	Montana	-2.9
Colorado	-1.4	Utah	-21.6
Idaho	-18.9	Wyoming	-13.1

Table 4.3
Support for Candidates by Selected Social Groups

Group	Clinton	Dole	Perot	Percent of Total
Men	43	44	10	48
Men—Married	40	48	10	33
Unmarried	49	35	12	15
Women	54	38	7	52
Women—Married	48	43	7	33
Unmarried	62	28	7	20
Women by Job Status				
Women Working	56	35	7	29
Women Not Working	46	43	9	71
Race and Ethnicity				
White	43	46	9	83
Black	84	12	4	10
Hispanic	72	21	6	5
Family Income				
Less than $15,000	59	28	11	11
$15–$30,000	53	36	9	23
$30–$50,000	48	40	10	27
$50–$75,000	47	45	7	21
$75–$100,000	44	48	7	9
Over $100,000	38	54	6	9
Union Member in Household	59	30	9	23
Partisanship				
Democrat	84	10	5	39
Independent	43	35	17	26
Republican	13	80	6	35
Ideology				
Liberal	78	11	7	20
Moderate	57	33	9	47
Conservative	20	71	8	33
Religion				
Jewish	78	16	3	3
Catholic	53	37	9	29
White Protestant	41	50	8	38
Community Size				
Population over 500,000	68	25	6	10
Population 50,000 to 500,000	50	39	8	21
Suburbs	47	42	8	39
Rural areas and towns	45	44	10	30

Source: Voter News Service National Exit Poll.

Table 4.4
Support for Candidates by Selected Attitudes

Attitude	Clinton	Dole	Perot	Percent of Total
Which candidate quality mattered most in deciding how you voted for President?				
He is in touch with the 1990s	89	8	4	10
He has a vision for the future	77	13	9	16
He cares about people like me	72	17	9	9
He stands up for what he believes in	42	40	16	13
He shares my view of government	41	46	10	20
He is honest and trustworthy	8	84	7	20
Which one issue mattered most in deciding how you vote for president?				
Education	78	16	4	12
Medicare/Social Security	67	26	6	15
Economy/Jobs	61	27	10	21
Crime/Drugs	40	50	8	7
Foreign Policy	35	56	8	4
Federal budget deficit	27	52	19	12
Taxes	19	73	7	11
When did you finally decide whom to vote for?				
In the last week	35	41	25	17
In the last month	47	36	13	13
Before last month	53	41	5	69
Compared to four years ago, is your family's financial situation				
Better today	66	26	6	33
Worse today	27	57	13	20
About the same	46	45	21	45
Do you think the condition of the nation's economy is				
Excellent	78	17	4	4
Good	62	31	6	51
Not so good	34	52	12	36
Poor	23	51	21	7

Source: Voter News Service National Exit Poll.

CHAPTER 5

CONCLUSIONS AND EPILOGUE

Despite several unique features, and particularly its extraordinary length of seven months, the election of 1996 conformed quite well with the recurring and predictable patterns that characterize television age elections with strong incumbents. The results of this election support the contention I raised earlier: the most important factor in determining the outcome of any modern presidential election in which the incumbent seeks another term of office is the strength of incumbency at the outset of the election year. Television news media respond to that strength in recurring and predictable ways and then transmit their interpretation directly to their viewing audiences. Their interpretation helps to create and perpetuate the context in which future events unfold and acquire meaning.

Television news media strive to depict an election as a dramatic story of the personal quest of a heroic individual for the nation's highest office. They assign the hero to the role of central actor in this drama and interpret events from the perspective of how those events might affect, or how they might be affected by, the hero. The incumbent is always the hero in this story. He does not always triumph in his quest, however: quite a number lose. Television news media treat the successful incumbents (those I call strong) as statesmen deserving of reelection, while viewing the unsuccessful ones (those I depict as weak) as political failures undeserving of additional terms of office. As I wrote in 1993 and restated at the beginning of chapter 1, we would know the name of the winner of this election by the Ides of March. By then, we knew it was Bill Clinton. He became the successful hero of the televised narrative of the election of 1996.

Clinton began the election campaign after defeating his Republican congressional adversaries in two highly televised battles over the levels of federal spending on Medicare, Medicaid, education, and the environment. He also reversed his political misfortunes from the previous year and seized the lead in public opinion surveys from all possible rivals. He was indeed a strong incumbent before the campaign began. Television news media responded in exactly the same ways they had done in previous elections when the incumbents were strong, they focused an unusual amount of attention on the most divisive features of the campaign for the nomination of the opposition party while illustrating the strong incumbent in a variety of scenes where he appeared statesmanlike. As I have demonstrated throughout this book, this pattern of coverage strengthened Clinton's lead while undermining Dole's candidacy. Moreover, the general election campaign followed this same pattern as television news media depicted Clinton as the deserving winner while simultaneously telling their audiences of how poorly Dole was running. Of course, Clinton led Dole in every national poll taken after the early weeks of January, 1996, and was never in any danger of losing the election.

I direct attention to two themes here, one being the instances where this campaign departed from the script of elections with strong incumbents that I outlined in the first chapter. In the second, I revisit the alternative scenario that I discussed at the end of the second chapter and emphasize the importance of the actions of an individual President in determining the strength of incumbency.

There was one major difference between the Republican nomination campaign of 1996 and the campaigns that occurred within the opposition parties in the three other elections with strong incumbents. This time, the battle ended before the national convention, and Dole's nomination was unanimous. In the previous election, Barry Goldwater and George McGovern had to confront very hostile factions at their conventions and attained their nominations only after several days of highly televised rancor within their parties. While Walter Mondale acquired his nomination at a relatively harmonious convention, he garnered the votes of only about 2,200 of the approximately 4,000 delegates in attendance. The harmony concealed deep divisions among Democrats. In contrast, Dole triumphed quite early in 1996, effectively ending the battle in South Carolina on March 2, and actually concluding it in California on March 26. This is not the usual scenario for the opposition party in strong incumbent elections. It is precisely the conclusion that characterizes opposition party campaigns in weak incumbent elections. In fact, Dole actually clinched his nomination at an earlier date than Carter (1976), Reagan (1980), or Clinton (1992), and each of them defeated the incumbent in the general election.

Unlike the previous strong incumbent years, there were no significant factional differences present in 1996 that would have helped perpetuate the opposition party's campaign until the convention. Dole united his party quite early in the year and then focused his attention on Clinton. Try as they might, television news media were unable to force the Republican campaign to conform to the two-candidate drama they prefer. They quite simply could not identify the one leading adversary of the front-runner, an essential feature for perpetuating a nomination campaign. Despite this unity, the Republican Party was not without divisions. Certainly, some became apparent in early 1997 when several young House members tried unsuccessfully to oust Gingrich as Speaker. Dole's dual presence as front-runner and major congressional leader suppressed any possible factional fights. Such fights will eventually occur, perhaps as early as 2000, and they will compromise Republican chances for victory. The strong unity within the Republican Party in 1996 helped make Dole a more competitive candidate than Goldwater, McGovern, or Mondale.

Clinton's margin of victory was substantial, but it was not as overwhelming as those of Johnson, Nixon, and Reagan. Those three presidents averaged 60.2 percent of the popular vote, eleven points ahead of Clinton's 49.2 percent. Clinton was clearly the weakest of the four strong incumbents of the television age, not only in terms of votes, but in terms of accomplishments as well. His policy successes prior to his reelection campaign were less impressive than those of the other strong incumbents. In addition, he faced a much more formidable rival. Clinton's victory in these circumstances helps demonstrate the importance of mediated incumbency in television age elections. Even though Clinton had been an active President with a substantial number of initiatives, he had attained little of what he wanted. He had lost his most important battles of 1994 and devoted most of 1995 and 1996 to stopping the Republicans. Clinton did not deliver a "New Deal," or a "Great Society" during his first term, but struggled to save them instead. The Republicans won control of Congress in 1994 by running against the government which they personified in Clinton. He responded by using the vast array of institutional and rhetorical powers that define the modern Presidency to seize that banner from them and win a second term.

The presence of a strong incumbent, or a weak one for that matter, in any given election is not deterministic. It varies across elections and is contingent on the nature of the times and the political skills of the incumbent. There was a distinct possibility throughout 1995 that the election could have ended much differently with Clinton losing. The factors that I examined above, of Clinton being the weakest of the strong incumbents and with Dole being an unusually strong challenger, may have combined into another scenario instead. I speculated earlier about what might have taken place if Clinton had performed less effectively than he did in the Medicare and budget battles. In that scenario, he had to engage in a lengthy and divisive battle with Richard Gephardt for the nomination. After winning that battle, he trailed Dole throughout the general election campaign and eventually lost. Dole had united his party relatively early during the year, a prerequisite for victory by a challenger in elections with weak incumbents. He campaigned from his Senate Majority Leader position while generating imagery where he appeared as a statesmanlike alternative to the embattled incumbent. Television news media responded in a predictable manner by treating Clinton as a loser and Dole as a qualified successor. In the actual scenario, Dole did not get that chance. Clinton eliminated that possibility when he became a strong incumbent in 1995.

The final chapter on the electoral effects of Clinton's incumbency and the responses of television news media to it is not yet complete. While Clinton cannot be a candidate in 2000, his incumbency will certainly be present. The fight for succession appears likely to include a great variety of candidates, including Clinton's surrogate and Vice President Albert Gore. While the context and outcome of that campaign is presently unclear, two features appear significant today. Gore will be a surrogate incumbent and his prospects will be related to Clinton's political strength as it appears at the beginning of 2000. The Vice Presidency has proven to be an ambiguous office from which to seek the White House, however, and does not usually provide a clear answer to the strength of incumbency in any given year. In each of the three television age elections with surrogate incumbents— 1960, 1968, and 1988—the Vice President won the nomination of the presidential party but encountered major difficulties in the general election. Bush was the only winner, although Nixon and Humphrey did not lose by much. Gore may very well face the same ambiguous fate, attaining a nomination victory with an uncertain general election outcome. Gore's chances of success will be contingent on four factors (1) the nature of Clinton's political strength at the beginning of 2000, (2) his own personal political skills, (3) the internal factionalism of the Republican Party, and (4) the ways in which television news media interpret each of these first three and transmit them to their viewers. Surrogate incumbency is a specialized version of presidential incumbency in the televised world of national politics.

BIBLIOGRAPHY

ABC World News Tonight.

Abramson, Paul R., John H. Aldrich, and David W. Rohde. *Change and Continuity in the 1980 Elections*. Washington, D.C.: Congressional Quarterly Press, 1982.

——— . *Change and Continuity in the 1984 Elections*. Washington, D.C.: Congressional Quarterly Press, 1986.

——— . *Change and Continuity in the 1988 Elections*. Washington, D.C.: Congressional Quarterly Press, 1990.

Agranoff, Robert. *The New Style in Elections Campaigns*. Boston: Holbrook Press, 1972.

Aldrich, John H. *Before the Convention: Strategies and Choices in Presidential Nomination Campaigns*. Chicago: University of Chicago Press, 1980.

——— . *Why Parties?* Chicago: University of Chicago Press, 1995.

Ansolabehere, Stephen, and Shaton Iyengar. *Going Negative*. New York: Free Press, 1995.

Asher, Herbert B. *Presidential Elections and American Politics: Voters, Candidates, and Campaigns Since 1952*. 5th edition. Pacific Grove, Calif.: Brooks/Cole, 1992.

Atherton, F. Christopher. *Media Politics: The News Strategies of Presidential Campaigns*. Lexington, Mass.: Lexington Books, 1984.

Balz, Dan. "In Control of His Own Fate: How Bob Dole's Campaign Has Carefully Nailed Down His Status as the GOP Front-Runner." *Washington Post National Weekly Edition*, 25–31 December 1995.

Barber, James David, ed. *Race for the Presidency: The Media and the Nominating Process*. Englewood Cliffs, N.J.: Prentice-Hall, 1978.

Barilleaux, Ryan J. *The Post-Modern Presidency*. New York: Praeger Press, 1988.

Barone, Michael, and Grant Ujifusa. *The Almanac of American Politics, 1996*. Washington, D.C.: National Journal, 1995.

Bartels, Larry M. *Presidential Primaries and the Dynamics of Public Choice*. Princeton: Princeton University Press, 1988.

Bass, Jack, and Walter DeVries. *The Transformation of Southern Politics: Social and Political Consequences Since 1945*. New York: Times-Mirror, 1977.

Bennett, W. Lance. *The Governing Crisis: Media, Money, and Marketing in American Elections*. New York: St. Martin's Press, 1992.

Berelson, Bernard R., Paul F. Lazersfeld, and William N. McPhee. *Voting*. Chicago: University of Chicago Press, 1954.

Black, Earl, and Merle Black. *The Vital South: How Presidents Are Elected*. Cambridge: Harvard University Press, 1992.

Blumenthal, Sidney. *The Permanent Campaign*. 2nd edition. New York: Touchstone Books, 1982.

Bond, Jon R., and Richard Fleisher. *The President in the Legislative Arena*. Chicago: University of Chicago Press, 1990.

Brace, Paul, and Barbara Hinckley. *Follow the Leader: Opinion Polls and the Modern Presidency*. New York: Basic Books, 1992.

Broder, David. "Bill Clinton's Free Ride: The Absence of any Serious Primary Challengers Is a Major Boost to His Prospects." *Washington Post National Weekly Edition*, 25–31 December 1995.

Buckley et al. v. Valeo, 424 U.S. 1 (1976).

Buell, Emmete H., Jr., and Lee Sigelman. *Nominating the President*. Knoxville: University of Tennessee Press, 1991.

Burke, John P. *The Institutional Presidency*. Baltimore, Md.: Johns Hopkins University Press, 1992.

Burnham, Walter Dean. *Critical Elections and the Mainsprings of American Politics*. New York: Norton, 1970.

Burns, James MacGregor. *The Deadlock of Democracy*. Englewood Cliffs, N.J.: Prentice-Hall, 1963.

Campbell, Angus. "A Classification of Presidential Elections." In *Elections and the Political Order*, by Angus Campbell, Philip E. Converse, Warren E. Miller, and Donald E. Stokes, pp. 963–977. New York: John Wiley and Sons, 1966.

Campbell, Angus, Philip E. Converse, Warren E. Miller, and Donald E. Stokes. *The American Voter*. New York: John Wiley and Sons, 1960.

Campbell, Colin, and Bert Rockman, eds. *The Clinton Presidency: First Appraisals*. Chatham, N.J.: Chatham House, 1995.

Carmines, Edward G., John P. McIver, and James A. Stimson, "Unrealized Partisanship: A Theory of Dealignment." *Journal of Politics*, 49 (May 1987), pp. 376–400.

CBS Evening News.

Ceaser, James W. *Reforming the Reforms*. Cambridge: Ballinger, 1982.

Ceaser, James W. et al. "The Rise of the Rhetorical Presidency." *Presidential Studies Quarterly*, 11 (Spring 1981), pp. 158–171.

Clubb, Jerome M., William H. Flanigan, and Nancy H. Zingale. *Partisan Realignment: Voters, Parties, and Government in American History*. Beverly Hills: Sage Publications, 1980.

Cogan, John. *The Budget Puzzle*. Stanford: Stanford University Press, 1994.

Converse, Philip E. "The Concept of the Normal Vote." In *Elections and the Political Order*, by Angus Campbell, Philip E. Converse, Warren E. Miller, and Donald E. Stokes, pp. 9–39. New York: John Wiley and Sons, 1966.

Converse, Philip E., Aage R. Clausen, and Warren E. Miller. "Electoral Myth and Reality: The 1964 Election." *American Political Science Review*, 59, 2 (June 1965), pp. 321–336.

Converse, Philip E., Angus Campbell, Warren E. Miller, and Donald E. Stokes. "Stability and Change in 1960: A Reinstating Election." *American Political Science Review*, 55, 2 (June 1961), pp. 269–280.

Converse, Philip E., Warren E. Miller, Jerrold G. Rusk, and Arthur C. Wolfe. "Continuity and Change in American Politics: Parties and Issues in the 1968 Election." *American Political Science Review*, 63, 4 (December 1969), pp. 1083–1105.

Corrado, Anthony J. *Creative Campaigning: PAC's and the Presidential Selection Process*. Boulder, Colo.: Westview Press, 1992.

Craig, Stephen C., ed. *Broken Contract: Changing Relationships Between Americans and Their Government*. Boulder, Colo.: Westview Press, 1995.

Cronin, Thomas E. *The State of the Presidency*. 2nd edition. Boston: Little, Brown and Company, 1980.

———. *Inventing the American Presidency*. Lawrence: University of Kansas Press, 1989.

Crotty, William J. *Decision for the Democrats: Reforming the Party Structure*. Baltimore, Md.: Johns Hopkins University Press, 1978.

———, ed. *America's Choice: The Election of 1992*. Guilford, Conn.: Dushkin Publishing Group, 1992.

Crotty, William J., and John S. Jackson, III. *Presidential Primaries and Nominations*. Washington, D.C.: Congressional Quarterly Press, 1985.

Crouse, Timothy. *The Boys on the Bus: Riding with the Campaign Press Corps*. New York: Ballantine, 1973.

Dalton, Russell J., Scott C. Flanagan, and Paul Allen Beck. *Electoral Change in Advanced Industrial Democracies: Realignment or Dealignment?* Princeton: Princeton University Press, 1984.

Darcy, R., Susan Welch, and Janet Clark. *Women, Elections, and Representation*. New York: Longman, 1987.

Davis, James W. *National Conventions in an Age of Party Reform*. Westport, Conn.: Greenwood Press, 1983.

Denton, Robert E. *The Symbolic Dimensions of American Politics*. Prospect Heights, Ill.: Waveland Press, 1982.

———. *The Primetime Presidency of Ronald Reagan*. New York: Praeger, 1988.

———, ed. *The 1992 Presidential Campaign: A Communication Perspective*. Westport, Conn.: Praeger, 1994.

DeVries, Walter, and Lance Tarrance. *The Ticket-Splitter: A New Force in American Politics*. Grand Rapids, Mich.: Eerdmans, 1972.

Diamond, Edwin, and Stephen Bates. *The Spot: The Rise of Political Advertising on Television*. Cambridge, Mass.: MIT Press, 1984.

Dionne, E. J. *Why Americans Hate Politics*. New York: Simon and Schuster, 1991.

———. *They Only Look Dead: Why Progressives Will Dominate the Next Political Era*. New York: Simon and Schuster, 1996.

Dover, E. D. "Presidential Elections in the Television Age: Realignment, Dealignment, and Incumbency." *Southeastern Political Review*, 15 (1987), pp. 27–43.

———. *Presidential Elections in the Television Age: 1960–1992*. Westport, Conn.: Praeger, 1994.

Edsell, Thomas B. "Adding Up Clinton's Numbers: The Polls Show He Has a Power Electoral College Base of Support." *Washington Post National Weekly Edition*, 25–31 December 1995.

Edwards, George C., III. *The Public Presidency: The Pursuit of Popular Support*. New York: St. Martin's Press, 1983.

———. *At the Margins: Presidential Leadership of Congress*. New Haven, Conn.: Yale University Press, 1989.

Edwards, George C., III, and Stephen J. Wayne. *Presidential Leadership: Politics and Policy Making*. New York: St. Martin's Press, 1990.

Ehrenhalt, Alan. *The United States of Ambition*. New York: Random House, 1992.

Eldersveld, Samuel, J. *Political Parties: A Behavioral Analysis*. Skokie, Ill.: Rand-McNally, 1964.

Entman, Robert M. *Democracy Without Citizens: Media and the Decay of American Politics*. New York: Oxford University Press, 1989.

———. "How the Media Affect What People Think: An Information Processing Approach." *Journal of Politics*, 51 (May 1989), pp. 347–370.

Epstein, Edward Jay. *News from Nowhere: Television and the News*. New York: Vintage, 1974.

Fallows, James. *Breaking the News: How the Media Undermine American Democracy*. New York: Vintage Books, 1997.

Fenno, Richard F. *Home Style: House Members in Their Districts*. Boston: Little, Brown, 1978.

Fiorina, Morris. *Retrospective Voting in American National Elections*. New Haven, Conn.: Yale University Press, 1981.

Fishel, Jeff, ed. *Parties and Elections in an Anti-Party Age*. Bloomington, Ind.: Indiana University Press, 1978.

Fisher, Louis. *The Politics of Shared Power: Congress and the Executive*. 3rd edition. Washington, D.C.: Congressional Quarterly Press, 1993.

Foote, Joe. *Television Access and Political Power: The Networks, the Presidency, and the "Loyal Opposition."* New York: Praeger, 1990.

Gais, Thomas L. *Improper Influence: Campaign Finance Law, Political Interest Groups, and the Problem of Equality*. Ann Arbor: University of Michigan Press, 1996.

Galderisi, Peter, Michael S. Lyons, Randy T. Simmons, and John G. Francis, eds. *The Politics of Realignment: Party Change in the Mountain West*. Boulder, Colo: Westview Press, 1987.

Gallup Poll.

Gallup–CNN–USA Today Poll.

Gans, Herbert J. *Deciding What's News*. New York: Vintage, 1980.

Germond, Jack W., and Jules Witcover. *Blue Smoke and Mirrors: How Reagan Won and Why Carter Lost the Election of 1980*. New York: Viking Press, 1981.

———. *Wake Us When It's Over: Presidential Politics of 1984*. New York: MacMillan, 1985.

———. *Whose Broad Stripes and Bright Stars: The Trivial Pursuit of the Presidency 1988*. New York: Warner Books, 1989.

Ginsberg, Benjamin. *The Captive Public: How Mass Opinion Promotes State Power*. New York: Basic Books, 1986.

Gitlin, Todd. *The Twilight of Common Dreams: Why America Is Wracked by Culture Wars*. New York: Henry Holt, 1995.

Graber, Doris A. *Verbal Behavior and Politics*. Urbana: University of Illinois Press, 1976.

———. *The President and the Public*. Philadelphia: Institute for the Study of Human Issues, 1982.

———. *Media Power in Politics*. 3rd edition. Washington, D.C.: Congressional Quarterly Press, 1993.

———. *Mass Media in American Politics*. 5th edition. Washington, D.C.: Congressional Quarterly Press, 1997.

Greer, John G. *Nominating Presidents: An Evaluation of Voters and Primaries*. Westport, Conn.: Greenwood Press, 1989.

Hadley, Arthur T. *The Invisible Primary*. Englewood Cliffs, N.J.: Prentice-Hall, 1973.

Hart, John. *The Presidential Branch: From Washington to Clinton*. 2nd edition. Chatham, N.J.: Chatham Hall, 1995.

Hart, Roderick P. *The Sound of Leadership: Presidential Communication in the Modern Age*. Chicago: University of Chicago Press, 1987.

Heard, Alexander. *Made in America: The Nomination and Election of Presidents*. New York: HarperCollins, 1991.

Hertsgaard, Mark. *On Bended Knee: The Press and the Reagan Presidency*. New York: Farrer, Straus, and Giroux, 1988.

Hinckley, Barbara. *The Symbolic Presidency: How Presidents Portray Themselves*. London: Routledge, 1990.

Hirschman, Albert O. *The Rhetoric of Reaction: Perversity, Futility, Jeopardy*. Cambridge: Harvard University Press, 1991.

Hodgson, Godfrey. *All Things to All Men*. New York: Touchstone Books, 1980.

Hoffstetter, Richard. *Bias in the News: Network Television Coverage of the 1972 Election Campaign*. Columbus: Ohio State University Press, 1976.

Hunter, James Davison. *Culture Wars: The Struggle to Define America*. New York: Basic Books, 1991.

Ippolito, Daniel. *Uncertain Legacies: Federal Budget Policy from Roosevelt through Reagan*. Charlottesville: University Press of Virginia, 1990.

Iyengar, Shanto. "Television News and Citizens' Explanations of National Affairs." *American Political Science Review*, 81 (September 1987), pp. 815–831.

———. *Is Anyone Responsible: How Television Frames Political Issues*. Chicago: University of Chicago Press, 1991.

Iyengar, Shanto, and Donald R. Kinder. *News That Matters: Television and American Public Opinion*. Chicago: University of Chicago Press, 1987.

Jacobson, Gary C. *The Electoral Origins of Divided Government*. Boulder, Colo.: Westview Press, 1990.

———. *The Politics of Congressional Elections*. 4th edition. New York: Longman, 1997.

Jamison, Kathleen Hall. *Eloquence in the Electronic Age: The Transformation of Political Speechmaking*. New York: Oxford University Press, 1988.

———. *Packaging the Presidency: A History and Criticism of Presidential Campaign Advertising*. Oxford: Oxford University Press, 1996.

Jones, Charles O. *The Presidency in a Separated System*. Washington, D.C.: Brookings Institution, 1994.

Just, Marion R. et al. *Crosstalk: Citizens, Candidates, and the Media in a Presidential Campaign*. Chicago: University of Chicago Press, 1996.

Keech, William R., and Donald R. Matthews. *The Party's Choice*. Washington, D.C.: Brookings Institution, 1977.

Keeter, Scott, and Cliff Zukin. *Uninformed Choice: The Failure of the New Presidential Nominating System*. New York: Praeger, 1983.

Keith, Bruce et al. *The Myth of the Independent Voter*. Berkeley: University of California Press, 1992.

Kellerman, Barbara. *The Political Presidency*. New York: Oxford University Press, 1984.

Kelley, Stanley. *Interpreting Elections*. Princeton: Princeton University Press, 1983.

Kerbel, Matthew Robert. *Edited for Television: CNN, ABC, and the 1992 Presidential Campaign*. Boulder, Colo.: Westview Press, 1994.

Kernall, Samual. *Going Public: New Strategies of Presidential Leadership*. 2nd edition. Washington, D.C.: Congressional Quarterly Press, 1993.

Kessel, John H. *The Goldwater Coalition: Republican Strategies in 1964*. Indianapolis: Bobbs-Merrill, 1968.

————. *Presidential Campaign Politics: Coalition Strategies and Citizen Response*. 4th edition. Homewood, Ill.: Dorsey Press, 1992.

Kettl, Donald. *Deficit Politics*. New York: MacMillan, 1992.

Key, V. O. *Southern Politics in State and Nation*. New York: Vintage Books, 1949.

————. "A Theory of Critical Elections." *Journal of Politics*, 17 (1955), pp. 3–18.

————. "Secular Realignment and the Party System." *Journal of Politics*, 21 (1959), p. 198.

————. *Politics, Parties, and Pressure Groups*. New York: Crowell, 1964.

————. *The Responsible Electorate*. Cambridge: Belknap Press, 1966.

Kiewiet, D. Roderick. *Macroeconomics and Micropolitics: The Electoral Effects of Economic Issues*. Chicago: University of Chicago Press, 1983.

Ladd, Everett Carll, Jr. *Where Have All the Voters Gone? The Fracturing of America's Political Parties*. 2nd edition. New York: Norton, 1982.

————. "Like Waiting for Godot: The Uselessness of Realignment for Understanding Change in Contemporary American Politics." *Polity*, 22 (1990), pp. 511–525.

Ladd, Everett Carll, Jr., and Charles D. Hadley. *Transformations of the American Party System*. Revised edition. New York: Norton, 1975.

Lamis, Alexander P. *The Two-Party South*. New York: Oxford University Press, 1984.

Lavrekas, Paul J., and Jack K. Holley, eds. *Polling and Presidential Election Coverage*. Newbury Park, Calif.: Sage, 1991.

Lazersfeld, Paul F., Bernard Berelson, and Hazel Gaudet. *The People's Choice: How the Voter Makes Up His Mind in a Presidential Campaign*. New York: Columbia University Press, 1944.

Lewis-Beck, Michael S. *Economics and Elections: The Major Western Democracies*. Ann Arbor: University of Michigan Press, 1988.

Lichter, S. Robert, Daniel Amundson, and Richard Noyes. *The Video Campaign: Network Coverage of the 1988 Primaries*. Washington, D.C.: American Enterprise Institute for Public Policy Research, 1988.

Lichter, S. Robert, and Richard Noyes. *Campaign '96: The Media and the Candidates*. Washington, D.C.: Center for Media and Public Affairs, 1996.

————. *Media Monitor*. Washington, D.C.: Center for Media and Public Affairs, 1996.

Light, Paul C. *The President's Agenda: Domestic Policy Choice from Kennedy to Reagan*. Baltimore, Md.: Johns Hopkins University Press, 1991.

Lowi, Theodore J. *The Personal President: Power Invested, Promise Unfulfilled*. Ithaca, N.Y.: Cornell University Press, 1985.

————. *The End of the Republican Era*. Norman: University of Oklahoma Press, 1995.

Maranto, Robert. *Politics and Bureaucracy in the Modern Presidency*. Westport, Conn.: Greenwood Press, 1993.

Marcus, Ruth. "Rolling in Campaign Dough: Clinton's Early Fund-Raising Sets the Stage for His Reelection Drive." *Washington Post National Weekly Edition*, 25–31 December 1995.

Mayer, William G. *The Divided Democrats: Ideological Unity, Party Reform, and Presidential Elections*. Boulder, Colo.: Westview Press, 1996.

———, ed. *In Pursuit of the White House: How We Choose Our Presidential Nominees*. Chatham, N.J.: Chatham House Publishers, 1996.

Mayhew, David R. *Divided We Govern: Party Control, Lawmaking, and Investigations, 1946–1990*. New Haven, Conn.: Yale University Press, 1991.

McCubbins, Mathew D., ed. *Under the Watchful Eye: Managing Presidential Campaigns in the Television Era*. Washington, D.C.: Congressional Quarterly Press, 1992.

McGinniss, Joe. *The Selling of the President 1968*. New York: Trident Press, 1969.

Milkis, Sidney M. *The President and the Parties: The Transformation of the American Party System Since the New Deal*. New York: Oxford University Press, 1993.

Milkis, Sidney M., and Michael Nelson. *The American Presidency: Origins and Development, 1776–1993*. Washington, D.C.: Congressional Quarterly Press, 1994.

Miller, Arthur H., Warren E. Miller, Aldern S. Raine, and Thad E. Brown. "A Majority Party in Disarray: Policy Polarization in the 1972 Election." *American Political Science Review*, 70 (1976), pp. 753–778.

Miller, Arthur H., and Martin P. Wattenberg. "Throwing the Rascals Out: Policy and Performance Evaluations of Presidential Candidates, 1952–1980." *American Political Science Review*, 79 (1985), pp. 359–368.

Miller, Warren E. "Party Identification, Realignment, and Party Voting: Back to Basics." *American Political Science Review*, 85 (1991), pp. 557–568.

Miroff, Bruce. "Presidential Campaigns: Candidates, Managers and Reporters." *Polity*, 12 (1980), p. 667.

Nathan, Richard. *The Administrative Presidency*. New York: MacMillan Publishing Company, 1983.

NBC Nightly News.

Nelson, Michael, ed. *The Elections of 1984*. Washington, D.C.: Congressional Quarterly Press, 1985.

———, ed. *The Elections of 1988*. Washington, D.C.: Congressional Quarterly Press, 1989.

———, ed. *The Elections of 1992*. Washington, D.C.: Congressional Quarterly Press, 1993.

———, ed. *The Election of 1996*. Washington, D.C.: Congressional Quarterly Press, 1997.

Neustadt, Richard. *Presidential Power*. New York: John Wiley and Sons, 1960.

————. *Presidential Power and the Modern Presidents: The Politics of Leadership from Roosevelt to Reagan*. New York: Free Press, 1990.

Nie, Norman, Sidney Verba, and John Petrocik. *The Changing American Voter*. Enlarged edition. Cambridge, Mass.: Harvard University Press, 1979.

Nimmo, Dan. *The Political Persuaders*. Englewood Cliffs, N.J.: Prentice-Hall, 1970.

Nimmo, Dan, and James E. Combs. *Mediated Political Realities*. New York: Longman, 1983.

Norpoth, Helmut. "Under Way and Here to Stay: Party Realignment in the 1980's?" *Public Opinion Quarterly*, 51 (Fall 1987), pp. 376–391.

Orren, Gary R., and Nelson W. Polsby. *Media and Momentum: The New Hampshire Primary and Nomination Politics*. Chatham, N.J.: Chatham House, 1987.

Owen, Diana. *Media Messages in American Presidential Elections*. Westport, Conn.: Greenwood Press, 1991.

Page, Benjamin I., and Robert Y. Shapiro. *The Rational Public: Fifty Years of Trends in Americans' Policy Preferences*. Chicago: University of Chicago Press, 1991.

Parenti, Michael. *Make-Believe Media: The Politics of Entertainment*. New York: St. Martin's Press, 1992.

Patterson, Thomas E. *The Mass Media Election: How Americans Choose Their President*. New York: Praeger, 1980.

————. *The American Democracy*. New York: McGraw-Hill, 1990.

————. *Out of Order*. New York: Knopf, 1993.

Patterson, Thomas E., and Robert D. McClure. *The Unseeing Eye: The Myth of Television Power in National Elections*. New York: G. P. Putnam's Sons, 1976.

Peterson, Mark. *Legislating Together*. Cambridge: Harvard University Press, 1990.

Petrocik, John R. "Realignment: New Party Coalitions and the Nationalization of the South." *Journal of Politics*, 49 (1987), p. 347.

Pfiffner, James P. *The Strategic Presidency*. 2nd edition revised. Lawrence: University of Kansas Press, 1992.

Phillips, Kevin P. *The Emerging Republican Majority*. Garden City, N.J.: Doubleday, 1969.

————. *Mediacracy: American Parties and Politics in the Communications Age*. New York: Doubleday and Company, 1975.

————. *The Politics of Rich and Poor: Wealth and the American Electorate in the Reagan Aftermath*. New York: Random House, 1990.

Polsby, Nelson W. *Consequences of Party Reform*. New York: Oxford University Press, 1983.

Pomper, Gerald M. "Classification of Presidential Elections." *Journal of Politics*, 29 (August 1967), pp. 535–566.

————. *Voter's Choice: Varieties of American Electoral Behavior*. New York: Dodd, Mead, and Company, 1975.

———. *The Election of 1980: Reports and Interpretations*. Chatham, N.J.: Chatham House Publishers, 1981.

———. *The Election of 1984: Reports and Interpretations*. Chatham, N.J.: Chatham House Publishers, 1985.

———. *The Election of 1988: Reports and Interpretations*. Chatham, N.J.: Chatham House Publishers, 1989.

———. *The Election of 1992: Reports and Interpretations*. Chatham, N.J.: Chatham House Publishers, 1993.

———. *The Elections of 1996: Reports and Interpretations*. Chatham, N.J.: Chatham House Publishers, 1997.

Popkin, Samuel L. *The Reasoning Voter: Communication and Persuasion in Presidential Campaigns*. Chicago: University of Chicago Press, 1991.

Riccards, Michael P. *The Ferocious Engine of Democracy: A History of the American Presidency*. New York: Madison Books, 1995.

Robinson, Michael J. "TV's Newest Program, the 'Presidential Nominations Game'." *Public Opinion*, 1 (May–June 1978), pp. 41–45.

Robinson, Michael J., and Margaret A. Sheehan. *Over the Wire and on TV: CBS and UPI in Campaign '80*. New York: Russell Sage, 1983.

Rosenstiel, Tom. *The Beat Goes On: President Clinton's First Year with the Media*. New York: Twentieth Century Fund, 1994.

Rubin, Richard. *Press, Party, and Presidency*. New York: W. W. Norton, 1981.

Sabato, Larry J. *The Rise of Political Consultants*. New York: Basic Books, 1981.

———. *Feeding Frenzy: How Attack Journalism Has Transformed American Politics*. New York: Free Press, 1991.

Salmore, Stephen A., and Barbara G. Salmore. *Candidates, Parties, and Campaigns*. Washington, D.C.: Congressional Quarterly Press, 1985.

Sandoz, Ellis, and Cecil V. Crabb, Jr., eds. *A Tide of Discontent*. Washington, D.C.: Congressional Quarterly Press, 1981.

Savage, James D. *Balanced Budgets and American Politics*. Ithaca, N.Y.: Cornell University Press, 1988.

Schick, Allan. *The Federal Budget: Politics, Policy, Process*. Washington, D.C.: Brookings Institution, 1994.

Schramm, Martin. *The Great American Video Game: Presidential Politics in the Television Age*. New York: Morrow, 1987.

Seligman, Lester G., and Cary R. Covington. *The Coalitional Presidency*. Chicago: The Dorsey Press, 1989.

Shafer, Byron. *Quiet Revolution: The Struggle for the Democratic Party and the Shaping of Post-Reform Politics*. New York: Russell Sage, 1983.

———. *Bifurcated Politics: Evolution and Reform in the National Party Convention*. Cambridge, Mass.: Harvard University Press, 1988.

Shafer, Byron, and William J. M. Claggett. *The Two Majorities: The Issue Context of Modern American Politics*. Baltimore, Md.: Johns Hopkins University Press, 1995.

Shull, Steven, ed. *The Two Presidencies*. Chicago: Nelson-Hall, 1991.

Skowronek, Stephen. *The Politics Presidents Make*. Cambridge, Mass.: Harvard University Press, 1993.

Smith, Larry David, and Dan Nimmo. *Cordial Concurrence: Orchestrating National Conventions in the Telepolitical Age*. New York: Praeger, 1991.

Smoller, Fred. "The Six o'clock Presidency: Patterns of Network News Coverage of the President." *Presidential Studies Quarterly*, xvi (1986), pp. 31–49.

Sorauf, Frank. *Inside Campaign Finance: Myths and Realities*. New Haven, Conn.: Yale University Press, 1992.

Spitzer, Robert. *The Presidential Veto*. Albany: State University of New York Press, 1988.

———. *President and Congress: Executive Hegemony at the Crossroads of American Government*. New York: McGraw-Hill, 1993.

Squire, Peverell. *The Iowa Caucuses and the Presidential Nominating Process*. Boulder, Colo.: Westview Press, 1989.

Stanley, Howard W., William T. Biance, and Richard G. Niemi. "Partisanship and Group Support Over Time: A Multivariate Analysis." *American Political Science Review*, 80 (Sept. 1986), pp. 969–976.

Stokes, Donald E. "Valence Politics." In *Electoral Politics*, Dennis Kavanagh, ed. pp. 141–164. New York: Clarendon Press, 1992.

Sundquist, James L. *Dynamics of the Party System: Alignment and Realignment of Political Parties in the United States*. Revised edition. Washington D.C.: Brookings Institution, 1983.

Taylor, Paul. *See How They Run: Electing the President in an Age of Mediaocracy*. New York: Knopf, 1990.

Teixeira, Ruy A. *The Disappearing American Voter*. Washington, D.C.: Brookings Institution, 1992.

Troy, Gil. *See How They Run: The Changing Role of the Presidential Candidate*. New York: Free Press, 1991.

Tulis, Jeffrey. *The Rhetorical Presidency*. Princeton: Princeton University Press, 1987.

Uslaner, Eric M. *The Decline of Comity in Congress*. Ann Arbor: University of Michigan Press, 1994.

Voter News Service. *National Exit Poll*. http//www.politics.com.

Waterman, Richard. *Presidential Influence and the Administrative State*. Knoxville: University of Tennessee Press, 1989.

Wattenberg, Martin P. *The Decline of American Political Parties: 1952–1980*. Cambridge, Mass.: Harvard University Press, 1990.

———. *The Rise of Candidate-Centered Politics: Presidential Elections in the 1980s*. Cambridge: Harvard University Press, 1991.

Wayne, Stephen J. *The Road to the White House 1996: The Politics of Presidential Elections*. New York: St. Martin's Press, 1996.

Wekon, Thomas J. *The Politicizing Presidency*. Lawrence: University of Kansas Press, 1995.

White, Theodore H. *The Making of the President 1960*. New York: Atheneum, 1961.

———. *The Making of the President 1964*. New York: Atheneum, 1965.

———. *The Making of the President 1968*. New York: Atheneum, 1969.

———. *The Making of the President 1972*. New York: Atheneum, 1973.

———. *America in Search of Itself: The Making of the President 1956–1980*. New York: Harper & Row, 1981.

Wilcox, Clyde. *The Latest American Revolution?* New York: St. Martin's Press, 1995.

Wildavsky, Aaron. *The Beleaguered Presidency*. Lawrence: University of Kansas Press, 1991.

Wildavsky, Aaron, and Naomi Caiden. *The New Politics of the Budgetary Process*. 3rd edition. New York: Longman, 1997.

Winebrenner, Hugh. "The Iowa Precinct Caucuses: The Making of a Media Event." *Southeastern Political Review*, 13 (1985), pp. 99–132.

Witcover, Jules. *Marathon: The Pursuit of the Presidency 1972–1976*. New York: Viking Press, 1977.

Wolfinger, Raymond J., and Steven J. Rosenstone. *Who Votes?* New Haven, Conn.: Yale University Press, 1980.

INDEX

Abortion, 107, 109, 122, 124, 140–141, 145, 148–149, 159, 161, 167

Alexander, Lamar, 89–94; invisible primary of 1995, 95–101; early weeks of 1996, 101–108; Iowa caucuses, 108–113; New Hampshire primary, 113–118; South Carolina primary, 118–125; final weeks of Republican campaign, 125–129

American Broadcasting Company (ABC), 7, 78–79, 82–86, 99–100; early weeks of 1996, 101–108; Iowa caucuses, 108–113; New Hampshire primary, 113–118; South Carolina primary, 118–125; final weeks of Republican campaign, 125–129; pre-convention campaign, 136–146; convention period, 146–155; post-convention campaign, 155–168

Arafat, Yasser, 138, 157, 162, 167

Barilleaux, Ryan, 10, 13, 15–17

Bloom, David (NBC), 107–108, 116, 153, 160, 165

Bosnia, 86, 129–130, 158

Braver, Rita (CBS), 77, 79, 82, 106, 151–152, 164

Brokaw, Tom (NBC), 112, 116, 148, 156, 160, 161

Brown, Jerry, 54–55, 57

Buchanan, Pat, 7, 40–41, 52–54, 58, 89, 91, 94, 141, 149, 166; invisible primary of 1995, 95–101; early weeks of 1996, 101–108; Iowa caucuses, 108–113; New Hampshire primary, 113–118; South Carolina primary, 118–125; final weeks of Republican campaign, 125–129

Budget, general, 6–7, 11–12, 15–17, 49, 51, 59–68, 73–74, 76, 79–87, 99–100, 102, 104, 107, 129, 131, 152, 159, 172, 175

Budget and Impoundment Control Act, 15, 60

Budget committees, 15–16, 61, 68, 74

Budget resolutions, 15–16, 61–62, 68, 74

Bush, George, 5, 13, 29, 37, 40–41, 48–49, 52–54, 58–59, 62–64, 68–69, 97–98, 103–104, 112, 125–126, 179

California primary, 8, 91–92, 94, 128–129, 133, 139

Capitol building, 25, 77–78, 81, 83–84, 128

Carter, Jimmy, 9, 27, 37, 39–41, 45, 49, 63, 179

Caucuses, 8, 26–28, 55, 91–93, 95, 97, 102–103, 108

Ceaser, James W., 18–19

Christian Coalition, 123–124, 141, 148

Clinton, Bill: election of 1992, 37, 39, 45, 52–59; election prospects for 1996, 3–9, 25, 29, 47–52, 66–72, 87–89; first two years in office, 49–51, 59–66; Medicare fight, 4–6, 51–52, 72–81; budget fight, 6–7, 51, 81–87, 91–92, 94, 98–101; Republican nomination campaign, 101–131; pre-convention campaign, 136–146; foreign policies, 137–139, 156–158; Democratic convention, 146, 150–153; general election campaign, 155–168; election results, 168–176; concluding remarks about, 178–180

Clinton, Hillary, 49, 56, 65, 78, 142, 151–152

Cochran, John (ABC), 106, 109–112, 115, 117, 123–124, 128, 131, 140–142, 146–147, 149, 153–154, 160, 164

Columbia Broadcasting System (CBS), 7, 56; Medicare fight, 74–79; budget fight, 82–85, 100; early weeks of 1996, 101–108; Iowa caucuses, 108–113; New Hampshire primary, 113–118; South Carolina primary, 118–125; final weeks of Republican campaign, 125–129; pre-convention campaign, 136–146; convention period, 146–155; post-convention campaign, 155–168

Congress, 4–5, 10–18, 22, 25–26, 30, 96–99, 120, 128, 136, 140, 145–146, 152, 154, 159–161, 164, 166

Contract With America, 50, 66–67, 75

Crier, Catherine (ABC), 111, 123

Cronin, Thomas, 12–14, 17, 20–21

D'Amato, Alfonse, 127, 142

Daschle, Tom, 78, 82, 87, 144

Debates, 58, 134–136, 155–156, 160–161, 163

Democratic Party, 1–2, 9, 16, 47, 50–51, 54–55, 61–72, 96, 134, 143, 146–153, 156, 165–166

Dole, Robert, 5–7, 47, 49–51, 59, 62–65, 73, 76, 89, 133–136; Medicare fight, 72–81; budget fight 81–87; invisible primary of 1995, 95–101; early weeks of 1996, 101–108; Iowa caucuses, 108–113; New Hampshire primary, 113–118; South Carolina Primary, 118–125; final weeks of Republican nomination campaign, 125–129; pre-convention campaign, 136–146; convention period, 146–155; post-convention campaign, 155–168; election results, 168–175; concluding remarks about, 178–180

Domenici, Pete, 83–86

Donvan, John (ABC), 110, 164–165

Dornan, Bob, 97–98

Douglass, Linda (CBS), 75–76, 83, 151

Dukakis, Michael, 49, 58, 69

Elections: with strong incumbents, 2, 4–5, 8, 28–37, 47–48, 80, 87, 92, 94, 129–131, 134, 139, 171, 177–180; with weak incumbents, 2, 4–5, 9, 28–29, 37–45, 52, 57, 88, 180

Electoral College, 49, 133, 136, 168, 170–171

Engberg, Eric (CBS), 107, 109

Executive Office of the President, 4, 9–17

Federal Election Campaign Act, 96, 98

Files controversy, 136, 141–143, 145, 165

Forbes, Steve, 89, 93–94, 129; invisible primary of 1995, 95–101; early weeks of 1996, 101–108; Iowa caucuses, 108–113; New Hampshire primary, 113–118; South Carolina primary, 118–125; final weeks of Republican nomination campaign, 125–129

Ford, Gerald, 37, 40–41, 68, 72, 97, 103

Foreman, Tom (ABC), 105, 121

Front-runner: references to, 3, 36–45, 48, 53–55, 57, 86, 89, 91, 93, 98–101, 104–119, 122–127, 166, 179; definition of, 26–29

Fund-raising, 55, 87, 95–96, 106, 136, 141, 155, 167

Gallup Poll, 5, 54, 58, 66–67, 73, 85, 99, 106, 113–114, 118, 131, 134, 153, 162–163, 167–168

Gender gap, 124, 146, 171–172

Gephardt, Richard, 54, 76–80, 86–89, 180

Gibbons, Sam, 76–77, 80, 82, 87

Gingrich, Newt, 6, 50, 71, 120, 124, 146, 152, 154, 160, 164, 178–179; Medicare battles, 72–81; budget battles, 81–87

Goldwater, Barry, 29–30, 36, 121, 178–179

Gore, Albert, Jr., 54, 64, 88, 152, 156, 180–181

Gramm, Phil, 63, 68, 119; invisible primary of 1995, 95–101; early weeks of 1996, 101–108; Iowa caucuses, 108–113; New Hampshire primary, 113–118

Greenfield, Jeff (ABC), 104, 127, 140, 160, 166

Harkin, Tom, 54–57

Hart, Gary, 27, 36, 104

Hart, John, 10, 12, 14–15, 17

Horse-race coverage, 37, 44, 57, 84, 107, 109, 111, 136, 152–154, 156, 161–165

House of Representatives, 13, 15, 25, 50–51, 61, 64, 82–85, 96–97, 144, 169–170; election of 1994, 66–72

Hume, Brit (ABC), 150–151, 161, 164

Humphrey, Hubert H., 36, 171, 180

Hyde, Henry, 141, 148

Ifill, Gwen (NBC), 100, 104–105, 107, 111–112, 116, 124, 127, 164

Invisible primary, 92–93, 95–101, 103

Iowa caucuses, 8, 27, 55, 93–119, 122, 125–126, 129–130

Jennings, Peter (ABC), 86, 116, 148, 162, 164

Johnson, Lyndon B., 9, 14, 29–32, 36–41, 52–53, 59, 171, 179

Jones, Phil (CBS), 100, 104, 107–
    117, 120–123, 126, 141, 145,
    160, 165
Judd, Jackie (ABC), 104, 142

Kasich, John, 79–80, 83, 86
Kemp, Jack, 62, 98, 127, 149–150,
    153, 163
Kennedy, Edward, 40–42
Kennedy, John F., 14, 27, 32, 95
Kennedy, Robert, 40–41, 53
Kerrey, Robert, 54, 57
Keyes, Alan, 97–98

Leading adversary: definition of, 28–
    30; references to, 36–39, 43, 53–
    54, 93, 101–105, 109–114,
    118–119, 126–129, 179
Lott, Trent, 71, 80, 88
Lowi, Theodore, 11–14, 19
Lugar, Richard, 97–98, 100, 106–
    107, 110, 113–114, 120, 126

McCurry, Mike, 80, 82
McGovern, George, 29–30, 36, 178–
    179
Mediated incumbency, 1–3, 80, 179
Medicaid, 63, 65, 76–77, 79, 128, 178
Medicare, 48, 51–52, 61, 63, 65, 99,
    128, 131, 152, 161, 172, 175, 178,
    180; battle over, 72–89
Midwestern states, 168–170, 173
Miklaszewski, Jim (NBC), 150, 158
Mitchell, Russ (CBS), 108, 110–111,
    116, 120, 127
Mondale, Walter, 27–31, 36, 104,
    178–179
Myers, Lisa (NBC), 107–108, 111,
    116, 122–124, 160, 163–164

National Broadcasting Company
    (NBC), 7, 78–79, 82–85, 99–100;
    early weeks of 1996, 101–108;

Iowa caucuses, 108–113; New
    Hampshire primary, 113–118;
    South Carolina primary, 118–125;
    final weeks of Republican cam-
    paign, 125–129; pre-convention
    campaign, 136–146; convention
    period, 146–155; post-convention
    campaign, 155–166
Netanyahu, Benjamin, 138, 157,
    162, 167
New Hampshire Primary, 8, 52–53,
    55, 57, 89, 93–94, 97, 99, 102–
    104, 107, 111–120, 122, 125–126,
    130
Nixon, Richard, 11–12, 14–15, 29–
    33, 36–37, 41, 49, 56–57, 59, 68,
    76, 103, 171, 179–180
Norris, Michelle (ABC), 110–111,
    115–117
Northeastern states, 168–170, 173

Office of Management and Budget,
    11–12, 14–15, 60
Opposition party, 2, 7–8, 28–36, 38–
    44, 54, 58, 61, 86, 89, 92, 94,
    129–131, 134, 178–179

Palmer, John (NBC), 130, 164
Panetta, Leon, 62, 78–80, 82–83
Perot, Ross, 48, 53–54, 58, 117, 126–
    127, 156, 160–165, 167–169, 174–
    175
Persian Gulf War, 54, 88, 117, 156
Phillips, Kevin (CBS), 108, 117
Political parties, general, 1–2, 8, 13,
    21–25, 28, 31, 34–35, 39–40, 67–
    68, 78, 96, 136–137
Powell, Colin, 98–99, 150, 156, 166
President and Presidency: Executive
    Office, 9–17; general, 28–35, 37–
    41, 45–48, 50–52, 55, 58–62, 68,
    77, 81, 87, 95, 97, 103, 131, 136,
    138–139, 143, 159, 171; Presi-

dency and television news, 21–26; rhetorical Presidency, 17–21
Presidential party, 2, 67–68, 180

Rabin, Yitzhak, 84, 128
Rather, Dan (CBS), 74–75, 82, 108, 116, 126, 148, 150, 161, 164–165
Reagan, Ronald, 5, 14, 16–17, 22, 27, 29–33, 36–42, 45, 49–50, 62–64, 67–68, 88, 97, 103, 107, 153–154, 158, 171, 179
Reconciliation procedure, 16–17, 62–64, 68, 79–80
Reed, Ralph, 141, 148–149
Republican Party, 1–3, 5–6, 47–54, 56, 61, 140–142, 164, 169, 179, 181; election of 1994, 66–72; Medicare fight, 72–81; budget fight, 81–87; nomination campaign of 1996, 91–131; national convention period, 146–155
Reynolds, Dean (ABC), 140, 161
Rhetorical Presidency, 4, 6, 8–9, 17–21
Roberts, Cokie (ABC), 146, 152
Rose Garden Strategy, 33, 37, 150

Schieffer, Bob (CBS), 76–78, 84, 105
Senate, 15, 25, 30, 92, 97, 135, 140–144
Shutdowns, government, 6–7, 48, 51, 73, 80–88, 100, 131, 161, 166
Social Security, 60, 63, 65, 83–84, 172, 175
South Carolina primary, 8, 94, 118–125
Southeastern states, 53, 71–72, 168–170, 173
Specter, Arlan, 97–98
Statesman, Clinton's role as, 3, 7, 31, 33, 36, 42, 44, 48, 135, 137–141, 146, 155–159, 162, 166–167, 178, 180

Taylor, Morley, 97–98

Television, 4, 6–7, 9, 14, 19–21, 34, 57
Television age, 1, 3–4, 7–8, 28–29, 37, 48, 52, 92, 177, 179
Television news media, 1–4, 6–9, 19–20, 31–34, 36–39, 47–48, 51, 92–94, 99–101, 133–136; coverage of Presidency, 21–26; coverage of nomination campaigns, 26–29; election of 1992, 52–59; Clinton's first two years, 59–66; Medicare fight, 72–81; budget fight, 81–87; early weeks of 1996, 101–108; Iowa caucuses, 108–113; New Hampshire primary, 113–118; South Carolina primary, 118–125; final weeks of Republican campaign, 125–129; pre-convention campaign, 136–146; convention period, 146–155; post-convention campaign, 155–168; concluding remarks about, 177–181
Tsongas, Paul, 54, 57
Tulis, Jeffrey, 18–20

Von Fremd, Mike (ABC), 121–122
Voter News Service, 136, 168, 170–171, 175

Western states, 168–170, 173
White, Theodore H., 20, 27, 37, 43
White House, 10–12, 17, 27, 43, 57, 63, 76, 78–80, 82–83, 86, 100, 135, 138–139, 141–143, 147, 150, 154, 157, 159, 162, 166, 180
Whitewater, 50, 136, 141–143, 163, 165
Wilson, Pete, 97–98, 148
Winnowing process, 26, 28, 43, 93–94, 102, 118
Wooten, Jim (ABC), 106, 109, 111, 117, 121, 124, 127, 163–165

About the Author

E. D. DOVER is Professor of Political Science, Public Policy and Administration at Western Oregon University. He is a long-time political and labor union activist. Among his earlier publications is *Presidential Elections in the Television Age: 1960–1992* (Praeger, 1994).

ISBN 0-275-96259-8

EAN

9 780275 962593

90000>

HARDCOVER BAR CODE